Edited by

John Daintith
Valerie Illingworth
Elizabeth Martin
Anne Stibbs
Market House Books Ltd.

Judy Pearsall
Sara Tulloch
Oxford University Press

DAMAGED

OXFORD UNIVERSITY PRESS

1993

Oxford University Press, Walton Street, Oxford OX2 6DP

Oxford New York Toronto
Delhi Bombay Calcutta Madras Karachi
Kuala Lumpur Singapore Hong Kong Tokyo
Nairobi Dar es Salaam Cape Town
Melbourne Auckland Madrid
and associated companies in
Berlin Ibadan

Oxford is a trade mark of Oxford University Press

Published in the United States by
Oxford University Press Inc., New York

British Library Cataloguing in Publication Data
A catalogue record of this book is
available from the British Library

Library of Congress Cataloging in Publication Data
The Oxford minidictionary of abbreviations
Data available

ISBN 0-19-863135-9

1 3 5 7 9 10 8 6 4 2

Text prepared by
Market House Books Ltd, Aylesbury

Printed in Great Britain by
Charles Letts (Scotland) Ltd.
Dalkeith, Scotland

Preface

During the last few decades abbreviations have p[ro]liferated to such an extent that they now fo[rm] a major part of the language. The *Oxford Minidic[tionary of Abbreviations* includes a wide variety of abbreviations commonly used today, ranging from the colloquial to the specialized worlds of computing and finance. Field labels or brief explanations are provided for abbreviations when necessary. The entries cover initialisms, such as BBC and FBI: acronyms (i.e. initialisms that are pronounced as words, such as Aids and NATO; shortenings, for example Gen. (for General, Geneva, etc.); and symbols for units of measurement, chemical elements, postal districts, and so on. A pronunciation guide (in brackets preceding the definition) is provided for acronyms; an explanation of this is given overleaf. In deciding the forms of the entry words in this dictionary, the editors have used a number of conventions. Points have been omitted for acronyms, for all-capital abbreviations, for degrees and other qualifications consisting of upper- and lower-case letters (e.g. BSc), and in other cases when this can be done without flouting convention of causing confusion with a real word (e.g. plc rather than p.l.c.). Shortenings are usually followed by a point unless the last letter of the shortened form is the last letter of the word (e.g. gdn = garden, guardian). When two or more forms are equally common, variants are included in brackets before the definition.

Pronunciation Guide

The symbols used are those of the International Phonetic Alphabet. The following consonants have their usual English sounds: b, d, f, h, k, l, m, n, p, r, s, t, v, w, z. Additional symbols are as follows:

ɑ: *as in* bar (bɑ:)
æ *as in* cat (kæt)
aɪ *as in* buy (baɪ)
aʊ *as in* gout (gaʊt)
tʃ *as in* cheese (tʃi:z)
ɛ *as in* get (gɛt)
ə *as in* paper ('peɪpə)
ᵊ *as in* able (eɪbᵊl)
ɜ: *as in* turn (tɜ:n)
eɪ *as in* pay (peɪ)
ɛə *as in* fair (fɛə)
ɪ *as in* pin (pɪn)
i: *as in* be (bi:)
ɪə *as in* hear (hɪə)

j *as in* yet (jɛt)
dʒ *as in* job (dʒɒb)
ŋ *as in* bring (brɪŋ)
ɒ *as in* got (gɒt)
əʊ *as in* go (gəʊ)
ɔ: *as in* law (lɔ:)
ɔɪ *as in* coin (kɔɪn)
ʃ *as in* shin (ʃɪn)
ʒ *as in* measure ('mɛʒə)
θ *as in* thaw (θɔ:)
ð *as in* then (ðɛn)
ʊ *as in* wool (wʊl)
u: *as in* new (nju:)
ʌ *as in* cup (kʌp)

For acronyms of two or more syllables the stressed syllables are preceded by the marks ' or ˌ in the pronunciation. The most strongly stressed syllable is preceded by ', as in 'peɪpə (paper); weakly stressed syllables are preceded by ˌ, as in 'kɒmiˌkɒm (Comecon).

A

a (ital.) *Physics, symbol for* acceleration • *symbol for* are(s) (metric measure of land) • *symbol for* atto- (prefix indicating 10^{-18}, as in **am**, attometre) • *indicating the* first vertical row of squares from the left on a chessboard

a. acre(s) • address • age • *Music* alto • amateur • anno (Latin: in the year) • answer • ante (Latin: before)

a 2 *Music* a due (Italian: for two (voices or instruments))

A *Physics, symbol for* absolute (temperature) • *Cards, symbol for* ace • *Biochem., symbol for* adenine • *Biochem., symbol for* adenosine • *Films* adult (former certification) • *Education* Advanced (in **A level**) • (ital.) *Chem., symbol for* affinity • *symbol for* ammeter (in circuit diagrams) • *Physics, symbol for* ampere(s) • (ital.) *Maths., symbol for* area • *symbol for* an arterial

road (as in **A1, A40**, etc.) • assault (in **A-day**) • atom(ic) (as in **A-bomb**) • austral (monetary unit of Argentina) • *international vehicle registration for* Austria • *Physics, symbol for* mass number • (ital.) *Physics, symbol for* nucleon number • *symbol for* ten (in hexadecimal notation) • *Med., indicating* a blood group or its associated antigen (*see also under* ABO) • *Education, indicating* the highest mark or grade for work • *indicating* managerial, professional (occupational grade) • *indicating* a musical note or key • *indicating* a standard paper size (*see under* A3–A5) • *Logic, indicating* a universal affirmative categorical proposition

Å *Physics, symbol for* angstrom unit

A. (*or* **A**) academy • acre(s) • adjutant • admiral • *Music* alto • America(n) • *Horticulture* annual • answer • April • assistant • associate • August

A1 *indicating* (in Lloyd's Register) ships maintained in good and efficient condition

A3 *indicating* a standard paper size, 297 × 420 mm

A4 *indicating* a standard paper size, 210 × 297 mm

A5 *indicating* a standard paper size, 148 × 210 mm

āa (*or* **āā**) *Med.* ana (Greek: of each; specifying quantities of ingredients in prescriptions)

a.a. after arrival • *Shipping* always afloat

AA administrative assistant • Alcoholics Anonymous • American Aviation (aircraft) • anti-aircraft • Architectural Association • Associate in Accounting • Associate in (*or* of) Arts • Augustinians of the Assumption • author's alteration • Automobile Association • *indicating* a certificate issued for a ship stating that all crew matters are in order • (formerly) *indicating* a film not be shown to a child under 14 unless accompanied by an adult •

Electricity, indicating a size of battery or cell

AA1 (*or* **AA-one**) *Finance, indicating* a very high quality rating for credit

AAA Amateur Athletic Association • (*or* **triple A**) anti-aircraft artillery • Australian Association of Accountants • Automobile Association of America • *Finance, indicating* the highest quality rating for credit

AA&QMG Assistant Adjutant and Quartermaster-General

AAC Army Air Corps

AACE Association for Adult and Continuing Education

AACR *Bibliog.* Anglo-American Cataloguing Rules

AAE American Association of Engineers

AAeE Associate in Aeronautical Engineering

AAEE (*or* **A&AEE**) Aircraft and Armament Experimental Establishment

AAFCE Allied Air Forces in Central Europe

AAgr Associate in Agriculture

AAG Assistant Adjutant-General

AAIB Associate of the Australian Institute of Bankers

AAM air-to-air missile · Association of Assistant Mistresses in Secondary Schools

AAMI *Med.* age-associated memory impairment

A & A additions and amendments

A&AEE Aeroplane and Armament Experimental Establishment

A & C addenda and corrigenda

A&E Accident and Emergency (department of a hospital)

a&h *Insurance* accident and health

a&i *Insurance* accident and indemnity

A & M Ancient and Modern (hymn book)

A & N Army and Navy (Club *or* Stores)

A & P advertising and promotion · (New Zealand) Agricultural and Pastoral (Association, Show, etc.)

A & R artists and repertoire *or* repertory (as in **A & R man**)

a&s *Insurance* accident and sickness

AAP Australian Associated Press

a.a.r. *Insurance* against all risks

AAS Associate in Applied Science

AASA Associate of the Australian Society of Accountants

AASC Australian Army Service Corps

A'asia Australasia

AAT *Med.* alpha-1-antitrypsin (treatment for cystic fibrosis)

ab. abridgment

a/b airborne

Ab (formerly) *Chem., symbol for* astatine (originally called alabamine; *see under* At)

AB *postcode for* Aberdeen · able-bodied seaman · airborne · Alberta (Canada) · ammonia for bees (applied for stings) · antiballistic (missile) · (USA) Bachelor of Arts (Latin *Artium Baccalaureus*) · *indicating* a human blood group containing A and B antigens (*see also under* ABO)

ABA Amateur Boxing Association · Antiquarian Booksellers' Association · Associate in Business Administration • Australian Bankers' Association

abbrev. (*or* **abbr.**) abbreviation

ABC Advance Booking Charter (airline ticket) • *Med.* airway, breathing, circulation (in first aid) • American Broadcasting Company • Argentina–Brazil–Chile • Associated British Cinemas • atomic, biological, and chemical (weapons or warfare) • Audit Bureau of Circulation • Australian Broadcasting Commission

ABCA Army Bureau of Current Affairs

ABCC Association of British Chambers of Commerce

abd. abdicate(d) • abdomen • abdominal

ABD all but dissertation (of a candidate reading for a higher degree) • (*or* **abd**) average body dose (of radiation)

ABE *Chem.* acetone–butanol–ethanol (solvent)

abf *Colloquial* absolute bloody final (drink)

ABFD Association of British Factors and Discounters

ABI Association of British Insurers

ABIA Association of British Introduction Agencies

ABINZ Associate of the Bankers' Institute of New Zealand

abl. ablative

ABM antiballistic missile

ABO *Med., indicating* a blood group system based on the presence or absence of antigens A and B (*see also under* A; AB; B; O)

A-bomb atom bomb

Abp Archbishop

ABP *Med.* arterial blood pressure • Associated British Ports

ABPI Association of the British Pharmaceutical Industry

ABPN Association of British Paediatric Nurses

abr. abridge(d) • abridgment

ABRC Advisory Board for the Research Councils

ABRSM Associated Board of the Royal Schools of Music

ABRV advanced ballistic re-entry vehicle

abs. abstract

ABS *Chem.* acrylonitrile–butadiene–styrene (type of plastic) • Antiblockiersystem (in **ABS brake**; German: antilocking system) • Australian Bureau of Statistics

abse. re. *Law* absente reo (Latin: the defendant being absent)

ABSM Associate of the Birmingham School of Music

abs. re. *Law* absente reo (*see* abse. re.)

abstr. abstract(ed)

abt about

ABTA ('æbtə) Association of British Travel Agents

ABTAC ('æbtæk) Australian Book Trade Advisory Committee

abv. above

a.c. *Physics* alternating current • *Med.* ante cibum (Latin: before meals; in prescriptions)

a/c account • account current

Ac *Chem., symbol for* acetyl (ethanoyl) group • *Chem., symbol for* actinium

AC air conditioning • Air Corps • Alcohol Concern (a charity) • *Physics* alternating current • analogue computer • ante Christum (Latin: before Christ) • *Law* Appeal Case(s) • appella-

tion contrôlée (*see under* AOC) • Assistant Commissioner • Athletic Club • Companion of the Order of Australia

A/C account • account current • air conditioning • aircraftman

ACA Associate of the Institute of Chartered Accountants • Australian Consumers' Association

ACAA Agricultural Conservation and Adjustment Administration

acac ('æk,æk) *Chem.* acetylacetonate ion (used in formulae)

acad. (*or* **Acad.**) academy

ACAS (*or* **Acas**; 'eɪkæs) Advisory Conciliation and Arbitration Service • Assistant Chief of Air Staff

ACB Australian Cricket Board

ACBSI Associate of the Chartered Building Societies Institute

acc. accelerate • acceleration • *Commerce* acceptance • *Commerce* accepted • *Music* accompanied (by) • *Music* accompaniment • according (to) • *Book-keeping* account • accountant • *Grammar* accusative

ACC (New Zealand) Accident Compensation Corporation • *Computing* accumulator • *Med.* acute cardiovascular collapse • Agricultural Credit Corporation Ltd • Anglican Consultative Council • Association of County Councils

ACCA Associate of the Chartered Association of Certified Accountants

acce. *Commerce* acceptance

accel. *Music* accelerando (Italian; with increasing speed)

ACCM Advisory Council for the Church's Ministry

accom. accommodation

accred. accredited

ACCS Associate of the Corporation of Secretaries (formerly Corporation of Certified Secretaries)

acct. account(ing) • accountant

ACCT Association of Cinematograph, Television, and Allied Technicians

accum. accumulative

ACD *Med.* acid citrate dextrose (as in **ACD solution**)

AC/DC (*or* **AC-DC**) *Physics* alternating current/direct current • *Colloquial, indicating* bisexual

ACDS Assistant Chief of Defence Staff

ACE *Engineering* advanced cooled engine • (EIS) Advisory Centre for Education • (EIS) Allied Command Europe • (EIS) *Biochem., Med.* angiotensin-converting enzyme (as in **ACE inhibitor**) • (Member of the) Association of Conference Executives • Association of Consulting Engineers

ACER Australian Council for Educational Research

ACET *Med.* Aids care, education, and treatment

ACF Army Cadet Force

ACFHE Association of Colleges of Further and Higher Education

ACFI Associate of the Clothing and Footwear Institute

ACG Assistant Chaplain-General

ACGI Associate of the City and Guilds Institute

ACGS Assistant Chief of the General Staff

ACh *Biochem.* acetylcholine

ACH *Banking* automated clearing house

ACI Associate of the Institute of Commerce

ACIA Associate of the Corporation of Insurance Agents

ACIArb Associate of the Chartered Institute of Arbitrators

ACIB Associate of the Chartered Institute of Bankers • Associate of the Corporation of Insurance Brokers

ACII Associate of the Chartered Insurance Institute

ACIS Associate of the Institute of Chartered Secretaries and Administrators (formerly Chartered Institute of Secretaries)

ACIT Associate of the Chartered Institute of Transport

ack. acknowledge • acknowledgment

ACK (or **ack**) *Computing, Telecom.* acknowledgment

ack-ack ('æk,æk) anti-aircraft (World War I phonetic alphabet for AA)

ackgt (or **ackt**) acknowledgment

ACM Air Chief Marshal • air combat manoeuvring • Association for Computing Machinery

ACMA Associate of the Institute of Cost and Management Accountants

a.c.n. all concerned notified

ACNS Assistant Chief of Naval Staff

ACORD (or **Acord**) (ə'kɔːd) Advisory Council on Research and Development

ACORN ('eɪkɔːn) (ital.) A Classification of Residential Neighbourhoods (directory) • *Computing* automatic checkout and recording network

ACOS Assistant Chief of Staff

ACOST (or **Acost**) (ə'kɒst) Advisory Council on Science and Technology

ACP African, Caribbean, and Pacific (countries) • Associate of the College of Preceptors • Association of Clinical Pathologists

ACPO (or **Acpo**) ('ækpəʊ) Association of Chief Police Officers

acpt. *Commerce* acceptance

ACR audio cassette recorder

ACRE ('eɪkə) Action with Rural Communities in England

ACRS *Taxation* Accelerated Cost Recovery System

ACS Additional Curates Society • advanced communications system • *Finance* automated confirmation service

ACSEA Allied Command South East Asia

ACSM Associate of the Camborne School of Mines

a/cs pay. accounts payable

a/cs rec. accounts receivable

act. acting • *Grammar* active • actor • actual • actuary

ACT advance corporation tax • Associate of the College of Technology • Association of Corporate Treasurers • Australian Capital Territory • Australian College of Theology

actg acting

ACTH *Biochem.* adrenocorticotrophic hormone

ACTT Association of Cinematograph, Television, and Allied Technicians (*see* BECTU)

ACTU Australian Council of Trade Unions

ACU Association of Commonwealth Universities

ACV (*or* **acv**) actual cash value • air-cushion vehicle

ACW aircraftwoman

ACWS aircraft control and warning system

ad (æd) advertisement • *Tennis* (North America) advantage

a.d. (*or* **A/d**) after date • ante diem (Latin: before the day) • autograph document

AD *Insurance* accidental damage • *Military* active duty • *Military* air defence • Algerian dinar (monetary unit; *see also under* DA) • (small caps.) anno Domini (Latin: in the year of the Lord) • Art Director • assembly district • Assistant Director • *Politics* Australian Democrat(s) • average deviation • Dame of the Order of Australia

A/D *Computing* analog–digital (conversion)

ADA (*or* **Ada**) ('eɪdə) *Computing, indicating* a programming language (after Ada Lovelace (1815–52), British mathematician)

adag. (*or* **adago**, **adgo**) *Music* adagio

Adapt (ə'dæpt) Access for Disabled People to Arts Today

ADAS ('eɪdæs) Agricultural Development and Advisory Service • *Computing* automatic data acquisition system

A-day assault day

ADB accidental death benefit • African Development Bank • Asian Development Bank • Associate of the Drama Board (Education)

ADC advanced developing country (*or* countries) • aide-de-camp • Aid to Dependent Children • *Computing* analogue-to-digital converter • *Scouting* Assistant District Commissioner

ADCM Archbishop of Canterbury's Diploma in Church Music

ADC(P) personal aide-de-camp to HM the Queen

add. *Med.* add *or* let there be added (in prescriptions; Latin *adde or addantur*) • addendum (*or* addenda) • addition(al) • address(ed)

ADD *Aeronautics* airstream direction detector

addl (*or* **addnl**) additional

addn addition

addsd addressed

ADDS Association of Directors of Social Services

ADEME Assistant Director, Electrical and Mechanical Engineering

ADF *Finance* (Australia) approved deposit fund • Asian Development Fund • Australian Defence Force • *Navigation* automatic direction finder

ad fin. ad finem (Latin: at *or* near the end)

ADFManc Art and Design Fellow, Manchester

ADFW Assistant Director of Fortifications and Works

ADG Assistant Director-General

ADGB Air Defence of Great Britain

ADGMS Assistant Director-General of Medical Services

ADH *Biochem.* antidiuretic hormone • Assistant Director of Hygiene

ADHD *Med.* attention deficit and hyperactivity disorder

ADI *Med.* acceptable daily intake (of a toxic substance in food)

ad inf. ad infinitum (Latin: to infinity)

ad init. ad initium (Latin: at the beginning)

ad int. ad interim (Latin: in the meantime)

adj. adjacent · adjective · adjoining · *Maths.* adjoint · adjourned · adjudged · adjunct · *Insurance, Banking, etc.* adjustment · adjutant

ADJAG Assistant Deputy Judge Advocate-General

adjt (*or* **Adjt**) adjutant

Adjt-Gen Adjutant-General

ADL *Computing* Ada design language

ad lib. ad libitum (Latin: according to pleasure, i.e. freely)

ad loc. ad locum (Latin: at the place)

adm. administration · administrative · administrator · admission · admitted

Adm. Admiral · Admiralty

admin. administration · (*or* **Admin.**) administrator

ADMS Assistant Director of Medical Services

ADN *international vehicle registration for* Yemen

ADNS Assistant Director of Nursing Services

ADOS Assistant Director of Ordnance Services

ADP *Biochem.* adenosine

diphosphate · automatic data processing

ADPA Associate Diploma of Public Administration

ADR *Law* alternative dispute resolution · *Stock exchange* American Depository Receipt

a.d.s. autograph document signed

ADS&T Assistant Director of Supplies and Transport

ADST *Finance* approved deferred share trust

ADTS Automated Data and Telecommunications Service

adv. advance · adverb(ial) · adversus (Latin: against) · advertisement · advertising · advice · advise · adviser · advisory · advocate

Adv. Advent · Advocate

ad val. ad valorem (Latin: according to value)

advb adverb

ADVS Assistant Director of Veterinary Services

advt advertisement

ADWE&M Assistant Director of Works, Electrical and Mechanical

ADX *Telecom.* automatic digital exchange

ae. aetatis (Latin: at the age of; aged)

AE account executive • *Taxation* age exemption • agricultural engineer(ing) • Air Efficiency Award • American English • Associate in Education • Associate in Engineering • *pseudonym of* George Russell, 1867–1935, Irish poet • *Insurance, indicating* (in Lloyd's Register) third-class ships

AEA Atomic Energy Authority

AEAF Allied Expeditionary Air Force

AE & P Ambassador Extraordinary and Plenipotentiary

AEB Associated Examining Board

AEC *Insurance* additional extended coverage • Agricultural Executive Council • (USA) Atomic Energy Commission

AECCG African Elephant Conservation Coordinating Group

AECI Associate of the Institute of Employment Consultants

AEd Associate in Education

AeE Aeronautical Engineer

AEEU Amalgamated Engineering and Electrical Union (formed from merger of AEU and EETPU)

AEF Allied Expeditionary Force

A-effect *Theatre* alienation effect

a.e.g. (*or* **aeg**) ad eundem gradum (Latin: to the same degree)

AEGIS ('iːdʒɪs) Aid for the Elderly in Government Institutions

AEI American Express International • Associated Electrical Industries

AEM Air Efficiency Medal

AEng Associate in Engineering

AEO Association of Exhibition Organizers

aeq. aequalis (Latin: equal)

AER Army Emergency Reserve

AERE Atomic Energy Research Establishment (Harwell)

AERO Air Education and Recreation Organization

aeron. aeronautical • aeronautics

aet. (*or* **aetat.**) aetatis (Latin: at the age of; aged)

AEU Amalgamated Engineering Union (formerly AUEW; *see* AEEU)

AEU(TASS) Amalgamated Engineering Union (Technical, Administrative, and Supervisory Section)

AEW airborne early warning (aircraft)

a.f. advanced freight • audiofrequency

Af *symbol for* afgháni (monetary unit of Afghanistan)

Af. Africa(n) • *symbol for* Aruban florin (monetary unit of Aruba)

AF Académie Française (French literary academy) • (*or* **A/F**) *Engineering* across flats (used in denoting sizes of nuts, as in ½AF) • air force • Anglo-French • audiofrequency • *Photog.* autofocus

A/F as found (in auction catalogues)

AFA Associate in Fine Arts • (Scotland) Associate of the Faculty of Actuaries

AFAM (*or* **AF & AM**) Ancient Free and Accepted Masons

AFB (USA) Air Force Base

AFBD Association of Futures Brokers and Dealers

AFBPsS Associate Fellow of the British Psychological Society

AFC Air Force Cross • Association Football Club • (*or* **a.f.c.**) automatic flight control • (*or* **a.f.c.**) automatic frequency control

AFCAI Associate Fellow of the Canadian Aeronautical Institute

AFCENT (*or* **AFCent**) ('æfsɛnt) Allied Forces in Central Europe (of NATO)

AFDCS Association of First Division Civil Servants

AFDS Air Fighting Development Squadron

aff. (*or* **affil.**) affiliate(d) • affix

afft affidavit

Afg. Afghanistan

AFG *international vehicle registration for* Afghanistan

Afgh. (*or* **Afghan.**) Afghanistan

AFHQ Allied Force(s) Headquarters

AFI American Film Institute

AFIA (Australia) Associate of the Federal Institute of Accountants

AFICD Associate Fellow of the Institute of Civil Defence

AFIIM Associate Fellow of the Institution of Industrial Managers

AFIMA Associate Fellow of the Institute of Mathematics and its Applications

AFL-CIO American Federation of Labor and Congress of Industrial Organizations

AFM Air Force Medal • *Chem., Physics* atomic force microscope (*or* microscopy) • *Telecom.* audio-frequency modulation

AFNOR ('æf,nɔː) Association française de normalisation (the standards organization of France)

AFOM Associate of the Faculty of Occupational Medicine

AFP (*or* afp) *Med.* alpha-fetoprotein

Afr. Africa(n)

AFr. (*or* A-Fr.) Anglo-French

AFR accident frequency rate (in industry)

AFRASEC ('æfrə,sɛk) Afro-Asian Organization for Economic Cooperation

AFRC Agricultural and Food Research Council

AFSLAET Associate Fellow of the Society of Licensed Aircraft Engineers and Technologists

aft. after • afternoon

AFTN Aeronautical Fixed Telecommunications Network

AFV armoured fighting vehicle

ag. agent • agreement • agriculture

Ag *Chem., symbol for* silver (Latin *argentum*)

Ag. August

AG Adjutant-General • (Germany) Aktiengesellschaft (public limited company; plc) • Attorney-General

Aga ('ɑːgə) Aktiebolaget Gasackumulator (cooker)

AGARD Advisory Group for Aerospace Research and Development (in NATO)

AGC (USA) advanced graduate certificate • (*or* a.g.c.) *Electronics* automatic gain control

agcy agency

agd agreed

AgE Agricultural Engineer

AGE Associate in General Education

AGH Australian General Hospital

AGI Associate of the Institute of Certificated Grocers

agit. *Med.* agitatum (Latin: shaken)

Agitprop ('ædʒɪt,prɒp) Agitpropbyuro (Soviet bureau in charge of agitation and propaganda)

AGM air-to-ground missile • annual general meeting

agr. agricultural • agriculture • agriculturist

AGR *Nuclear physics* advanced gas-cooled reactor • Association of Graduate Recruiters

AGRA Army Group Royal Artillery • Association of Genealogists and Record Agents

agric. agricultural • agriculture • agriculturist

agron. agronomy

AGS Associate in General Studies

AGSM Associate of the Guildhall School of Music and Drama • Australian Graduate of the School of Management

agst against

agt agent • agreement

a.g.w. (*or* **AGW**) actual gross weight

AGWI *Marine insurance* Atlantic, Gulf, West Indies

agy agency

a.h. *Shipping* aft (*or* after) hatch • ampere-hour

AH (small caps.) anno Hegirae (Latin: in the year of the Hegira; in the Muslim calendar) • (*or* **A/H**) *Marine insurance* Antwerp–Hamburg coastal ports

AHA Australian Hotels Association

AH & FITB Agricultural, Horticultural, and Forestry Industry Training Board

AHAUS Amateur Hockey Association of the United States

AHC Accepting Houses Committee

AHF *Med.* antihaemophilic factor

AHG *Med.* antihaemophilic globulin

AHH *Med., Biochem.* aryl hydrocarbon hydroxylase (used in tobacco research)

AHQ Air Headquarters • Army Headquarters

AHRIH(NZ) Associate of Honour of the Royal Institute of Horticulture (New Zealand)

AHSM Associate of the Institute of Health Services Management

a.i. ad interim (Latin: for the meantime)

AI Amnesty International • Army Intelligence • artificial insemination • artificial intelligence

AIA Associate of the Institute of Actuaries • Association of International Artists

AIAgrE Associate of the Institution of Agricultural Engineers

AIAL Associate Member of the International Institute of Arts and Letters

AIAS Associate Surveyor Member of the Incorporated Association of Architects and Surveyors

AIBD Associate of the Institute of British Decorators

AIBP Associate of the Institute of British Photographers

AIBScot Associate of the Institute of Bankers in Scotland

AIC Agricultural Improvement Council

AICA Associate Member of the Commonwealth Institute of Accountants

AICC All India Congress Committee

AICE Associate of the Institution of Civil Engineers

AICeram Associate of the Institute of Ceramics

AICS Associate of the Institute of Chartered Shipbrokers

AID acute infectious disease • *Med.* artificial insemination (by) donor

AIDA *Advertising* attention, interest, desire, action (of the customer)

Aids (*or* **AIDS**) (eɪdz) acquired immune deficiency syndrome

AIE Associate of the Institute of Education

AIEE Associate of the Institution of Electrical Engineers

AIF (formerly) Australian Imperial Forces

AIFireE Associate of the Institution of Fire Engineers

AIG Adjutant (*or* Assistant) Inspector-General

AIGCM Associate of the Incorporated Guild of Church Musicians

AIH *Med.* artificial insemination (by) husband

AIHsg Associate of the Institute of Housing

AIIA Associate of the Indian Institute of Architects • Associate of the Insurance Institute of America

AIInfSc Associate of the Institute of Information Scientists

AIL Associate of the Institute of Linguists

AILocoE Associate of the Institution of Locomotive Engineers

AIM Australian Institute of Management

AIMarE Associate of the Institute of Marine Engineers

AIMechE Associate of the Institution of Mechanical Engineers

AIMI Associate of the Institute of the Motor Industry

AIMinE Associate of the Institution of Mining Engineers

AIMSW Associate of the Institute of Medical Social Workers

AInstCE Associate of the Institution of Civil Engineers

AInstFF Associate of the Institute of Freight Forwarders Ltd

AInstP Associate of the Institute of Physics

AInstPI Associate of the Institute of Patentees and Inventors

AINucE Associate of the Institution of Nuclear Engineers

AIP Associate of the Institute of Plumbing • Association of Independent Producers

AIPA Associate Member of the Institute of Practitioners in Advertising

AIPR Associate of the Institute of Public Relations

AIProdE Associate of the Institution of Production Engineers

AIQS Associate Member of the Institute of Quantity Surveyors

AIR All India Radio

AIRTE Associate of the Institute of Road Transport Engineers

AIRTO Association of Independent Research and Technology Organizations

AISA Associate of the Incorporated Secretaries Association

AIStructE Associate of the Institution of Structural Engineers

AIT Association of HM Inspectors of Taxes

AITC Association of Investment Trust Companies

AITI Associate of the Institute of Translators and Interpreters

AIWEM Associate of the Institution of Water and Environmental Management

AJA American of Japanese ancestry • Australian Journalists' Association

AJAG Assistant Judge Advocate-General

AJC Australian Jockey Club

AJEX Association of Jewish Ex-Service Men and Women

AK US *postcode for* Alaska • automatic Kalashnikov (rifle) • Knight of the Order of Australia

a.k.a. (*or* **AKA**) also known as

AKC Associate of King's College, London

al. alcohol(ic) • alia (Latin: other things)

a.l. *Finance* allotment letter • autograph letter

Al *Chem., symbol for* aluminium

AL US *postcode for* Alabama • *international vehicle*

registration for Albania • Anglo-Latin • *postcode for* St Albans

Ala (*or* **ala**) *Biochem.* alanine

Ala. Alabama

ALA (*or* **ala**) all letters answered • Associate in Liberal Arts • Associate of the Library Association • Association of London Authorities

ALAA Associate of Library Association of Australia

ALAM Associate of the London Academy of Music and Dramatic Art

Alap (*or* **ALAP**) ('ælæp) as low as practicable (describing radiation doses or levels)

Alara (*or* **ALARA**) ('ælərə) as low as reasonably achievable (describing radiation doses or levels)

Alas. Alaska

alb. *Med.* albumin

Alb. Albania(n) • (*or* **Alba.**) Alberta

ALBM air-launched ballistic missile

alc. alcohol

ALCD Associate of the London College of Divinity

ALCM air-launched cruise

missile · Associate of London College of Music

ALCS Authors' Lending and Copyright Society

Ald. (or **Aldm.**) Alderman

ALE *Insurance* additional living expense

A level *Education* Advanced level

ALF Animal Liberation Front · Arab Liberation Front (Iraq)

ALFSEA Allied Land Forces South-East Asia

alg. algebra(ic)

Alg. Algeria(n)

Algol (or **ALGOL**) ('ælgɒl) *Computing* algorithmic language

ALI Argyll Light Infantry · Associate of the Landscape Institute

ALICE ('ælɪs) Autistic and Language-Impaired Children's Education

ALJ Australian Law Journal

alk. alkali

ALLC Association for Literary and Linguistic Computing

ALM audiolingual method (in teaching a foreign language)

ALP Australian Labor Party

ALPSP Association of Learned and Professional Society Publishers

ALS Associate of the Linnean Society · (or **a.l.s.**) autograph letter signed

al seg. *Music* al segno (Italian: to (or at) the sign)

alt. alteration · alternate · alternative · alternator · altimeter · altitude · alto

ALT *Biochem., Med.* alanine aminotransferase

Alta. Alberta

alt. dieb. *Med.* alternis diebus (Latin: every other day)

alt. hor. *Med.* alternis horis (Latin: every other hour)

alt. noct. *Med.* alternis noctibus (Latin: every other night)

ALU *Computing* arithmetic and logic unit

alum. aluminium

am *Physics, symbol for* attometre(s)

a.m. amplitude modulation · ante meridiem (Latin: before noon)

a/m above mentioned

Am *Chem., symbol for* americium

Am. America(n)

AM air mail · Albert

Medal • *Radio* amplitude modulation • ante meridiem (*see under* a.m.) • assistant manager • Associate Member • (USA) Master of Arts (Latin *Artium Magister*) • Member of the Order of Australia

AMA Assistant Masters Association • Associate of the Museums Association • Association of Metropolitan Authorities • Australian Medical Association

AMAusIMM Associate Member of the Australasian Institute of Mining and Metallurgy

Amb. (*or* **Ambas.**) Ambassador • ambulance

AMC Agricultural Mortgage Corporation Ltd • Association of Municipal Corporations

AMCIB Associate Member of the Corporation of Insurance Brokers

AMCIOB Associate Member of the Chartered Institute of Building

AMCT Associate of the Manchester College of Technology

AMDEA Association of Manufacturers of Domestic Electrical Appliances

AMDG ad majorem Dei gloriam (Latin: to the greater glory of God; the Jesuit motto)

amdt amendment

AME Association of Municipal Engineers

AMEME Association of Mining Electrical and Mechanical Engineers

AMet Associate of Metallurgy

Amex ('æmɛks) American Express

AMF Australian Military Forces

AMG Allied Military Government

AMGOT Allied Military Government of Occupied Territory (in World War II)

AMI *Med.* acute myocardial infarction

AMIAE Associate Member of the Institution of Automobile Engineers

AMIAP Associate Member of the Institution of Analysts and Programmers

AMIBF Associate Member of the Institute of British Foundrymen

AMIChemE Associate Member of the Institution of Chemical Engineers

AMICW Associate Member of the Institute of Clerks of Works of Great Britain

AMIE Associate Member of the Institute of Engineers and Technicians

AMIE(Aust) Associate Member of the Institution of Engineers, Australia

AMIED Associate Member of the Institute of Engineering Designers

AMIElecIE Associate Member of the Institution of Electrical and Electronic Incorporated Engineers

AMIERE Associate Member of the Institute of Electronic and Radio Engineers

AMIEx Associate Member of the Institute of Export

AMIFireE Associate Member of the Institution of Fire Engineers

AMIGasE Associate Member of the Institution of Gas Engineers

AMIH Associate Member of the Institute of Housing

AMIHT Associate Member of the Institution of Highways and Transportation

AMIIM Associate Member of the Institution of Industrial Managers

AMILocoE Associate Member of the Institution of Locomotive Engineers

AMIMarE Associate Member of the Institute of Marine Engineers

AMIMGTechE Associate Member of the Institution of Mechanical and General Technician Engineers

AMIMI Associate Member of the Institute of the Motor Industry

AMIMinE Associate Member of the Institution of Mining Engineers

AMIMM Associate Member of the Institution of Mining and Metallurgy

AMInstBE Associate Member of the Institution of British Engineers

AMInstR Associate Member of the Institute of Refrigeration

AMInstTA Associate Member of the Institute of Traffic Administration

AMINucE Associate Member of the Institution of Nuclear Engineers

AMIOP Associate Member of the Institute of Printing

AMIPA Associate Member of the Institute of Practitioners in Advertising

AMIPE Associate Member of the Institution of Production Engineers

AMIPM Associate Member of the Institute of Personnel Management

AMIProdE Associate Member of the Institution of Production Engineers

AMIRSE Associate Member of the Institute of Railway Signalling Engineers

AMIStructE Associate Member of the Institution of Structural Engineers

AMIWEM Associate Member of the Institution of Water and Environmental Management

AMMA (*or* **Amma**) ('æmə) Assistant Masters' and Mistresses' Association

AMNECInst Associate Member of the North East Coast Institution of Engineers and Shipbuilders

AMNZIE Associate Member of the New Zealand Institution of Engineers

AMORC Ancient Mystical Order Rosae Crucis (Rosicrucians)

amort. amortization

amp. ampere • amplified • amplifier

AMP *Biochem.* adenosine monophosphate • Associated Master Plumbers and Domestic Engineers • Australian Mutual Provident Society

Amraam ('æm,rɑːm) advanced medium-range air-to-air missile

AMRINA Associate Member of the Royal Institution of Naval Architects

AMS American Musicological Society • army medical services (*or* staff) • Assistant Military Secretary • automatic music search

AMSE Associate Member of the Society of Engineers

AMSO Association of Market Survey Organizations

amt amount

AMT (*or* **a.m.t.**) airmail transfer • Associate in Mechanical Technology • Associate in Medical Technology

AMTE Admiralty Marine Technology Establishment

AMTRI Advanced Manufacturing Technology Research Institute

amu (or **a.m.u.**) *Physics* atomic mass unit

AMus Associate in Music

AMVETS ('æmvets) American Veterans (of World War II and subsequent wars)

an. anno (Latin: in the year)

a.n. above named

An *Chem., symbol for* actinon

AN *Chem.* acid number • Anglo-Norman • *Med.* antenatal • Associate in Nursing

A/N advice note

ANA All Nippon Airways • *Commerce* Article Number Association

anal. analogous • analogy • analysis • analytic

anat. anatomical • anatomy

anc. ancient

ANC African National Congress • Army Nurse Corps

anch. anchored

AND (ænd) *Computing, Electronics* and (from its sense in logic, as in **AND gate**, **AND operation**) • *international vehicle registration for Andorra*

ANECInst Associate of the North-East Coast Insti-

tution of Engineers and Shipbuilders

ANF *Med.* atrial natriuretic factor

Angl. Anglican • Anglicized

Anh. Anhang (German: appendix; of a book, etc.)

anhyd. (or **anhydr.**) *Chem.* anhydrous

anim. *Music* animato (Italian: in a lively manner)

ann. annals • anni (Latin: years) • annual • annuity

anniv. anniversary

anon. anonymous(ly)

ANOVA ('ænəʊvə) *Maths.* analysis of variance

ANS *Anatomy, Zoology* autonomic nervous system

ANSI ('ænsɪ) American National Standards Institute

ant. antenna • anterior • antonym

Ant. Antarctica

ANTA ('æntə) Australian National Travel Association

anthrop. (or **anthropol.**) anthropological • anthropology

antilog ('æntɪ,lɒg) antilogarithm

antiq. antiquarian • antiquity

ANU Australian National University

ANZ Australia and New Zealand Banking Group

ANZAAS ('ænzəs, -zæs) Australian and New Zealand Association for the Advancement of Science

Anzac ('ænzæk) Australian and New Zealand Army Corps (in World War I)

ANZIA Associate of the New Zealand Institute of Architects

ANZIC Associate of the New Zealand Institute of Chemistry

ANZUS ('ænzəs) Australia, New Zealand, and the United States (referring to the security alliance between them)

AO Australian Opera • Officer of the Order of Australia

A/O (or **a/o**) *Accounting* account of • and others

AOA Air Officer in charge of Administration

AOB (or **a.o.b.**) any other business

AOC Air Officer Commanding • (or **AC**) appellation (d'origine) contrôlée (French: controlled place of origin; wine classification)

AOCB any other competent business

AOD Army Ordnance Department

AOER Army Officers' Emergency Reserve

AOH Ancient Order of Hibernians

A-OK (USA) all (systems) OK

AONB area of outstanding natural beauty

a/or and/or

AOR *Music* adult-oriented rock • *Music* album-oriented rock

a.p. additional premium • *Med.* ante prandium (Latin: before a meal; in prescriptions) • author's proof

Ap. apostle

AP (or **A/P**) *Insurance* additional premium • *Grammar* adjective phrase • (USA) Air Police • (Spain) Alianza Popular (Popular Alliance; political party) • Associated Press • *Insurance* average payable

APA Associate in Public Administration

APACS Association for Payment Clearing Services

APB all-points bulletin (police alert) • Auditing Practices Board

APC armoured personnel carrier

APCK Association for Promoting Christian Knowledge (in the Church of Ireland)

APD Army Pay Department

APEC ('eɪpɛk) Asia-Pacific Economic Cooperation Conference

APEX ('eɪpɛks) Advance-Purchase Excursion (reduced airline or rail fare) • Association of Professional, Executive, Clerical, and Computer Staff (now amalgamated with GMB)

APH *Obstetrics* antepartum haemorrhage

API American Petroleum Institute (*see also* API scale) • *Computing* application programmer interface

APIS Army Photographic Intelligence Service

API scale American Petroleum Institute scale (for measuring the specific gravity of petroleum products)

APL *Computing* A Programming Language

APLA Azanian People's Liberation Army

APM Assistant Provost-Marshal

APMI Associate of the Pensions Management Institute

apmt appointment

APO Armed Forces (*or* Army) Post Office

Apoc. Apocalypse • (*or* **Apocr.**) Apocrypha(l)

app. apparatus • apparent(ly) • appendix (of a book) • applied • appointed • apprentice • approved • approximate(ly)

appar. apparatus • apparent(ly)

appd approved

appl. appeal • applicable • applied

appro ('æprəʊ) approval

approx. approximate(ly)

APPU Australian Primary Producers' Union

appx appendix (of a book)

Apr. April

APR Accredited Public Relations Practitioner • annual percentage rate (of interest)

APRI Associate of the Plastics and Rubber Institute

APS (Australia) Aborigines' Protection Society

APSE (æps) *Computing*

Ada programming support environment

APsSI Associate of the Psychological Society of Ireland

APSW Association of Psychiatric Social Workers

apt. apartment

APT advanced passenger train • *Med.* alum-precipitated (diphtheria) toxoid

APTC Army Physical Training Corps

APU acute psychiatric unit (of a prison, etc.) • *Education* Assessment of Performance Unit (body monitoring pupil performance)

aq. aqua (Latin: water) • aqueous

AQ *Psychol.* accomplishment (*or* achievement) quotient • *Military* Administration and Quartering

aq. bull. *Pharmacol.* aqua bulliens (Latin: boiling water)

aq. cal. *Pharmacol.* aqua calida (Latin: warm water)

aq. com. *Pharmacol.* aqua communis (Latin: tap water)

aq. dest. *Pharmacol.* aqua destillata (Latin: distilled water)

aq. ferv. *Pharmacol.* aqua fervens (Latin: hot water)

aq. frig. *Pharmacol.* aqua frigida (Latin: cold water)

AQMG Assistant Quartermaster-General

aq. pur. *Pharmacol.* aqua pura (Latin: pure water)

aq. tep. *Pharmacol.* aqua tepida (Latin: tepid water)

ar. arrival • arrive(s) *or* arrived

a.r. (*or* a/r, A/r) *Insurance* all risks • anno regni (Latin: in the year of the reign)

Ar *Chem.*, symbol for argon • *Chem.*, symbol for aryl group

Ar. Arabia(n) • Arabic • Aramaic

AR *Psychol.* accomplishment (*or* achievement) ratio • (*or* A/R) account receivable • *Chem.* analytical reagent • Anna Regina (Latin: Queen Anne) • *Taxation* annual return • *US postcode for* Arkansas • Army Regulations • Associated Rediffusion • Autonomous Region

ARA Associate of the Royal Academy

Arab. Arabia(n) • Arabic

ARACI Associate of the Royal Australian Chemical Institute

ARAD Associate of the Royal Academy of Dancing

ARAeS Associate of the Royal Aeronautical Society

ARAIA Associate of the Royal Australian Institute of Architects

Aram. Aramaic

ARAM Associate of the Royal Academy of Music

ARAS Associate of the Royal Astronomical Society

arb. arbitrager • arbitration • arbitrator

ARBA Associate of the Royal Society of British Artists

ARBS Associate of the Royal Society of British Sculptors

arc. *Music* arcato *or* coll'arco (Italian: with the bow)

ARC Aeronautical Research Council • Agricultural Research Council (now the AFRC) • *Med.* Aids-related complex • Archaeological Resource Centre (York) • Architects' Registration Council

ARCA (*or* **ARCamA**) Associate of the Royal Cambrian Academy • Associate of the Royal Canadian Academy (of Arts) • Associate of the Royal College of Art

arccos ('ɑː,kɒs) *Maths.* arc (inverse) cosine

arccosec ('ɑːkəʊ,sɛk) *Maths.* arc (inverse) cosecant

arccot ('ɑː,kɒt) *Maths.* arc (inverse) cotangent

arch (ɑːtʃ) *Maths.* arc (inverse) hyperbolic cosine

arch. archaic • archaism • archery • archipelago • architect • architectural • architecture

Arch. Archbishop

archaeol. archaeology

Archbp Archbishop

Archd. Archdeacon • Archduke

archit. architecture

archt. architect

ARCIC Anglican/Roman Catholic International Commission

ARCM Associate of the Royal College of Music

ARCO Associate of the Royal College of Organists

ARCO(CHM) Associate of the Royal College of Organists with Diploma in Choir Training

arcos ('ɑː,kɒs) *Maths.* arc (inverse) cosine

ARCPsych Associate of the Royal College of Psychiatrists

ARCS Associate of the Royal College of Science • Associate of the Royal College of Surgeons (of England)

arcsec (ˈɑːkˌsɛk) *Maths.* arc (inverse) secant

arcsin (ˈɑːkˌsaɪn) *Maths.* arc (inverse) sine

ARCST Associate of the Royal College of Science and Technology (Glasgow)

arctan (ˈɑːkˌtæn) *Maths.* arc (inverse) tangent

ARCUK Architects' Registration Council of the United Kingdom

ARCVS Associate of the Royal College of Veterinary Surgeons

ARE Admiralty Research Establishment • Arab Republic of Egypt • Associate of the Royal Society of Painter-Etchers and Engravers

ARELS Association of Recognized English Language Schools

ARF *Med.* acute respiratory failure

Arg (*or* **arg**) *Biochem.* arginine

Arg. Argentina • Argentine (*or* Argentinian)

ARIAS Associate of the Royal Incorporation of Architects in Scotland

ARIBA Associate of the Royal Institute of British Architects (now Member; *see* RIBA)

ARICS Professional Associate of the Royal Institution of Chartered Surveyors

ARINA Associate of the Royal Institution of Naval Architects

Ariz. Arizona

Ark. Arkansas

Arm. Armenia(n) • Armoric(an)

ArM Master of Architecture (Latin *Architecturae Magister*)

ARM Australian Republican Movement

ARMCM Associate of the Royal Manchester College of Music

ARMS (ɑːmz) Action for Research into Multiple Sclerosis • Associate of the Royal Society of Miniature Painters

arp. *Music* arpeggio

ARP air-raid precautions

ARPANET (*or* **Arpanet**)

('ɑːpə,nɛt) *Computing* Advanced Research Projects Agency Network

ARPS Associate of the Royal Photographic Society

arr. *Music* arrangement • *Music* arranged (by) • arrival • arrive(s) • (*or* **arrd**) arrived

ARR accounting rate of return • Association of Radiation Research

ARSA Associate of the Royal Scottish Academy

ARSCM Associate of the Royal School of Church Music

arsech ('ɑː,sɛtʃ) *Maths.* arc (inverse) hyperbolic secant

arsh ('ɑː,ʃ) *Maths.* arc (inverse) hyperbolic sine

ARSH Associate of the Royal Society for the Promotion of Health

arsinh ('ɑː,saɪn) *Maths.* arc (inverse) hyperbolic sine

ARSL Associate of the Royal Society of Literature

ARSM Associate of the Royal School of Mines

art. article • artificial • artillery

artanh ('ɑː,tæn) *Maths.*

arc (inverse) hyperbolic tangent

arth (ɑːθ) *Maths.* arc (inverse) hyperbolic tangent

arty artillery

ARV *Bible* American (Standard) Revised Version

ARVIA Associate of the Royal Victoria Institute of Architects

ARWA Associate of the Royal West of England Academy

ARWS Associate of the Royal Society of Painters in Water-Colours

As *Chem., symbol for* arsenic

As. Asia(n) • Asiatic

AS *Education* Advanced Supplementary (in **AS level**) • *Music* al segno (Italian: to (*or* at) the sign) • (*or* **A-S**) Anglo-Saxon • antisubmarine • Associate in Science

A/S account sales • *Education* Advanced Supplementary (in **A/S level**) • *Banking* after sight • alongside

ASA Advertising Standards Authority • Amateur Swimming Association • Army Sailing Association • Associate Member of the Society of Actuaries • Australian Society of Accountants

ASAA Associate of the Society of Incorporated Accountants and Auditors

ASAI Associate of the Society of Architectural Illustrators

ASAM Associate of the Society of Art Masters

AS&TS of SA Associated Scientific and Technical Societies of South Africa

a.s.a.p. as soon as possible

ASAT (*or* **Asat**) ('eɪsæt) *Military* antisatellite (interceptor)

asb. asbestos

ASBAH Association for Spina Bifida and Hydrocephalus

ASBM air-to-surface ballistic missile

ASBSBSW Amalgamated Society of Boilermakers, Shipwrights, Blacksmiths, and Structural Workers

Asc. *Astrology* Ascendant

ASC Administrative Staff College, Henley • altered state of consciousness

ASCA Associate of the Society of Company and Commercial Accountants

ASCAB Armed Services Consultant Approval Board

ASCAP ('æskæp) American Society of Composers, Authors, and Publishers

ASCII ('æskɪt) *Computing* American Standard Code for Information Interchange

ASD Armament Supply Department

ASDC Associate of the Society of Dyers and Colourists

ASDE Airport Surface Detection Equipment

ASE American Stock Exchange

ASEAN ('æsɪˌæn) Association of South East Asian Nations

ASF Associate of the Institute of Shipping and Forwarding Agents

ASH (æʃ) Action on Smoking and Health

ASI airspeed indicator

ASIAD Associate of the Society of Industrial Artists and Designers

ASIA(Ed) Associate of the Society of Industrial Artists (Education)

ASIO Australian Security Intelligence Organization

ASL American Sign Language

ASLEF (*or* **Aslef**) ('æzlɛf)

Associated Society of Locomotive Engineers and Firemen

A/S level (*or* **AS level**) *Education* Advanced Supplementary level

ASLIB (*or* **Aslib**) ('æzlɪb) Association for Information Management (formerly Association of Special Libraries and Information Bureaux)

ASM air-to-surface missile • Association of Senior Members

ASME Association for the Study of Medical Education

Asn (*or* **asn**) *Biochem.* asparagine

ASN army service number

ASO Air Staff Officer

Asp (*or* **asp**) *Biochem.* aspartic acid

ASP (æsp) (USA) Anglo-Saxon Protestant

ASPAC ('æz,pæk) Asian and Pacific Council

ass. assembly • assistant • association

ASSC Accounting Standards Steering Committee

AsslE Associate of the Institute of Engineers and Technicians

assn association

assoc. associate(d) • association

AssocIMinE Associate of the Institution of Mining Engineers

AssocISI Associate of the Iron and Steel Institute

AssocMCT Associateship of Manchester College of Technology

AssocMIAeE Associate Member of the Institution of Aeronautical Engineers

AssocSc Associate in Science

ASSR (formerly) Autonomous Soviet Socialist Republic

asst (*or* **ass/t**) assistant

asstd assorted

assy assembly

Assyr. Assyrian

AST *Biochem., Med.* aspartate aminotransferase • Atlantic Standard Time • automated screen trading

ASTC Administrative Service Training Course

ASTM American Society for Testing Materials

ASTMS ('æztɛmz *or* 'eɪ 'es 'tiː 'em 'es) Association of Scientific, Technical, and Managerial Staffs (now part of the MSF)

astr. astronomer • astronomical • astronomy

astrol. astrologer • astrological • astrology

astron. astronomer • astronomical • astronomy

ASU Arab Socialist Union

ASV *Bible* American Standard Version

ASVA Associate of the Incorporated Society of Valuers and Auctioneers

ASVU Army Security Vetting Unit

ASW antisubmarine work • Association of Scientific Workers

ASWDU Air Sea Warfare Development Unit

ASWE Admiralty Surface Weapons Establishment

at. atmosphere • atomic

At *symbol for* ampere-turn (unit) • *Chem., symbol for* astatine • (æt) *Colloquial* (a member of the) Auxiliary Territorial Service

AT achievement test • alternative technology • anti-tank • Atlantic Time • *Education* attainment target

ATA Air Transport Auxiliary • Associate Technical Aide

ATAE Association of Tutors in Adult Education

ATAF Allied Tactical Air Force

ATB advanced technology bomber

ATC air-traffic control • Air Training Corps • Air Transport Command • Art Teacher's Certificate • *Computing* authorization to copy (of software) • automatic train control

ATCL Associate of Trinity College of Music, London

ATCRBS Air Traffic Control Radar Beacon System

ATD Art Teacher's Diploma

ATE *Electronics* automatic test equipment

a tem. *Music* a tempo (Italian: in time)

ATI Associate of the Textile Institute

ATII Associate Member of the Institute of Taxation

Atl. Atlantic

ATL *Insurance* actual total loss • *Med.* adult T-cell leukaemia

atm *symbol for* atmosphere (unit of pressure)

atm. atmospheric

ATM *Banking* automated teller machine

ATN *Maths.* arc tangent • *Telecom.* augmented transition network

at. no. atomic number

ATO (*or* **ato**) Ammunition Technical Officer (bomb-disposal officer in the RAOC) • *Aeronautics* assisted takeoff

A to J (New Zealand) Appendices to Journals (of the House of Representatives or Parliament)

ATOL ('ætɒl) Air Travel Organizers' Licence

ATP *Biochem.* adenosine triphosphate • Association of Tennis Professionals • *Railways* automatic train protection

ATPL(A) Airline Transport Pilot's Licence (Aeroplanes)

ATPL(H) Airline Transport Pilot's Licence (Helicopters)

ATS automated trade system • Auxiliary Territorial Service (in World War II)

att. attached • attention • attorney

ATT antitetanus toxoid

Att-Gen. Attorney-General

attn attention • for the attention of

attrib. attribute • attributed (to) • attribution • attributive(ly)

atty. (*or* **Atty.**) attorney

Atty-Gen. Attorney-General

ATV all-terrain vehicle • Associated Television

at. wt. atomic weight

Au *Chem., symbol for* gold (Latin *aurum*)

AU angstrom unit • astronomical unit

AUA *Finance* agricultural unit of account (in the EC)

AUC ab urbe condita *or* anno urbis conditae (Latin: (in the year) from the founding of the city; indicating years numbered from the founding of Rome) • Australian Universities Commission

AUCAS Association of University Clinical Academic Staff

aud. audit • auditor

AUEW Amalgamated Union of Engineering Workers (*see under* AEU)

aug. *Grammar* augmentative • augmented

Aug. August

AULLA ('aʊlə) Australasian Universities Language and Literature Association

AUM air-to-underwater missile

AUP Aberdeen University Press

Aus. Australia(n) • Austria(n)

AUS *international vehicle registration for* Australia

Aust. Australia(n) • Austria(n)

Austral. Australasia • Australia(n)

aut. autumn

AUT Association of University Teachers

auth. author(ess) • authority • authorize(d)

Auth. Ver. Authorized Version (of the Bible)

auto. automatic • automobile • automotive

autobiog. autobiographical • autobiography

aux. auxiliary

AUX *Linguistics* auxiliary verb

av. avenue • average • avoirdupois

a.v. (*or* **a/v**) *Finance* ad valorem (Latin: according to value)

Av. Avenue

AV *Chem.* acid value • (*or*

A/V) *Finance* ad valorem (Latin: according to value) • Artillery Volunteers • *Med.* atrioventricular (as in **AV bundle, AV node**) • audiovisual • Authorized Version (of the Bible)

AVA audiovisual aids

AVC additional voluntary contribution (in pension schemes) • *Electronics* automatic volume control

AVCM Associate of Victoria College of Music

AVD Army Veterinary Department

avdp. avoirdupois

ave. (*or* **Ave.**) avenue

avg. average

AVI *Computing* audio visual interleaved

AVLA Audio Visual Language Association

AVLIS atomic vapour laser isotope separation

AVM Air Vice-Marshal

avn aviation

avoir. avoirdupois

AVR Army Volunteer Reserve

AVRO ('ævrəʊ) *Aeronautics* A. V. Roe and Co

a.w. actual weight • *Shipping* all water

AW Articles of War

AWA Amalgamated Wireless (Australasia) Ltd

AWACS (*or* **Awacs**) ('erwæks) airborne warning and control system

AWB (South Africa) Afrikaner Weerstandsbeweging (right-wing political party)• Australian Wool Board

AWC Australian Wool Corporation

AWE Atomic Weapons Establishment

AWeldI Associate of the Welding Institute

AWJ *Engineering, Building trades* abrasive water jet

AWL (*or* **awl**) absent with leave

AWO Association of Water Officers

AWOL (*or* **awol**) ('eɪwɒl) absent without (official) leave

AWRE Atomic Weapons Research Establishment

aws Graduate of Air Warfare Course

AWU Australian Workers' Union

AWW (South Africa) Afrikaner Weerstandsbeweging (right-wing political party)

ax. axiom

AXAF Advanced X-ray Astrophysical Facility (at NASA)

az. azimuth

AZ *US postcode for* Arizona

AZT azidothymidine (drug used in treating Aids)

B

b *indicating* the second vertical row of squares from the left on a chessboard

b. bag • bale • ball • base • *Music* bass (*or* basso) • billion • bloody (euphemism) • book • born • *Cricket* bowled by • breadth • brother • *Cricket* bye

B *symbol for* baht (Thai

monetary unit) • *symbol for* balboa (Panamanian monetary unit) • *Physics, symbol for* baryon number • *international vehicle registration for* Belgium • *postcode for* Birmingham • *Chess, symbol for* bishop • black (indicating the degree of softness of lead in a pencil; also in **BB** (or **2B**), double black, etc.) • *symbol for* bolívar (Venezuelan monetary unit; *see also under* Bs) • (USA) bomber (as in **B-52**) • *Chem., symbol for* boron • breathalyzer (as in **B-test**) • *symbol for* eleven (in hexadecimal notation) • (bold ital.) *Physics, symbol for* magnetic flux density • *symbol for* secondary road (as in **B405**, etc.) • (ital.) *Physics, symbol for* susceptance • *indicating* administrative, professional, (occupational grade) • *Med., indicating* a blood group or its associated antigen (*see also under* ABO) • *indicating* a musical note or key • *indicating* a standard paper size (*see under* B4, B5) • *indicating* something of secondary importance or interest (as in **B-film, B-road**)

B. (*or* **B**) Bachelor (in academic degrees) • *Music* bass (or basso) • *Cartography* bay • Bible • billion • book • breadth • British

B4 *indicating* a standard paper size, 250 × 353 mm

B5 *indicating* a standard paper size, 176 × 250 mm

Ba *Chem., symbol for* barium

BA Bachelor of Arts • *Finance* bank (or banker's) acceptance • *postcode for* Bath • British Academy • British Airways • British Association (for the Advancement of Science) • British Association (pitch of screw thread, as in **4BA**)

BAA British Airports Authority

BAAB British Amateur Athletic Board

BAAF British Agencies for Adoption and Fostering

BAAL British Association for Applied Linguistics

BAAS British Association for the Advancement of Science

BABIE ('beɪbɪ) British Association for Betterment of Infertility and Education

Bac. (France) baccalauréat (school examination)

BAc Bachelor of Acupuncture

BAC biologically active compound(s) • blood-alcohol concentration (*or* content) • British Aircraft Corporation • Business Archives Council

BACAT (bæ'kæt) barge aboard catamaran

BAcc Bachelor of Accountancy

BACM British Association of Colliery Management

BACO British Aluminium Company Ltd

BACS Bankers' Automated Clearing Service

bact. bacteria(l)

bacteriol. bacteriological • bacteriology

BADA British Antique Dealers' Association

BAe British Aerospace

BAE Bachelor of Aeronautical Engineering • Bachelor of Arts in Education • (USA) Bureau of Agricultural Economics

BAEA British Actors' Equity Association

BA(Econ) Bachelor of Arts in Economics

BA(Ed) Bachelor of Arts in Education

BAED Bachelor of Arts in Environmental Design

BAFO British Air Forces of Occupation

BAFTA ('bæftə) British Academy of Film and Television Arts

BAGA ('bɑːgə) British Amateur Gymnastics Association

BAgEc Bachelor of Agricultural Economics

BAgr Bachelor of Agriculture

BAgrSc Bachelor of Agricultural Science

BAHOH British Association for the Hard of Hearing

BAI Bachelor of Engineering (Latin *Baccalaureus Artis Ingeniariae*)

BAIE British Association of Industrial Editors

BA(J) (*or* **BAJour**) Bachelor of Arts in Journalism

bal. *Book-keeping* balance

BAL blood-alcohol level • British anti-lewisite (dimercaprol; antidote to war gas and metal poisoning)

ball. ballast

BALPA ('bælpə) British Airline Pilots' Association

Balt. Baltic

BAM Bachelor of Applied

Mathematics • Bachelor of Arts in Music

BAMA British Aerosol Manufacturers' Association

b. and b. (*or* **B & B**) bed and breakfast

B & C *Insurance* building and contents

B & D (*or* **B and D**) bondage and discipline (*or* domination)

B&FBS British and Foreign Bible Society

B and S (*or* **B & S**) brandy and soda

B&W (*or* **b&w**) *Photog.* black and white

BAO Bachelor of Arts in Obstetrics

BAOMS British Association of Oral and Maxillo-Facial Surgeons

BAOR British Army of the Rhine

bap. baptized

BAPC British Aircraft Preservation Council

BAppArts Bachelor of Applied Arts

BAppSc(MT) Bachelor of Applied Science (Medical Technology)

bapt. baptism • baptized

Bapt. Baptist

bar. barometer • baromet-

ric • barrel (container or unit of measure) • barrister

Bar. baritone

BAR Browning Automatic Rifle

BARB (baːb) Broadcasters' Audience Research Board

BARC British Automobile Racing Club

BArch Bachelor of Architecture

BArchE Bachelor of Architectural Engineering

barg. bargain

barit. baritone

Bart. Baronet

Bart's St Bartholomew's Hospital, London

BAS Bachelor in Agricultural Science • Bachelor of Applied Science

BASc Bachelor of Agricultural Science • Bachelor of Applied Science

BASC British Association for Shooting and Conservation

BASCA British Academy of Songwriters, Composers, and Authors

Basic ('beɪsɪk) (*or* **BASIC**) *Computing* beginners' all-purpose symbolic instruction code (program-

ming language) • (or **basic**)
British-American scientific
international commercial
(in **Basic English**)

BASMA ('bæsmə) Boot
and Shoe Manufacturers'
Association and Leather
Trades Protection Society

BASW ('bæzwə) British
Association of Social Workers

batt. *Military* battery

Bav. Bavaria(n)

b.b. ball bearing • bearer
bonds

BB bail bond • bed and
breakfast • *postcode for*
Blackburn • Blue Book (the
HMSO publication *UK Na-
tional Accounts*) • B'nai
B'rith (Jewish international
society) • Boys' Brigade •
Brigitte Bardot (1934– ,
French film actress) • (or
2B) double black (indicating a very soft lead pencil)

BBA Bachelor of Business
Administration • Big Brothers of America • *Obstetrics*
born before arrival • British
Bankers' Association • British Board of Agreement

BBB (or **3B**) treble black
(indicating a very soft lead
pencil)

BBBC (or **BBB of C**)

British Boxing Board of
Control

BBC British Broadcasting
Corporation

BBFC British Board of
Film Censors

bbl. barrel (container or
unit of measure for oil, etc.)

BBMA British Brush
Manufacturers' Association

BBQ barbecue

BBS Bachelor of Business
Science (or Studies) • *Computing* bulletin board system

BBSF British Brain and
Spine Foundation

BBV Banco Bilbao Vizcaya
(Spanish bank)

b.c. (or **bc**) *Music* basso
continuo • blind copy

BC Bachelor of Chemistry • Bachelor of Com-
merce • bank clearing •
bankruptcy court • Battery
Commander • (small caps.)
before Christ (following a
date) • (or **B/C**) bills for collection • *Med.* blood consumption • borough coun-
cil • British Coal • British
Columbia

BCA (New Zealand) Bachelor of Commerce and Ad-
ministration • British Chiropractic Association

BCAP British Code of Advertising Practice

BCAR British Civil Airworthiness Requirements

BCAS British Compressed Air Society

b.c.c. (*or* **bcc**) blind carbon copy • *Crystallog.* body-centred cubic

BCC British Coal Corporation • British Council of Churches

BCCI Bank of Credit and Commerce International

BCD *Computing* binary-coded decimal • *Astronomy* blue compact dwarf (type of star)

BCE Bachelor of Chemical Engineering • Bachelor of Civil Engineering • (small caps.) before common (or Christian) era (following a date; the non-Christian equivalent of bc) • Board of Customs and Excise

BCF billion cubic feet • British Chess Federation • British Cycling Federation

BCG *Med.* bacille Calmette–Guérin (anti-tuberculosis vaccine)

BCh (*or* **BChir**) Bachelor of Surgery (Latin *Baccalaureus Chirurgiae*)

BCL Bachelor of Civil Law

BCM British Commercial Monomark

BCMF British Ceramic Manufacturers' Federation

BCMG Birmingham Contemporary Music Group

BCMS Bible Churchmen's Missionary Society

BCNZ Broadcasting Corporation of New Zealand

BCom (*or* **BComm**) Bachelor of Commerce

BComSc Bachelor of Commercial Science

BCPL Basic Computer Programming Language

BCS Bachelor of Chemical Science • Bachelor of Commercial Science • Bengal Civil Service • British Cardiac Society • British Computer Society

BCSA British Constructional Steelwork Association

BCURA British Coal Utilization Research Association

BCYC British Corinthian Yacht Club

bd board • *Insurance, Finance* bond • *Bookbinding* bound • bundle

b.d. *Commerce* bill(s) discounted

b/d *Book-keeping* brought down

Bd *Computing*, symbol for baud • Board • Boulevard

BD Bachelor of Divinity • *symbol for* Bahrain dinar (monetary unit) • *international vehicle registration for* Bangladesh • *Commerce* bill(s) discounted • *postcode for* Bradford • Bundesrepublik Deutschland (Federal Republic of Germany)

B/D bank draft • *Commerce* bill(s) discounted • *Book-keeping* brought down

BDA Bachelor of Domestic Arts • Bachelor of Dramatic Art • British Deaf Association • British Dental Association • British Diabetic Association

Bde Brigade

BDes Bachelor of Design

bd.ft. board foot (measure of timber)

b.d.i. both dates (*or* days) included

BDI (Germany) Bundesverband der Deutschen Industrie (Federal Association of German Industry)

bdl. (*or* **bdle**) bundle

bdrm bedroom

bds *Bookbinding* boards • bundles

BDS Bachelor of Dental Surgery • *international vehicle registration for* Barbados • British Driving Society

BDSc Bachelor of Dental Science

b.d.v. (*or* **BDV**) *Physics* breakdown voltage

b.e. bill of exchange

Be *Chem.*, symbol for beryllium

Bé Baumé (temperature scale)

BE Bachelor of Education • Bachelor of Engineering • Bank of England • *Physics* Barkhausen emission • best estimate • bill of exchange • British Element • British Empire

BEA British East Africa • British Epilepsy Association

BEAB British Electrical Approvals Board

BEAMA (Federation of) British Electrotechnical and Allied Manufacturers' Associations

BEAS British Educational Administration Society

BEc Bachelor of Economics

BEC Building Employers' Confederation

BECTU Broadcasting, Entertainment, and Cinematograph Technicians Union (formed by amalgamation of BETA with ACTT)

BEd Bachelor of Education

Beds Bedfordshire

BEE Bachelor of Electrical Engineering

BEF British Equestrian Federation • British Expeditionary Force (in World Wars I and II)

BEI Banque européenne d'investissement (French: European Investments Bank)

Bel. Belgian • Belgium

Belg. Belgian • Belgium

BEM British Empire Medal • bug-eyed monster

BEMA British Essence Manufacturers' Association • Business Equipment Manufacturers' Association

BEMAS British Education Management and Administration Society

BEME ('biːˈmiː) Brigade Electrical and Mechanical Engineer

Benelux ('bɛnɪˌlʌks) Belgium, Netherlands, Luxembourg (customs union)

Beng. Bengal(i)

BEng Bachelor of Engineering

BEngr Bachelor of Engraving

BEO Base Engineer Officer

Berks Berkshire

BES Bachelor of Engineering Science • Biological Engineering Society • British Ecological Society • Business Expansion Scheme

BESO British Executive Service Overseas

BEST (best) British Expertise in Science and Technology (database)

bet. between

BEUC ('bɛruːk) Bureau européen des unions de consommateurs (French: European Bureau of Consumers' Unions)

BeV (USA) billion electronvolts

BEXA British Exporters Association

bf (or **bf.**) brief

b.f. (or **bf**) *Colloquial* bloody fool • *Printing* bold face

b/f *Book-keeping* brought forward

BF Bachelor of Forestry • Banque de France (Bank of France) • *symbol for* Belgian

franc • *Colloquial* bloody
fool • body fat • breathing
frequency

B/F *Book-keeping* brought
forward

BFA Bachelor of Fine Arts

BFBS (*or* **B & FBS**) British and Foreign Bible Society

BFI British Film Institute

BFMIRA British Food
Manufacturing Industries'
Research Association

b.f.o. (*or* **BFO**) *Electronics*
beat-frequency oscillator

BFPO British Forces Post
Office

BFr Belgian franc

BFSS British Field Sports
Society

bg *Commerce* bag

b/g bonded goods

BG *international vehicle registration for* Bulgaria

BGCS Botanic Gardens
Conservation Secretariat

BGenEd Bachelor of General Education

BGS Brigadier General
Staff • British Geological
Survey • British Geriatrics
Society • British Goat Society

BH *international vehicle registration for* Belize (formerly
British Honduras) • *Astronomy* black hole • *postcode for*
Bournemouth

B/H bill of health

B'ham Birmingham

BHE Bachelor of Home
Economics

B'head Birkenhead

BHF British Heart Foundation

bhp brake horsepower

BHRA British
Hydromechanics' Research
Association

BHRCA British Hotels,
Restaurants, and Caterers'
Association

BHS British Home
Stores • British Horse Society

Bi *Chem.*, *symbol for* bismuth

Bib. Bible • Biblical

bibl. (*or* **bibliog.**) bibliographer • bibliographical •
bibliography

BIBRA British Industrial
Biological Research Association

BICERI British Internal
Combustion Engine Research Institute

b.i.d. *Med.* bis in die
(Latin: twice a day; in prescriptions)

BID Bachelor of Industrial Design

BIE Bachelor of Industrial Engineering

BIEE British Institute of Energy Economics

BIF British Industries Fair

BIFFEX ('brfeks) Baltic International Freight Futures Exchange

BIFU ('brfuː) Banking, Insurance, and Finance Union

BIH Bureau international de l'heure (French: International Time Bureau)

BIIBA British Insurance and Investment Brokers' Association

BIM British Institute of Management

biog. biographic(al) • biography

biol. biological • biology

BIOS ('baɪɒs) *Computing* basic input-output system

BIR British Institute of Radiology

BIS Bank for International Settlements • British Interplanetary Society

BISF British Iron and Steel Federation

BISFA British Industrial and Scientific Film Association

BISPA British Independent Steel Producers' Association

BISRA British Iron and Steel Research Association

bit (bɪt) *Computing, Maths.* binary digit

BJ Bachelor of Journalism • bubblejet (printer)

BJSM British Joint Services Mission

bk backwardation • bank • book

Bk *Chem., symbol for* berkelium

bkcy bankruptcy

bkg banking

bkpt (*or* **bkrpt**) bankrupt

bks barracks • books

BKSTS British Kinematograph, Sound, and Television Society

bl barrel (container *or* unit of measure)

bl. bale • black • blue

b.l. (*or* **b/l**) bill of lading • breech-loading (rifle)

BL Bachelor of Law • Bachelor of Literature (*or* Letters) • Barrister-at-Law • bill lodged • bill of lading • *Physics* Bloch lines • *postcode for* Bolton • (*formerly*) British Leyland • British Library

B/L bill of lading

BLA Bachelor of Landscape Architecture • Bachelor of Liberal Arts • British Liberation Army

bldg building

BLESMA ('blɛsmə) British Limbless Ex-Servicemen's Association

BLEU Belgo-Luxembourg Economic Union

BLit Bachelor of Literature

BLitt Bachelor of Letters (Latin *Baccalaureus Litterarum*)

blk black • block • bulk

BLL Bachelor of Laws

BLOX (blɒks) *Finance* block order exposure system

BLS Bachelor of Library Science

BLT bacon, lettuce, and tomato (sandwich)

Blvd Boulevard

b.m. board measure (measurement of wood)

BM Bachelor of Medicine • Bachelor of Music • base metal • *Surveying* benchmark • *Med.* bone marrow • brigade major • British Monomark • British Museum

BMA British Medical Association

BMC British Medical Council • (formerly) British Motor Corporation

BME Bachelor of Mechanical Engineering • Bachelor of Mining Engineering • Bachelor of Music Education • *Med.* benign myalgic encephalomyelitis

BMedSci Bachelor of Medical Science

BMEO British Middle East Office

BMet Bachelor of Metallurgy

BMetE Bachelor of Metallurgical Engineering

BMEWS (biː'mjuːz) ballistic missile early-warning system

BMH British Military Hospital

BMI body-mass index • Broadcast Music Incorporated

BMJ (ital.) British Medical Journal

BMM British Military Mission

BMR *Physiol.* basal metabolic rate

BMRA Brigade Major Royal Artillery

BMS Bachelor of Marine Science

BMT basic motion time-study

BMus Bachelor of Music

BMW Bayerische Motorenwerke (German: Bavarian Motor Works)

BMX bicycle motocross

bn bassoon • battalion • billion

Bn Baron • Battalion

BN Bachelor of Nursing • bank note • *postcode for* Brighton

BNAF British North Africa Force

BNEC British National Export Council

BNF *Computing* Backus–Naur (*or* Backus normal) form • (*or* **BNFL**) British Nuclear Fuels (Limited)

BNFC British National Film Catalogue

bnkg banking

BNOC British National Oil Corporation • British National Opera Company

BNP Banque nationale de Paris (French: National Bank of Paris)

BNS buyer no seller

BNSc Bachelor of Nursing Science

BNSC British National Space Centre

BNTA British Numismatic Trade Association

BNurs Bachelor of Nursing

b.o. back order • branch office • broker's order • buyer's option

b/o *Book-keeping* brought over

BO *Colloquial* body odour • box office

B/O *Book-keeping* brought over • buyer's option

BOA British Olympic Association • British Orthopaedic Association

BOAC (formerly) British Overseas Airways Corporation

BOC British Oxygen Corporation

BOCE Board of Customs and Excise

Bod. (*or* **Bodl.**, **Bodley**) Bodleian Library (Oxford)

BOD biochemical oxygen demand

BOF *Computing* beginning of file

B of E Bank of England

BoJ (*or* **BOJ**) Bank of Japan

Bol. Bolivia(n)

BOLTOP ('bɒl,tɒp) better on lips than on paper

(written on the back of envelopes containing love letters)

BONUS ('bəʊnəs) *Fi-
nance* Borrower's Option
for Notes and Underwrit-
ten Standby

bor. borough

bos'n boatswain

BOSS (bɒs) (South Af-
rica) Bureau of State Security

bot. botanic(al) • botany •
bottle • bought

BOT *Computing* beginning of tape (in **BOT
marker**) • (or **BoT**) Board
of Trade (now part of DTI)

BOTB British Overseas
Trade Board

BOT marker *Computing*
beginning of tape marker

bp (or **b.p.**) below proof (of
alcohol density) • bills payable • *Chem.* boiling point

bp. baptized • birthplace

Bp Bishop

BP Bachelor of Pharmacy •
Bachelor of Philosophy • (or
B-P) (Robert) Baden-
Powell (1857–1941,
founder of the Boy Scout
movement • barometric
pressure • *Finance* basis
point • (small caps.) before
present (following a num-
ber of years) • *Med.* blood

pressure • *Chem.* boiling
point • British Petroleum •
British Pharmacopoeia

B/P bills payable

BPA Bachelor of Professional Arts • British Paediatric Association

BPAS British Pregnancy
Advisory Service

BPC British Pharmaceutical Codex

BPE (or **BPEd**) Bachelor
of Physical Education

b.p.f. *Commerce* bon pour
francs (French: value in
francs)

BPG Broadcasting Press
Guild

BPH Bachelor of Public
Health

BPharm Bachelor of
Pharmacy

BPhil Bachelor of Philosophy

bpi *Computing* bits per inch

BPIF British Printing
Industries' Federation

bpm *Music* beats per minute

BPMF British Postgraduate Medical Federation

bps *Computing* bits per second

BPS British Pharmacologi-
cal Society

BPsS British Psychological Society

b.pt. boiling point

bpy *Chem.* bipyridine (used in formulae)

Bq *Physics, symbol for* becquerel

br. branch • bronze • (*or* **br**) brother

b.r. bank rate • (*or* **b/r**) bills receivable

Br *symbol for* birr (Ethiopian monetary unit) • Bombardier • *Chem., symbol for* bromine • *RC Church* Brother • Bugler

Br. Branch • Breton • Britain • British

BR *Med.* blink reflex • *international vehicle registration for* Brazil • British Rail • *postcode for* Bromley

B/R bills receivable

BRA Brigadier Royal Artillery • British Records Association • British Rheumatism and Arthritis Association

BRAD (bræd) (*ital.*) British Rates and Data (publications directory)

Braz. Brazil(ian)

BRCS British Red Cross Society

BRE Bachelor of Religious Education • Building Research Establishment

b. rec. bills receivable

Brig. Brigadier

Brig. Gen. Brigadier General

Brit. Britain • British

BRM British Racing Motors

BRMA British Rubber Manufacturers' Association

BRMCA British Ready-Mixed Concrete Association

BRN *international vehicle registration for* Bahrain

BRNC Britannia Royal Naval College

bro. (brəʊ) brother

brom. *Chem.* bromide

bros. (*or* **Bros.**) (brɒs) brothers

BRS British Road Services

BRU *international vehicle registration for* Brunei

bs bags • bales

b.s. balance sheet • bill of sale

Bs *symbol for* bolívars (*see under* B) • *symbol for* boliviano (Bolivian monetary unit)

BS Bachelor of Surgery • *international vehicle registration for* Bahamas • Bibliographical Society • bill of sale • Biochemical Society • *postcode for* Bristol • British Standard (indicating the catalogue or publication number of the British Standards Institution) • British Steel plc • Budgerigar Society • building society • *Slang* bullshit

B/S bill of sale • *Commerce* bill of store

BSA Bachelor of Science in Agriculture • Bachelor of Scientific Agriculture • *Med.* body surface area • Boy Scouts' Association

BSAA Bachelor of Science in Applied Arts

BSAdv Bachelor of Science in Advertising

BSAE (*or* **BSAeEng**) Bachelor of Science in Aeronautical Engineering • (*or* **BSAgE**) Bachelor of Science in Agricultural Engineering

BSAgr Bachelor of Science in Agriculture

BSB British Satellite Broadcasting (*see* BSkyB) • British Standard brass (type of screw thread)

BSBA Bachelor of Science in Business Administration

BSBI Botanical Society of the British Isles

BSBus Bachelor of Science in Business

BSc Bachelor of Science

BSC Bachelor of Science in Commerce • British Steel Corporation • British Sugar Corporation • Broadcasting Standards Council

BScA (*or* **BSc(Ag)**) Bachelor of Science in Agriculture

BScApp Bachelor of Applied Science

BSCC British Society of Clinical Cytology

BSCE Bachelor of Science in Civil Engineering

BSChE Bachelor of Science in Chemical Engineering

BScD Bachelor of Dental Science

BSc(Dent) Bachelor of Science in Dentistry

BSc(Econ) Bachelor of Science in Economics

BSc(Ed) Bachelor of Science in Education

BSc(Hort) Bachelor of Science in Horticulture

BScMed Bachelor of Medical Science

BSc(Nutr) Bachelor of Science in Nutrition

BScSoc Bachelor of Social Sciences

BSD (*or* **BSDes**) Bachelor of Science in Design • British Society of Dowsers

BSE (*or* **BSEd**) Bachelor of Science in Education • (*or* **BSEng**) Bachelor of Science in Engineering • bovine spongiform encephalopathy

BSEc Bachelor of Science in Economics

BSEE (*or* **BSEEng**) Bachelor of Science in Electrical Engineering • Bachelor of Science in Elementary Education

BSEIE Bachelor of Science in Electronic Engineering

BSEM Bachelor of Science in Engineering of Mines

BSES Bachelor of Science in Engineering Sciences • British Schools Exploring Society

BSF Bachelor of Science in Forestry • British Salonica Force • British Standard fine (type of screw thread)

BSFA British Science Fiction Association

BSFM Bachelor of Science in Forestry Management

BSFor Bachelor of Science in Forestry

BSFS Bachelor of Science in Foreign Service

BSFT Bachelor of Science in Fuel Technology

BSGE Bachelor of Science in General Engineering

BSH British Society of Hypnotherapists

BSHA Bachelor of Science in Hospital Administration

BSHE (*or* **BSHEc**) Bachelor of Science in Home Economics

BSHyg Bachelor of Science in Hygiene

BSI British Standards Institution

BSIA British Security Industry Association

BSIE Bachelor of Science in Industrial Engineering

BSIS Business Sponsorship Incentive Scheme

BSJ Bachelor of Science in Journalism

BSJA British Show Jumping Association

BSkyB British Sky Broadcasting (formed by merger of BSB with Sky Television)

Bs/L bills of lading

BSL Bachelor of Sacred Literature • Bachelor of Science in Linguistics

BSLS Bachelor of Science in Library Science

BSM Bachelor of Sacred Music • Bachelor of Science in Medicine • British School of Motoring

BSME Bachelor of Science in Mechanical Engineering • Bachelor of Science in Mining Engineering

BSMet Bachelor of Science in Metallurgy

BSMetE Bachelor of Science in Metallurgical Engineering

BSMT (or **BSMedTech**) Bachelor of Science in Medical Technology

BSN Bachelor of Science in Nursing

BSNS Bachelor of Naval Science

BSocSc Bachelor of Social Science

BSOT Bachelor of Science in Occupational Therapy

BSP (or **BSPhar**, **BSPharm**) Bachelor of Science in Pharmacy • British Standard pipe (type of screw thread) • business systems planning

BSPA Bachelor of Science in Public Administration

BSPE Bachelor of Science in Physical Education

BSPH Bachelor of Science in Public Health

BSPT (or **BSPhThR**) Bachelor of Science in Physical Therapy

BSRA British Ship Research Association

BSRT Bachelor of Science in Radiological Technology

BSS Bachelor of Secretarial Science • Bachelor of Social Science • basic safety standards • British Standards Specification

BSSc Bachelor of Social Science

BSSE Bachelor of Science in Secondary Education

BSSO British Society for the Study of Orthodontics

BSSS Bachelor of Science in Secretarial Studies • Bachelor of Science in Social Science

BST Bachelor of Sacred Theology • *Agriculture* bovine somatotrophin • British Summer Time

B/St bill of sight

BSU *Engineering* bench scale unit

BSW British Standard Whitworth (type of screw thread)

bt bought

Bt Baronet • *Military* brevet

BT Bachelor of Teaching • Bachelor of Theology • *Psychol.* behaviour therapy • *postcode for* Belfast • *Med.* benign tumour • British Telecom (*or* Telecommunications)

BTA British Theatre Association • British Tourist Authority (formerly British Travel Association)

BTB *Med.* breakthrough bleeding

BTC British Transport Commission

BTCh Bachelor of Textile Chemistry

BTCV British Trust for Conservation Volunteers

BTE Bachelor of Textile Engineering

BTEC (*or* **BTec**) Business and Technician Education Council

BTech Bachelor of Technology

BTEX *Chem.* benzene, toluene, ethylbenzene, and xylene (solvents)

BTG British Technology Group

bth bath(room)

BTh Bachelor of Theology

BTHMA British Toy and Hobby Manufacturers' Association

BThU British thermal unit

btl. bottle

btm bottom

BTN Brussels Tariff Nomenclature

BTP Bachelor of Town Planning

btry *Military* battery

BTS British Telecommunications Systems

Btss Baroness

Btu British thermal unit

BTU Board of Trade unit • (USA) British thermal unit

BTW by the way (used in electronic mail)

bty *Military* battery

bu. (*or* **bu**) bushel(s)

Bu *Chem.*, *symbol for* butyl group (in formulae)

BUAV British Union for the Abolition of Vivisection

Bucks Buckinghamshire

bul. bulletin

Bulg. Bulgaria(n)

bull. bulletin

BUNCH (bʌntʃ) Burroughs, Univac, NCR, Control Data, Honeywell (computer manufacturers)

BUPA ('buːpə) British United Provident Association (health-insurance company)

bur. buried

Bur. Burma

BUR *international vehicle registration for* Burma

bus. business

bush. bushel

b.v. *Accounting* book value

BV bene vale (Latin: farewell) • Blessed Virgin (Latin *Beata Virgo*) • *Med.* blood volume

BVA British Veterinary Association

BVetMed Bachelor of Veterinary Medicine

BVM Bachelor of Veterinary Medicine • Blessed Virgin Mary (Latin *Beata Virgo Maria*)

BVMS Bachelor of Veterinary Medicine and Surgery

b/w *Photog., etc.* black and white

BW biological warfare • *Photog., etc.* black and white • *Med.* body weight • bonded warehouse • British Waterways

B/W *Photog., etc.* black and white

BWA Baptist World Alliance

BWG *Engineering* Birmingham Wire Gauge

BWI British West Indies

BWM British War Medal

BWR *Nuclear physics* boiling-water reactor

BWV *Music* Bach Werke-Verzeichnis (German: Catalogue of Bach's Works; precedes the catalogue number of a work by J. S. Bach)

bx box

b.y. billion years

BYOB bring your own beer (booze, *or* bottle)

Byz. Byzantine

Bz (*or* **bz**) *Chem., symbol for* benzene (in formulae)

C

c *symbol for* centi- (prefix indicating 10^{-2}, as in **cm**, centimetre) • *Chem.*, *symbol for* concentration • *Maths.*, *symbol for* constant • cubic (in **cc**, cubic centimetre) • (ital.) *Physics*, *symbol for* specific heat capacity • (ital.) *Physics*, *symbol for* speed of light in a vacuum • *indicating* the third vertical row of squares from the left on a chessboard

c. canine (tooth) • caput (Latin: chapter) • carat • carbon (paper) • case • cathode • *Cricket* caught • cent(s) • *Currency* centavo(s) • centime(s) • centre • century (*or* centuries) • chairman • chairwoman • chapter • child • church • (ital.) circa (Latin: about; preceding a date) • city • colt • contralto • copyright • cousin • cycle(s)

c/- (Australia, New Zealand) care of (in addresses)

C *Geology* Cambrian • (ital.) *Physics*, *symbol for* capacitance • *Chem.*, *symbol for* carbon • *Geology* Carboniferous • (USA) cargo transport (specifying a type of military aircraft, as in **C-5**) • Celsius (in °**C**, degree Celsius; formerly degree centigrade) • *Theatre* centre (of stage) • century • *Colloquial* cocaine • cold (water) • *Parliamentary procedure* Command Paper (prefix to serial number, 1870–99). *See also under* Cd; Cmd; Cmnd • Companion (in British Orders of Chivalry) • *Physics*, *symbol for* coulomb • crown (a standard paper size; *see under* C4; C8) • *international vehicle registration for* Cuba • *Biochem.*, *symbol for* cytidine • *Biochem.*, *symbol for* cytosine • (ital.) *Physics*, *symbol for* heat capacity • *Roman numeral for* hundred • (ital.) *Chem.*, *symbol for* molecular concentration • *Computing*, *indicating* a programming language (developed from B) • *indicating* a musical note or key

C. (*or* **C**) Cape (on maps) • Catholic • Celtic • *Cards* clubs • Conservative • Corps • council • *Music* counter-tenor • county

C1 *indicating* supervisory, clerical (occupational grade)

C2 *indicating* skilled manual (occupational grade)

C3 *indicating* a low standard of physical fitness; hence inferior (originally a military grade)

C4 *Television* Channel Four • crown 4to (a standard paper size, 7½ × 10 in)

C8 crown 8vo (a standard paper size, 5 × 7½ in)

ca. *Med.* carcinoma • (ital.) circa (*see under* c.)

c.a. *Commerce* capital asset • *Music* coll' arco (Italian: with the bow)

Ca *Chem., symbol for* calcium

CA *postcode for* California • *postcode for* Carlisle • Central America • Chartered Accountant • Chief Accountant • civil aviation • clean air • coast artillery • commercial agent • Consular Agent • Consumers' Association • Controller of Accounts • Cooperative Agreement • County Alderman • *Commerce* current assets

C/A (*or* **CA**) capital account • credit account • current account

CAA Civil Aviation Authority • Clean Air Act

CAAV Central Association of Agricultural Valuers

cab. cabin

CAB Citizens' Advice Bureau • Commonwealth Agricultural Bureaux

CABEI (*or* **Cabei**) Central American Bank for Economic Integration

CABG *Med.* coronary artery bypass graft(ing)

CABS *Med.* coronary artery bypass surgery

CACM Central American Common Market

CAD (*or* **c.a.d.**) cash against documents • (kæd) computer-aided design • *Med.* coronary artery disease

CADCAM (*or* **CAD/CAM**) ('kæd,kæm) computer-aided design, computer-aided manufacturing

CADMAT ('kæd,mæt) computer-aided design, manufacturing, and testing

CADS computer-aided design system

CAE (Australia) College of Advanced Education • computer-aided engineering

CAER Conservative Action for Electoral Reform

CAF charities aid fund (or foundation) • (or **c.a.f.**) Commerce cost and freight

CAI computer-aided (or -assisted) instruction

cal symbol for calorie

cal. calendar • calibre

Cal symbol for kilocalorie (or Calorie)

Cal. California

CAL computer-aided (or -assisted) learning

calc. calculate(d)

Calif. California

Caltech ('kæltɛk) California Institute of Technology

Cam. Cambridge

CAM (kæm) communication, advertising, and marketing (as in **CAM Foundation**) • computer-aided (or -assisted) manufacture

Camb. Cambridge

Cambs Cambridgeshire

CAMC Canadian Army Medical Corps

cAMP Biochem. cyclic

AMP (adenosine 3'-5'-phosphate)

CAMRA ('kæmrə) Campaign for Real Ale

CAMS Certificate of Advanced Musical Study

CAMW Central Association for Mental Welfare

can. Music canon • canto

Can. Canada • Canadian • Ecclesiast. Canon(ry)

CAN customs-assigned number

canc. cancellation • cancelled

c & b Cricket caught and bowled (by)

c & c carpets and curtains

c & d collection and delivery

C & E Customs and Excise

c & f cost and freight

C & G City and Guilds

c & i cost and insurance

C & I commerce and industry

c & m care and maintenance

C & W country and western (music)

Cant. Canterbury • Bible Canticles

Cantab. (kæn'tæb) Cantabrigiensis (Latin: of Cambridge; used with academic awards)

Cantuar. ('kæntjʊ,ɑː) Cantuariensis (Latin: (Archbishop) of Canterbury)

CANUS *Military* Canada–United States

cap. capacity • *Med.* capiat (Latin: let him (*or* her) take; in prescriptions) • capital • capitalize • capital letter • capitulum *or* caput (Latin: chapter *or* heading)

CAP Common Agricultural Policy (in the EC) • computer-aided production

CAPE Clifton Assessment Procedures for the Elderly

caps. capital letters • capsule

Capt. Captain

car. carat

c.a.r. compounded annual rate (of interest)

CAR Central African Republic • *Finance* compound annual return (*or* rate)

carb. *Chem.* carbon • *Chem.* carbonate

Card. *RC Church* Cardinal

CARD (kɑːd) Campaign Against Racial Discrimination

CARE (kɛə) Christian Action for Research and Edu-

cation • Cooperative for American Relief Everywhere • Cottage and Rural Enterprises

CARICOM ('kærɪ,kɒm) Caribbean Community and Common Market

CARIFTA (kæ'rɪftə) Caribbean Free Trade Area

carn. carnival

carp. carpentry

carr. fwd *Commerce* carriage forward

CAS Chief of Air Staff • *Aeronautics* collision avoidance system

ca. sa. (keɪ seɪ) *Law* capias ad satisfaciendum (a writ of execution)

CASE computer-aided (*or* -assisted) software (*or* system) engineering • Confederation for the Advancement of State Education • Cooperative Awards in Science and Engineering

casevac ('kæsɪ,væk) *Military* casualty evacuation

CASI Canadian Aeronautics and Space Institute

cat. catalogue • catamaran • *Christianity* catechism • category

CAT Centre for Alternative Technology • *Genetics* chloramphenicol acetyl transfer-

ase (as in **CAT assay**) · *Aeronautics* clear-air turbulence · College of Advanced Technology · computer-aided (*or* -assisted) teaching · computer-aided (*or* -assisted) testing · computer-aided (*or* -assisted) trading · computer-aided (*or* -assisted) typesetting · (kæt) *Med.* computerized axial (*or* computer-assisted) tomography

Catal. Catalan

Cath. Cathedral · Catholic

CATI computer-assisted telephone interviewing

CATS *Education* credit accumulation transfer scheme

CATV cable television · community antenna television

caus. causative

cav. *Law* caveat

Cav. (*or* **cav.**) cavalry

CAV (*or* **c.a.v.**) *Law* curia advisari vult (Latin: the court wishes to consider it; used in law reports when the judgment was given after the hearing)

c.b. cash book · centre of buoyancy (of a boat, etc.)

c/b *Cricket* caught and bowled

Cb *Chem.*, symbol for columbium

CB *postcode for* Cambridge · Cape Breton (Canada) · carbon black · *Theatre* centre back (of stage) · chemical and biological (weapons *or* warfare) · *Radio* Citizens' Band · Companion of the (Order of the) Bath · confined to barracks · county borough

CBA cost benefit analysis

CBC Canadian Broadcasting Corporation · Central Buying Company · (*or* **c.b.c.**) *Med.* complete blood count · County Borough Council

CBD cash before delivery · central business district

CBE Commander of the Order of the British Empire

CBEL Cambridge Bibliography of English Literature

CBI Confederation of British Industry

CBIM Companion of the British Institute of Management

CBiol Chartered Biologist

CBL computer-based learning

CBNS Commander British Navy Staff

CBOE Chicago Board of Options Exchange

CBOT Chicago Board of Trade

CBR chemical, bacteriological, and radiation (weapons or warfare)

CBS (USA) Columbia Broadcasting System · *RC Church* Confraternity of the Blessed Sacrament

CBSA Clay Bird Shooting Association

CBSI Chartered Building Societies Institute

CBSO City of Birmingham Symphony Orchestra

CBT computer-based training

c.b.u. (or **CBU**) *Commerce* completely built-up (of goods for immediate use)

CBW chemical and biological warfare

CBX company branch (telephone) exchange

CBZ *Chem.* carbobenzyloxy

cc carbon copy (or copies) · cubic centimetre(s)

cc. chapters

c.c. carbon copy (or copies) · contra credit · cubic centimetre(s)

CC City Council · City Councillor · civil commo-

tion · civil court · closed circuit (transmission) · collision course · *Photog.* colour correction (or conversion; as in **CC filter**) · Companion of the Order of Canada · company commander · County Clerk · County Commissioner · County Council · County Court · cricket club

C–C *Chem.* carbon–carbon (as in **C–C bond**)

CCA current-cost accounting

CCAB Consultative Committee of Accountancy Bodies

CCAHC Central Council for Agricultural and Horticultural Cooperation

CCB (South Africa) Civil Cooperation Bureau

CCBI Council of Churches for Great Britain and Ireland

CCBN Central Council for British Naturism

CCC Central Criminal Court · Commodity Credit Corporation · County Cricket Club · Customs Cooperation Council

CCCI *Military* command, control, communications, and intelligence

CCCP Soyuz Sovetskikh Sotsialisticheskikh Respublik (Russian: Union of Soviet Socialist Republics)

CCD Central Council for the Disabled • *Electronics* charged-coupled device

CCE Chartered Civil Engineer

CCF Combined Cadet Force • *Med.* congestive cardiac failure

CCFD *Statistics* complementary cumulative frequency distribution

CCFM Combined Cadet Forces Medal

CCFP Certificate of the College of Family Physicians

CCG Control Commission for Germany

CCGT combined-cycle gas turbine

CCHE Central Council for Health Education

CChem Chartered Chemist

CCHMS Central Committee for Hospital Medical Services

CCIA Commission of the Churches on International Affairs

CCITT Comité consultatif international télégraphique et téléphonique (French: International Telegraph and Telephone Consultative Committee)

CCJ Circuit Court Judge • Council of Christians and Jews

CCM *Med.* caffeine clearance measurement

c.c.p. *Crystallog.* cubic close-packed

CCP Chinese Communist Party • Code of Civil Procedure • Court of Common Pleas

CCPR Central Council of Physical Recreation

CCR cassette camera recorder

CCRA Commander Corps of Royal Artillery

CCRE Commander Corps of Royal Engineers

CCREME Commander Corps of Royal Electrical and Mechanical Engineers

CCRSigs Commander Corps of Royal Signals

CCS casualty clearing station

CCSU Council of Civil Service Unions

CCTA Central Computer

and Telecommunications Agency

CCTS Combat Crew Training Squadron

CCTV closed-circuit television

CCU *Med.* coronary care unit

CCV *Aeronautics* control-configured vehicle

ccw. counterclockwise

CCW Curriculum Council for Wales

cd *Physics, symbol for* candela • cord

c.d. (*or* **c/d**) *Book-keeping* carried down • cash discount • *Finance* cum dividend (i.e. with dividend)

Cd *Chem., symbol for* cadmium • *Parliamentary procedure* Command Paper (prefix to serial number, 1900–18). *See also under* C; Cmd; Cmnd

CD Canadian Forces Decoration • certificate of deposit • Civil Defence • civil disobedience • closing date • *Electronics* compact disc • Conference on Disarmament (of the UN) • *Med.* contagious disease • Corps Diplomatique (French: Diplomatic Corps)

C/D consular declaration

CDA Copper Development Association

CDC Control Data Corporation (computer manufacturers)

CDE (*or* **CD-E**) compact disc erasable • Conference on Confidence- and Security-Building and Disarmament in Europe (as in **CDE treaty**)

c.d.f. *Statistics* cumulative distribution function

cd fwd *Book-keeping* carried forward

CDH *Med.* congenital dislocation of the hip

CDI (*or* **CD-I**) compact-disc interactive

CDipAF Certified Diploma in Accounting and Finance

c. div. *Finance* cum dividend (i.e. with dividend)

CDM *Astronomy* cold dark matter (as in **CDM theory**)

Cdn Canadian

CDN *international vehicle registration for* Canada

cDNA *Biochem.* complementary DNA

Cdo Commando

CDP Committee of Directors of Polytechnics

Cdr *Military* Commander

CDR (*or* **CD-R**) compact-disc recordable

CDRA Committee of Directors of Research Associations

Cdre *Military* Commodore

CD-ROM (ˌsiːˌdiːˈrɒm) *Computing* compact disc read-only memory

CDS Chief of the Defence Staff

CDSO Companion of the Distinguished Service Order

CDT (USA and Canada) Central Daylight Time • Craft, Design, and Technology (a subject on the GCSE syllabus)

CDTV *Computing* Commodore Dynamic Total Vision • compact-disk television

CDU Christlich-Demokratische Union (Christian Democratic Union; German political party)

CDV CD-video (compact-disc player) • Civil Defence Volunteers • current domestic value

c.e. *Law* caveat emptor (Latin: let the buyer beware) • compass error

Ce *Chem., symbol for* cerium

CE Chemical Engineer • Chief Engineer • Christian Endeavour • (small caps.) Christian Era (following a date) • Church of England • Civil Engineer • *Education* Common Entrance • (small caps.) Common Era (following a date) • Communauté européenne (French: European Community, EC; now often used in place of CEE) • Corps of Engineers • Council of Europe

CEA Central Electricity Authority • Cinematograph Exhibitors Association • Combustion Engineering Association • Confédération européenne de l'agriculture (French: European Confederation of Agriculture)

CED Committee for Economic Development

CEDO Centre for Educational Development Overseas

CEDR (ˈsiːdə) Centre for Dispute Resolution

CEE Communauté économique européenne (French: European Economic Community; *see also under* CE)

CEED Centre for Economic and Environment Development

CEGB Central Electricity Generating Board

CEI Council of Engineering Institutions

CEIR Corporation for Economic and Industrial Research

cel. *Music* celesta

Celt. Celtic

CEMA Council for Economic Mutual Assistance • Council for the Encouragement of Music and the Arts

CEMR Council of European Municipalities and Regions

CEMS Church of England Men's Society

cen. central • century

CEN ('sɛn) Comité européen de normalisation (French: European Standardization Committee)

CENELEC ('sɛnə,lɛk) Comité européen normalisation électrotechnique (French: European Electrotechnical Standardization Committee)

CEng Chartered Engineer

cent. *Currency* centavo • *Currency* centesimo • centi-

grade • central • centum (Latin: hundred) • century

CENTAG ('sɛntæg) Central (European) Army Group (in NATO)

CENTO (*or* **Cento**) ('sɛntəʊ) Central Treaty Organization

CEO Chief Executive Officer

CER (Australia and New Zealand) Closer Economic Relations

CERG *Politics* Conservative European Reform Group

CERL (sɜːl) Central Electricity Research Laboratories

CERN (sɜːn) Conseil européen pour la recherche nucléaire (French: European Organization for Nuclear Research; now called European Laboratory for Particle Physics)

cert. certificate(d) • certification • certified • certify

CERT Charities Effectiveness Review Trust

Cert Ed Certificate in Education

CertHE Certificate in Higher Education

certif. certificate

CES Christian Evidence Society

CEST Centre for Exploitation of Science and Technology

Cestr. Cestrensis (Latin: (Bishop) of Chester)

CET Central European Time • Common External Tariff • Council for Educational Technology

cet. par. ceteris paribus (Latin: other things being equal)

CETS Church of England Temperance Society

Ceyl. Ceylon

cf. *Bookbinding* calfskin • compare (Latin *confer*)

c.f. *Music* cantus firmus (Latin: fixed song) • (*or* **c/f**) *Book-keeping* carried forward • (*or* **c/f**) cost and freight

Cf *Chem., symbol for* californium

Cf. *RC Church* Confessions

CF Canadian Forces • *postcode for* Cardiff • *Commerce* carriage forward • Chaplain to the Forces • *symbol for* Comorian franc (monetary unit of Comoros) • compensation fee • *Med.* conventional fractionation radiotherapy • cost

and freight • *Chem.* crystal field (as in **CF theory**) • *Med.* cystic fibrosis

CFA Canadian Field Artillery • Communauté financière africaine (French: African Financial Community, as in **CFA franc**) • Council for Acupuncture

CFAF CFA (Communauté financière africaine) franc

CFC *Chem.* chlorofluorocarbon (*or* chlorinated fluorocarbon) • Common Fund for Commodities (in the UN)

c.f.d. cubic feet per day

CFD *Engineering* computational fluid dynamics

CFE Central Fighter Establishment • College of Further Education • *Military* Conventional Forces in Europe (as in **CFE treaty**)

c.f.h. cubic feet per hour

CFI (*or* **c.f.i.**) cost, freight, and insurance

c.f.m. cubic feet per minute

CFM Cadet Forces Medal • *Chem.* chlorofluoromethane

CFO *Meteorol.* Central Forecasting Office • Chief Financial Officer

CFP Common Fisheries

Policy (of the EC) • Communauté financière du Pacifique (French: Pacific Financial Community)

CFPF CFP (Communauté financière du Pacifique) franc

CFR Commander of the Order of the Federal Republic of Nigeria • *Nuclear engineering* commercial fast reactor • *Engineering* Cooperative Fuel Research (Committee) (as in **CFR engine**)

c.f.s. cubic feet per second

CFS Central Flying School • *Med.* chronic fatigue syndrome

CFT *Med.* complement fixation test

CFTC (USA) Commodity Futures Trading Commission

cg *symbol for* centigram(s) • (*or* **c.g.**) centre of gravity

CG Captain-General • Captain of the Guard • centre of gravity • coastguard • Coldstream Guards • Consul-General

CGA *Computing* colour graphics adapter • Community of the Glorious Ascension • Country Gentlemen's Association

CGBR Central Government Borrowing Requirement

cge carriage

CGE *Politics* Conservative Group for Europe

CGH Cape of Good Hope

CGI City and Guilds Institute • computer graphics interface

CGLI City and Guilds of London Institute

cgm centigram(s)

CGM Conspicuous Gallantry Medal

cgo cargo

CGRM Commandant-General of the Royal Marines

cgs (*or* **c.g.s.**) centimetre, gram, second (in **cgs units**)

CGS Chief of General Staff

CGT capital-gains tax

CGT-FO (France) Confédération général du travail-force ouvrière (General Confederation of Labour-Workers' Force)

ch *Maths.* cosh

ch. chain (unit of measure; crochet stitch) • chaldron • chaplain • chapter • charge(s) • *Chess* check • *Horse racing* chestnut •

cheval-vapeur (French: horsepower) • chief • child(ren) • church

c.h. candle hour(s) • central heating • court house • custom(s) house

Ch. Chaldean • Chaldee • Champion • Chancellor • China • Chinese • Chirurgiae (Latin: of surgery; in academic degrees) • Church

CH *postcode for* Chester • Companion of Honour • corporate hospitality • custom(s) house • *international vehicle registration for* Switzerland (French *Confédération Helvétique*)

C/H central heating

Chal. (*or* **Chald.**) Chaldaic (*or* Chaldee) • Chaldean

Chamb. Chamberlain

Chan. (*or* **Chanc.**) Chancellor • Chancery

chap. (*or* **Chap.**) chaplain • chapter

CHAPS (tʃæps) Clearing House Automatic Payments System

char. character • charter

CHAR Campaign for Homeless People (originally Campaign for the Homeless and Rootless)

charact. characterize

ChB Bachelor of Surgery (Latin *Chirugiae Baccalaureus*)

CHB Companion of Honour of Barbados

CHC child health clinic • Community Health Council

ChD Doctor of Surgery (Latin *Chirugiae Doctor*)

Ch. D. *Law* Chancery Division

CHD coronary heart disease

CHDL computer hardware description language

ChE Chemical Engineer

CHE Campaign for Homosexual Equality

chem. chemical(ly) • chemist(ry)

ChemE Chemical Engineer

Ches. Cheshire

ch. fwd charges forward

chg. (*or* **chge**) *Commerce, Finance* charge

Ch. hist. Church history

Chin. China • Chinese

CHINA *Colloquial* Come home, I need action (on letters)

CHIPS (tʃips) Clearing House Inter-Bank Payments System

CHIRP (tʃɜːp) *Civil avia-*

tion Confidential Human Incidence Reporting Programme (pilots' comments on safety trends)

Ch. J. Chief Justice

Chl *Botany, Biochem.* chlorophyll (as in **Chl a**)

ChLJ Chaplain of the Order of St Lazarus of Jerusalem

chm. (*or* **Chm.**, **chmn**) chairman • checkmate

ChM Master of Surgery (Latin *Chirurgiae Magister*)

choc. chocolate

chor. choral • chorus

CHP combined heat and power (energy use)

ch. pd charges paid

ch. ppd. charges prepaid

chq. cheque

CHQ *Military* Corps Headquarters

Chr. Christ • Christian(ity) • *Bible* Chronicles

chron. chronicle • (*or* **chronol.**) chronological(ly) • (*or* **chronol.**) chronology

Chron. *Bible* Chronicles

chs chapters

CHSA Chest, Heart, and Stroke Association

CHSC Central Health Services Council

c.h.w. constant hot water

Ci *Physics, symbol for* curie

CI Channel Islands • Chief Inspector • *Astronomy* Colour Index • *Chem.* combustion index • compression-ignition (as in **CI engine**) • continuous improvement (in management) • *Photog.* contrast index • *international vehicle registration for* Côte d'Ivoire (Ivory Coast) • (Imperial Order of the) Crown of India

C³I *Military* command, control, communications, and intelligence

CIA (USA) Central Intelligence Agency • Chemical Industries' Association

CIAgrE Companion of the Institution of Agricultural Engineers

CIAL Corresponding Member of the International Institute of Arts and Letters

CIArb Chartered Institute of Arbitrators

CIB Central Intelligence Board • Chartered Institute of Bankers • (New Zealand) Criminal Investigation Branch

CIBSE Chartered Institution of Building Services

Engineers (formerly Chartered Institute of Building Services, **CIBS**)

CIC Commander-in-Chief

Cicestr. Cicestrensis (Latin: (Bishop) of Chichester)

CICHE Committee for International Cooperation in Higher Education

CICI Confederation of Information Communication Industries

CID Committee for Imperial Defence • Council of Industrial Design • Criminal Investigation Department

Cie Compagnie (French: Company; Co.)

CIE Commission internationale de l'éclairage (French: International Commission on Illumination; ICI) • Companion of the Order of the Indian Empire (former honour) • (Ireland) Córas Iompair Éireann (Irish Gaelic: Transport Organization of Ireland)

c.i.f. (*or* **CIF**) *Commerce* cost, insurance, and freight (as in **c.i.f. contract**)

c.i.f.c. *Commerce* cost, insurance, freight, and commission

c.i.f.c.i. *Commerce* cost, insurance, freight, commission, and interest

c.i.f.e. *Commerce* cost, insurance, freight, and exchange

CIFE Colleges and Institutes for Further Education

c.i.f.i. *Commerce* cost, insurance, freight, and interest

CIGasE Companion of the Institute of Gas Engineers

CIGS Chief of the Imperial General Staff

CIH Certificate in Industrial Health

CII Chartered Insurance Institute

CIM China Inland Mission • Commission for Industry and Manpower • computer input on (*or* from) microfilm • computer-integrated manufacture (*or* manufacturing)

CIMA Chartered Institute of Management Accountants

CIMarE Companion of the Institute of Marine Engineers

CIMechE Companion of the Institution of Mechanical Engineers

CIMEMME Companion

of the Institute of Mining Electrical and Mining Mechanical Engineers

CIMGTechE Companion of the Institution of Mechanical and General Technician Engineers

CIN *Med.* cervical intra-epithelial neoplasia (in grading cervical smears)

C-in-C (*or* **C in C**) Commander-in-Chief

CIO (USA) Congress of Industrial Organizations

CIOB Chartered Institute of Building

CIPA Chartered Institute of Patent Agents

CIPFA (*or* **Cipfa**) Chartered Institute of Public Finance and Accountancy

CIPM Commission internationale des poids et mesures (French: International Committee on Weights and Measures) • Companion of the Institute of Personnel Management

CIPS Choice in Personal Safety (organization)

CIPW *Geol.* Cross, Iddings, Pirsson, Washington (rock classification; named after its devisers)

cir. (ital.) circa (*see under* c.) • circular • circulation • circumference

CIR Commission (*or* Council) on Industrial Relations

circ. (ital.) circa (*see under* c.) • circular • circulation • circumcision • circumference

circum. circumference

CIRIA Construction Industry Research and Information Association

CIS *Med.* combined-injury syndrome • Commonwealth of Independent States (the former Soviet republics)

CISAC Centre for International Security and Arms Control

CISC complex instruction-set computer

CIS-COBOL *Computing* compact interactive standard COBOL

CISL Confédération internationale des syndicats libres (French: International Confederation of Free Trade Unions)

CISTI Canadian Institute for Scientific and Technological Information

cit. citation • cited • citizen • citrate

CIT (New Zealand) Central Institute of Technology • Chartered Institute of Transport

CITES (ˈsaɪtiːz) Convention on International Trade in Endangered Species

CIU Club and Institute Union

civ. civil • civilian

CIV City Imperial Volunteers

CIWF Compassion in World Farming

CJ Chief Justice

CJD Creutzfeldt–Jakob disease

CJM *RC Church* Congregation of Jesus and Mary

ck cask • check • cook

CKD (*or* **c.k.d.**) *Commerce* completely knocked down (i.e. in parts; of goods for sale)

ckw. clockwise

cl *symbol for* centilitre(s)

cl. claim • clarinet • (*or* **Cl.**) class • classification • clause • clearance • clergy(man) • clerk • close • cloth

c.l. carload • cum laude (Latin: with praise)

c/l (*or* **C/L**) cash letter

Cl *Chem., symbol for* chlorine

CL civil law • common law • *international vehicle reg-*

istration for Sri Lanka (formerly Ceylon)

CLA Country Landowner's Association

class. classic(al) • classification • classified

clav. *Music* clavier

cld *Stock exchange* called • cleared

CLIMAP (ˈklaɪmæp) Climate: Long-range Interpretation, Mapping, and Prediction (international project)

CLit (*or* **CLitt**) Companion of Literature

CLJ Commander of the Order of St Lazarus of Jerusalem

Cllr Councillor

clo. clothing

CLP Constituency Labour Party

CLPT computer language(s) for the processing of text

CLR computer-language recorder

CLRAE Conference of Local and Regional Authorities of Europe

CLT computer-language translator

clvd clavichord

cm *symbol for* centimetre(s)

c.m. carat métrique (French: metric carat) • causa mortis (Latin: by reason of death) • *Music* common metre • court martial

cM *Genetics, symbol for* centimorgan

Cm *Chem., symbol for* curium

CM carboxymethyl (in **CM-cellulose**) • Certificated (or Certified) Master • *postcode for* Chelmsford • church mission(ary) • command module (spacecraft) • *Music* common metre • *RC Church* Congregation of the Mission • Corresponding Member • Master of Surgery (Latin *Chirurgiae Magister*) • Member of the Order of Canada

CMA Canadian Medical Association • Communication Managers' Association

CMAC Catholic Marriage Advisory Council

CMB Central Midwives Board (superseded by UKCC)

CMC Conservation Monitoring Centre

CMChM Master of Surgery

Cmd *Parliamentary procedure* Command Paper

(prefix to serial number, 1919–56). *See also under* C; Cd; Cmnd

CMD *Music* common metre double • conventional munitions disposal (type of bomb disposal)

Cmdr *Military* Commander

Cmdre Commodore

CMEA Council for Mutual Economic Assistance (i.e. COMECON)

CMF Central Mediterranean Force • Commonwealth Military Forces

CMG Companion of the Order of St Michael and St George

CMI *Med.* cell-mediated immunity • computer-managed instruction

cml commercial

CML chronic myelocytic (or myelogenous, myeloid) leukaemia

CMLJ Commander of Merit of the Order of St Lazarus of Jerusalem

Cmnd *Parliamentary procedure* Command Paper (prefix to serial number since 1957). *See also under* C; Cd; Cmd

CMOS (or **C/MOS**) ('siːmɒs) *Electronics* complementary metal oxide semiconductor (*or* silicon)

Cmpn Companion

CMS Certificate in Management Studies · Church Missionary Society · *Computing* conversational monitor system

CMV *Med., Microbiol.* cytomegalovirus

CN Canadian National (Railway)

C/N *Biochem., Ecology* carbon–nitrogen (in **C/N ratio**) · *Insurance* cover note · *Commerce* credit note

CNAA Council for National Academic Awards

CNAR *Finance* compound net annual rate

CNC computer numerical control

CND Campaign for Nuclear Disarmament

CNES Centre national d'études spatiales (French space agency)

CNF Commonwealth Nurses' Federation

CNG compressed (*or* consolidated) natural gas

CNI Companion of the Nautical Institute

CNN Cable News Network · Certified Nursery Nurse

CNO Chief Nursing Officer · Chief of Naval Operations

cnr corner

CNR Canadian National Railway

CNRS (France) Centre national de la recherche scientifique (National Centre for Scientific Research)

CNS *Anatomy* central nervous system

c.o. *Med.* complains of

c/o care of · *Book-keeping* carried over

Co *Chem., symbol for* cobalt

Co. Coalition · Colorado · Company · County

CO Cabinet Office · *Med.* cardiac output · *postcode for* Colchester · *international vehicle registration for* Colombia · *US postcode for* Colorado · *Military* combined operations · Commanding Officer · Commonwealth Office (now part of the FCO) · conscientious objector · criminal offence · Crown Office · *Electronics* current oscillations

C/O cash order · certificate of origin

CoA *Biochem.* coenzyme A

COA change of address

coad. coadjutor

Cobol (*or* **COBOL**) ('kəʊ,bɒl) *Computing* common business-oriented language

COC *Med.* combined oral contraceptive

coch. (*or* **cochl.**) *Med.* cochleare (Latin: spoonful)

coch. amp. *Med.* cochleare amplum (Latin: heaped spoonful)

coch. mag. *Med.* cochleare magnum (Latin: tablespoonful)

coch. med. *Med.* cochleare medium (Latin: dessertspoonful)

coch. parv. *Med.* cochleare parvum (Latin: teaspoonful)

COCOM (*or* **CoCom**) ('kəʊ,kɒm) Coordinating Committee for Multinational Export Controls

COCOMO (*or* **CoCoMo**) (kɒ'kəʊməʊ) *Computing* constructive cost model

c.o.d. cash on delivery

Cod. (*or* **cod.**) codex

COD cash on delivery · chemical oxygen demand · (USA) collect on delivery ·

(ital.) Concise Oxford Dictionary

CODAN ('kəʊdæn) *Telecom.* carrier-operated device anti-noise

CODASYL ('kəʊdəsɪl) *Computing* Conference on Data Systems Languages

codec ('kəʊdɛk) *Computing* coder-decoder

Codesh ('kəʊdɛʃ) Convention for a Democratic South Africa

co-ed (,kəʊ'ɛd) coeducational

CoEnCo Committee for Environmental Conservation

C of A Certificate of Airworthiness

C of C Chamber of Commerce

C of E Church of England · Council of Europe

C of I Church of Ireland

C of M *Aeronautics* Certificate of Maintenance

C of S Chief of Staff · Church of Scotland

cog. cognate

CoG (*or* **c.o.g.**) centre of gravity

COGB certified official government business

COHSE (*or* **Cohse**)

('kaʊzɪ) Confederation of Health Service Employees

COI Central Office of Information

col. collect(ed) • collector • college • collegiate • colonial • colour(ed) • column

Col. Colombia(n) • Colonel • Colorado • *Bible* Colossians

COL computer-oriented language • cost of living

coll. collateral • colleague • collect(ed) • collection • collector • (*or* **Coll.**) college • collegiate • colloquial(ism) • *Med.* collyrium (eyewash)

collab. (in) collaboration (with)

collat. collateral(ly)

collect. collective(ly)

colloq. colloquial(ly) • colloquialism

coll'ott. (*or* **col 8ᵛᵃ**) *Music* coll'ottava (Italian: in octaves)

collr collector

Colo. Colorado

Coloss. *Bible* Colossians

cols columns

Col-Sergt (*or* **Col-Sgt**) Colour-Sergeant

com. comedy • comic • commerce • commercial • commission(er) • commit-

tee • common(ly) • commune • communication(s)

Com. Commander • Commissioner • Committee • Commodore • Communist

COM computer output on microfilm (*or* microfiche)

COMA (*or* **Coma**) ('kaʊmə) Committee on Medical Aspects of Food Policy

COMAL ('kaʊmæl) *Computing* common algorithmic language

comb. combination • combining • combustion

Comdg *Military* Commanding

Comdr *Military* Commander

Comdt *Military* Commandant

COMECON ('kɒmɪˌkɒn) Council for Mutual Economic Assistance

Comet (*or* **COMET**) ('kɒmɪt) Committee for Middle East Trade

COMEX ('kaʊˌmɛks) (USA) Commodity Exchange (New York)

Cominform ('kɒmɪnˌtɔːm) Communist Information Bureau

COMINT ('kɒmɪnt) communications intelligence

Comintern ('kɒmɪnˌtɜːn) Communist International

coml commercial

comm. commentary • commerce • commercial(ly) • committee • commonwealth • communication

commem. commemoration

Commissr (or **Commr**) Commissioner

Commn Commission

Commnd Military Commissioned

Commy Commissary

COMO Committee of Marketing Organizations

comp. companion • comparative • compare • compensation • compilation • compiled • compiler • complete • composition • compositor • compound(ed) • comprehensive • comprising

Comp Companion (of an institution; as in **CompIMechE**, Institution of Mechanical Engineers)

compar. comparative • comparison

Comp-Gen Comptroller-General

compo. composition

Comr Commissioner

comsat ('kɒmsæt) communications satellite

Com. Ver. Common Version (of the Bible)

Comy-Gen Commissary-General

con. concerto • conclusion • conjunx (Latin: wife) • connection • consolidate(d) • continue(d) • contra (Latin: against) • convenience • conversation

Con. Conformist • Conservative • Finance Consols • Consul • Music contralto

conc. concentrate(d) • concentration • concerning • concerto

con. cr. Book-keeping contra credit

cond. (or **condr**) conductor

conf. Med. confection • confer (Latin: compare) • conference • confessor

Confed. Confederacy • Confederate • Confederation

cong. Pharmacol. congius (Latin: gallon) • congregation(ist)

Cong. Congregational(ist) • Congress • Congressional

con. inv. consular invoice

conj. conjugation • conjunction • conjunctive

conn. connect(ed) • connection • connotation

Conn. Connecticut

cons. conservation • *Med.* conserve • consigned • consignment • consolidated • consonant • constable • constitution(al) • construction • consul • consult(ing)

Cons. Conservative • Conservatoire (*or* Conservatorium, Conservatory) • Constable • Constitution • Consul

con. sec. conic section

Conserv. Conservatoire (*or* Conservatorium, Conservatory)

consgt consignment

Consols ('kɒnsɒlz) consolidated annuities (*or* stock)

const. constable • constant • (*or* **Const.**) constitution

constr. construct(ion) • construe

cont. container • containing • contents • (*or* **Cont.**) continent(al) • continue(d) • (*or* **cont**) *Music* continuo • contra (Latin: against) • contract • contraction • control(ler)

contd continued

contemp. contemporary

contg containing

contr. contract(s) • contracted • contraction • contralto • contrary • contrast(ed) • control(ler)

contr. bon. mor. contra bonos mores (Latin: contrary to good manners)

contrib. contributing • contribution • contributor

CONUS continental United States

conv. convention(al) • convertible

Conv. Convocation

co-op. (*or* **coop.**) cooperative

cop. copper • copyright(ed)

Cop. Copernican • Coptic

COP *Thermodynamics* coefficient of performance

COPA Comité des organisations professionnelles agricoles de la CE (French: Committee of Agricultural Organizations in the EC)

COPD chronic obstructive pulmonary disease

Copec ('kɒpɛk) Conference on Christian Politics, Economics, and Citizenship

Copt. Coptic

COPUS (*or* **Copus**) ('kəʊpəs) Committee on the Public Understanding of Science

cor. corner • cornet • coroner • corpus (Latin: the body) • correct(ed) • correction • correlative • correspondence • correspondent • corresponding

Cor. *Bible* Corinthians

CORE (kɔː) (USA) Congress of Racial Equality

CORGI ('kɔːgɪ) Confederation for Registration of Gas Installers

Cor. Mem. Corresponding Member

Corn. Cornish • Cornwall

corol. (*or* **coroll.**) corollary

Corp. (*or* **Corpl**) Corporal • (*or* **Corpn**) Corporation

corr. correct(ed) • correction • corrective • correspond(ent) • correspondence • corresponding • corrupt(ed) • corruption

correl. correlative

corresp. correspondence

Corresp. Mem. Corresponding Member

Cor. Sec. Corresponding Secretary

cos (kɒz) *Maths.* cosine

c.o.s. *Commerce* cash on shipment

Cos. (*or* **cos.**) Companies • Counties

COS *Commerce* cash on shipment • Charity Organization Society • (*or* **CoS**) Chief of Staff

COSA Colliery Officials and Staffs Association

cosec ('kəʊsɛk) *Maths.* cosecant

cosech ('kəʊʃɛk) *Maths.* hyperbolic cosecant

cosh (kɒʃ) *Maths.* hyperbolic cosine

COSHH Control of Substances Hazardous to Health

CoSIRA (kəʊ'saɪrə) Council for Small Industries in Rural Areas

COSLA (*or* **Cosla**) ('kɒzlə) Convention of Scottish Local Authorities

cosmog. cosmography

COSPAR ('kəʊ,spɑː) Committee on Space Research

Coss. Consules (Latin: Consuls)

COSSAC Chief of Staff to Supreme Allied Commander

cot (kɒt) *Maths.* cotangent

cotan (ˈkəʊˌtæn) *Maths.* cotangent

COTE (*or* **Cote**) Committee for the Accreditation of Teacher Education

coth (kɒθ) *Maths.* hyperbolic cotangent

COV (*or* **Cov**) *Statistics* covariance • *Genetics* crossover value

covers (ˈkəʊvɜːs) *Maths.* coversed sine

Coy. *Military* company

cp. compare

c.p. candlepower

CP Canadian Pacific (Railway) • Canadian Press • (South Africa) Cape Province • *Surveying* change point • chemically pure • Chief Patriarch • Clerk of the Peace • College of Preceptors • colour printing (as in **CP filter**) • *Military* Command Post • commercial paper • Common Pleas • Common Prayer • Communist Party • Community Programme (employment scheme) • corpo-

ral punishment • Court of Probate

CPA (USA) Certified Public Accountant • Chartered Patent Agent • *Insurance* claims payable abroad • Commonwealth Parliamentary Association

CPAC Consumer Protection Advisory Committee

CPAG Child Poverty Action Group

CPAS Church Pastoral Aid Society

CPB Communist Party of Britain

CPC Clerk of the Privy Council • *Med.* clinicopathological conference • Communist Party of China • Conservative Political Centre

cpd compound

CPGB Communist Party of Great Britain

c.p.h. cycles per hour

CPH Certificate in Public Health

CPhys Chartered Physicist

cpi *Printing* characters per inch

Cpl *Military* Corporal

CPL Commercial Pilot's Licence

CPM Colonial Police Medal

CP/M *Computing, trademark* Control Program Monitor

CPO Chief Petty Officer • compulsory purchase order • County Planning Officer

CPP current purchasing power (in **CPP accounting**)

CPR Canadian Pacific Railway • *Med.* cardiopulmonary resuscitation

CPRE Council for the Protection of Rural England

CPRS Central Policy Review Staff

cps *Computing* characters per second • *Physics* cycles per second

CPS Centre for Policy Studies • cents per share • Crown Prosecution Service • Custos Privati Sigilli (Latin: Keeper of the Privy Seal)

CPSA Civil and Public Services Association (clerical civil servants' union)

CPSU (formerly) Communist Party of the Soviet Union

CPsychol Chartered Psychologist

CPU (*or* **c.p.u.**) *Computing* central processing unit • Commonwealth Press Union

CQ *Military* charge of quarters

CQSW Certificate of Qualification in Social Work

cr. (*or* **Cr.**) credit(or) • crown

Cr *Chem.*, symbol for chromium • Councillor

CR Carolina Regina (Latin: Queen Caroline) • Carolus Rex (Latin: King Charles) • carriage return • carrier's risk • cash receipts • Civis Romanus (Latin: Roman citizen) • *Anglican Church* Community of the Resurrection • company's risk • *Med.* complete regression (*or* remission) • *Psychol.* conditioned reflex (*or* response) • Costa Rica (abbrev. *or* IVR) • credit report • *Statistics* critical ratio • *postcode for* Croydon • current rate • Custos Rotulorum (Latin: Keeper of the Rolls)

CRA Commander of the Royal Artillery

CRAC Careers Research and Advisory Centre

CRAeS Companion of

the Royal Aeronautical Society

CRAMRA Convention on the Regulation of Antarctic Mineral Resource Activities

CRASC Commander of the Royal Army Service Corps

CRC *Printing* camera-ready copy • Cancer Research Campaign • Community Relations Council • *Computing* cyclic redundancy check (*or* code)

CRCP Certificant of the Royal College of Physicians

CRCS Certificant of the Royal College of Surgeons

CRE Commander of the Royal Engineers • Commercial Relations and Exports • Commission for Racial Equality

cres. (*or* **cresc.**) *Music* crescendo

Cres. Crescent (in street names)

CRF *Finance* capital recovery factor

CRIB Current Research in Britain (publication)

crim. criminal

crim. con. *Law* criminal conversation (i.e. adultery)

crit. critic • critical(ly) • criticism

CRMF Cancer Relief Macmillan Fund

CRMP Corps of Royal Military Police

CRNCM Companion of the Royal Northern College of Music

CRO cathode-ray oscilloscope (*or* oscillograph) • community relations officer • Criminal Records Office

CRP (India) Central Reserve Police

CRT cathode-ray tube • composite rate tax

cryst. crystalline • (*or* **crystallog.**) crystallography

cs. case

c.s. capital stock

c/s cases • cycles per second

Cs *Chem., symbol for* caesium

CS capital stock • Chartered Surveyor • Chemical Society • Chief of Staff • Christian Science (*or* Scientist) • Civil Service • Clerk to the Signet • Court of Session • *international vehicle registration for* Czechoslovakia • *see* CS gas

C/S cycles per second

CSA Confederate States of America

CSB Bachelor of Christian Science • *Med.* chemical stimulation of the brain

CSBM *Military* Confidence- and Security-Building Measures

csc *Maths.* cosecant

CSC Civil Service Commission • Congregation of the Holy Cross • Conspicuous Service Cross (replaced by the DSC)

CSCE Conference on Security and Cooperation in Europe

CSD Chartered Society of Designers • Civil Service Department • Cooperative Secretaries Diploma

CSE Certificate of Secondary Education (replaced by General Certificate of Secondary Education, GCSE)

CSEU Confederation of Shipbuilding and Engineering Unions

CSF *Med.* cerebrospinal fluid • *Med.* colony-stimulating factor (as in **G-CSF**, granulocyte CSF)

CSG Companion of the Order of the Star of Ghana

CS gas *indicating* a tear gas (surname initials of its US inventors, Ben Carson and Roger Staughton)

CSI *Image technol.* compact source iodide (as in **CSI lamp**) • Companion of the Order of the Star of India

CSIRO Commonwealth Scientific and Industrial Research Organization (Australia)

CSM cerebrospinal meningitis • Committee on Safety of Medicines • Company Sergeant-Major

CSO Central Statistical Office • Chief Scientific Officer • Chief Signal Officer • Chief Staff Officer • *Image technol.* colour separation overlay • community service order

CSP Chartered Society of Physiotherapists (*or* Physiotherapy) • Civil Service of Pakistan • Council for Scientific Policy

CSR combat-stress reaction

CSS Certificate in Social Service • (*or* **CSSp**) (member of the) Congregation of the Holy Ghost (Sanctus Spiritus); Holy Ghost Father • Council for Science and Society

CSSB Civil Service Selection Board

CSSR *RC Church* Congregatio Sanctissimi Redemptoris (Latin: Congregation of the Most Holy Redeemer; Redemptorists)

CST (USA) Central Standard Time

CSTI Council of Science and Technology Institutes

CStJ Commander of the Most Venerable Order of the Hospital of St John of Jerusalem

CSU *Med.* catheter specimen of urine • Christlich-Soziale Union (Christian Social Union; German political party) • Civil Service Union

CSV community service volunteer

CSYS (Scotland) Certificate of Sixth Year Studies

ct carat • caught • cent • court • crate

ct. centum (Latin: hundred) • certificate

Ct. Connecticut • Count • (or **Ct**) *Music* countertenor • Court

CT cable transfer • *postcode for* Canterbury • *Med.* cell therapy • (USA) Central Time • *Med.* computerized (*or* computed) tomography (as in **CT scanner**) • *US postcode for* Connecticut • corporation tax • counter trade

CTC city technology college • Commando Training Centre • crushing, tearing, and curling (machine) • Cyclists' Touring Club

CText Chartered Textile Technologist

CTF coal-tar fuels

ctge cartage • cartridge

CTL *Insurance* constructive total loss

CTM *Med.* computerized (*or* computed) tomographic myelography

ctn carton • *Maths.* cotangent

CTO *Philately* cancelled to order (of postage stamps)

CTOL ('siːtɒl) conventional takeoff and landing

ctr. centre

CTR controlled thermonuclear research

cts centimes • cents • certificates • crates

CTS Catholic Truth Society • *Med.* computerized (*or* computed) tomographic scanner

CTT capital-transfer tax

CTV cable television • Canadian Television Network Limited

CTZ control traffic zone (around an aerodrome or airport)

cu. cubic

Cu *Chem.*, symbol for copper (Latin *cuprum*)

CU Cambridge University • *Photog.* close-up

cub. cubic

CUF common university fund

cum. *Finance* cumulative

cum div. *Finance* cum dividend (i.e. with dividend)

cum. pref. *Finance* cumulative preference (shares)

CUNA Credit Union National Association

CUP Cambridge University Press • *symbol for* Cuban peso (monetary unit)

cur. currency • current

cur. adv. vult *Law* curia advisari vult (*see under* CAV)

curt. current (i.e. this month)

CUSO ('kju:səʊ) Canadian University Services Overseas

CUTS (kʌts) Computer Users' Tape System

c.v. cheval-vapeur (French: horsepower) • curriculum vitae

CV calorific value • *Med.* cardiovascular • Common Version (of the Bible) • *Finance* convertible • *postcode for* Coventry • (Canada) Cross of Valour • curriculum vitae

2CV 2 cheval-vapeur (deux chevaux; two-horse-power French car)

CVA *Med.* cerebrovascular accident

CVCP Committee of Vice-Chancellors and Principals (of the Universities of the United Kingdom)

c.v.d. *Commerce* cash versus documents

CVD *Electronics* chemical vapour deposition

CVEsc *symbol for* escudo (monetary unit of Cape Verde)

CVI *Med.* common variable immunodeficiency

CVJ constant velocity joint (in vehicles)

CVO Commander of the Royal Victorian Order

C.voc. *Music* colla voce

(Italian: with the voice; instruction to accompanist)

CVS *Med.*, *Zoology* cardiovascular system • *Med.* chorionic villus sampling • Council of Voluntary Service

CVSNA Council of Voluntary Service National Association

CVT constant variable transmission (in vehicles)

cw. clockwise

c.w. *Physics* carrier wave

CW chemical weapons (*or* warfare) • Cockcroft–Walton (as in **CW generator**) • continuous wave(s) (as in **CW radar**; also indicating Morse code, as in **CW speed**) • *postcode for* Crewe • *Physics* Curie–Weiss (in **CW law**)

CWA Crime Writers' Association

CWGC Commonwealth War Graves Commission

Cwlth Commonwealth

c.w.o. cash with order

CWO Chief Warrant Officer

CWS Cooperative Wholesale Society • Court Welfare Service

cwt *symbol for* hundredweight

cx *Med.* cervix

cy capacity • currency • *Chem.*, *symbol for* cyanide (in formulae) • cycle(s)

CY calendar year • *international vehicle registration for* Cyprus

cyc. (*or* **cyclo.**) cyclopedia

cyl. cylinder • cylindrical

Cym. Cymric

Cys (*or* **cys**) *Biochem.* cysteine

Cz *Geology* Cenozoic

CZ Canal Zone

Czech. Czechoslovak • Czechoslovakia(n)

D

d *symbol for* day • *symbol for* deci- (prefix indicating 0.1, as in **dB**, decibel) • *Physics,* symbol for deuteron • (ital.) *Chem.* dextrorotatory (as in **d-tartaric acid**) • (ital.) *symbol for* diameter • *Music* doh (in tonic sol-fa) • (ital.) *symbol for* relative density • (ital.) *symbol for* thickness • *Maths.,* indicating a small increment in a given variable or function (as in **d**y/**d**x) • *indicating* the fourth vertical row of squares from the left on a chessboard

d. dam (in animal pedigrees) • date • daughter • day • *Dentistry* deciduous • degree • delete • depart(s) • diameter • died • dime • *Currency* dinar(s) (*see also under* D; DA; Din; JD) • dividend • dollar(s) (symbol **$**) • *Med.* dose • *Currency* drachma(s) (*see also under* Dr) • (formerly) penny *or* pennies (Latin *denarius*)

D (ital.) *Physics, Med.,* symbol for absorbed dose (of radiation) • *symbol for* dalasi (Gambian monetary unit) • defence (in **D notice**) • *Chem., symbol for* deuterium • (ital.) *symbol for* diameter • *symbol for* dinar (Tunisian monetary unit) • *symbol for* dong (Vietnamese monetary unit) • (ital.) *Aeronautics, symbol for* drag • (bold ital.) *Physics, symbol for* electric flux density (*or* displacement) • *Roman numeral for* five hundred • *international vehicle registration or civil aircraft marking for* Germany • *Maths.,* indicating the first derivative of a function (in **D operator**) • (small cap.) *Chem.,* indicating an optically active compound having a configuration related to dextrorotatory glyceraldehyde (as in **D-glucose**) • *indicating* a musical note or key

D. (*or* **D**) December • (USA) Democrat(ic) • Deus (Latin: God) • *Cards* diamonds • Director • doctor • Dominus (Latin: God or Christ) • Don (Spanish title) • Duchess • Duke • Dutch

da *symbol for* deca- (prefix indicating 10, as in **dam**, decametre)

d/a *Commerce* days after acceptance • *Commerce* documents against acceptance

Da *Biochem., symbol for* dalton(s)

D/a deposit account • discharge afloat

DA *postcode for* Dartford • deed of arrangement • delayed action (bomb) • *symbol for* dinar (Algerian monetary unit) • Diploma in Anaesthesia (*or* Anaesthetics) • Diploma in Art • direct action • (USA) District Attorney • doesn't answer • duck's arse (hairstyle)

D/A *Commerce* days after acceptance • deposit account • (*or* **D-A**) *Computing, Electronics* digital-to-analogue • *Commerce* documents against acceptance (as in **D/A bill**)

DAA&QMG Deputy Assistant Adjutant and Quartermaster-General

DAAG Deputy Assistant Adjutant-General

DA&QMG Deputy Adjutant and Quartermaster-General

DAB digital audio broadcasting

DAc Doctor of Acupuncture

DAC Development Assistance Committee (of the OECD) • *Computing* digital-to-analogue converter

DACG Deputy Assistant Chaplain-General

DAD Deputy Assistant Director (as in **DADMS**, Deputy Assistant Director of Medical Services; **DADOS**, Deputy Assistant Director of Ordnance Services; **DADQ**, Deputy Assistant Director of Quartering; **DADST**, Deputy Assistant Director of Supplies and Transport)

DADG Deputy Assistant Director General (as in **DADGMS**, Deputy Assistant Director General of Medical Services)

DAdmin Doctor of Administration

DAE (ital.) Dictionary of American English

DAFS Department of Agriculture and Fisheries for Scotland

DAG Deputy Adjutant-General

DAGMAR ('dægmɑː) *Commerce* defining advertising goals for measured advertising results

DAgr Doctor of Agriculture

Dak. Dakota

dal *symbol for* decalitre(s)

dam *symbol for* decametre(s)

DAMS Deputy Assistant Military Secretary

Dan. *Bible* Daniel • Danish

D&AD Designers and Art Directors Association

D&B discipline and bondage

D & C *Med.* dilatation and curettage (of the uterus)

d and d drunk and disorderly

D & D death and dying

D and V *Med.* diarrhoea and vomiting

d.a.p. documents against payment

DAP *Computing* distributed array processor

DAP&E Diploma in Applied Parasitology and Entomology

DAppSc Doctor of Applied Science

DAQMG Deputy Assistant Quartermaster-General

DAR Daughters of the American Revolution

DArt Doctor of Art

d.a.s. *Commerce* delivered alongside ship

DASc Doctor of Agricultural Science(s)

dat. dative

DAT *Med.* dementia of the Alzheimer type • digital audio tape

DATEC ('deɪtɛk) Art and Design Committee, Technician Education Council

Datel ('deɪ,tɛl) *Trademark* data telex (data transmission service)

DATV digitally assisted television

dau. daughter

DAvMed Diploma in Aviation Medicine

DAX *Stock exchange* Deutsche Aktienindex (German share price index)

d.b. *Music* double bass

dB *symbol for* decibel(s)

Db *symbol for* dobra (monetary unit of São Tomé and Príncipe)

DB Bachelor of Divinity (Latin *Divinitatis Baccalaureus*) • (*or* **D/B**) Book-

keeping daybook • *Radio, Television* delayed broadcast • (Germany) Deutsche Bundesbank (German Federal Bank) • Domesday Book

dBA (*or* **dBa**) *symbol for* decibel A (decibels above reference noise, adjusted: unit for measuring noise)

DBA Doctor of Business Administration • (*or* **d.b.a.**) doing business as (*or* at)

DBC Deaf Broadcasting Council

DBE Dame Commander of the Order of the British Empire

DBib Douay Bible

dbk drawback

dbl. (*or* **dble**) double

DBMS *Computing* database management system

DBO Diploma of the British Orthoptic Board

DBS direct broadcast(ing by) satellite

DC *Music* da capo (Italian: from the head; i.e. repeat from the beginning) • Daughters of Charity of St Vincent de Paul • (*or* **DC.**) *Botany* de Candolle (indicating the author of a species, etc.) • Detective Con-

stable • (*or* **d.c.**) *Physics* direct current • District Commissioner • district council • District of Columbia (abbrev. *or* postcode) • Doctor of Chiropractic • *Commerce* documents (against) cash • Douglas Commercial (aircraft, as in **DC10**) • *Theatre* down centre (of stage)

D/C *Marine insurance* deviation clause

DCAe Diploma of the College of Aeronautics

DCAS Deputy Chief of the Air Staff

DCB Dame Commander of the Order of the Bath

DCC digital compact cassette • Diploma of Chelsea College

DCE *Computing* data-communication equipment • domestic credit expansion

DCF *Accounting* discounted cash flow

DCG Deputy Chaplain-General

DCGS Deputy Chief of the General Staff

DCh Doctor of Surgery (Latin *Doctor Chirurgiae*)

DCH Diploma in Child Health

DChD Doctor of Dental Surgery

DChE Doctor of Chemical Engineering

DCI Detective Chief Inspector • (*or* **d.c.i.**) double column inch (in advertisements)

DCL Doctor of Civil Law

DCLI Duke of Cornwall's Light Infantry

DCLJ Dame Commander of the Order of St Lazarus of Jerusalem

DCM Diploma in Community Medicine • *Military* Distinguished Conduct Medal

DCMG Dame Commander of the Order of St Michael and St George

DCnL Doctor of Canon Law

DCO Duke of Cambridge's Own (regiment)

DComm Doctor of Commerce

DCP Diploma in Conservation of Paintings • Diploma in Clinical Pathology

DCPath Diploma of the College Pathologists

DCR Diploma of the College of Radiographers (as in **DCR(MU)**, medical ultrasound; **DCR(NM)**, nuclear medicine; **DCR(R)**, diagnostic radiography; **DCR(T)**, radiotherapy)

DCrim Doctor of Criminology

DCS Deputy Chief of Staff • Deputy Clerk of Sessions • digital camera system • Doctor of Christian Science • Doctor of Commercial Sciences

DCSO Deputy Chief Scientific Officer

DCT Doctor of Christian Theology

DCVO Dame Commander of the Royal Victorian Order

dd dated • delivered

d.d. days after date • delayed delivery • *Commerce* delivered dock • demand draft • dry dock • today's date (Latin *de dato*)

D/d days after date • *Commerce* delivered

DD *Insurance* damage done • *Banking* demand draft • *Finance* direct debit • dishonourable discharge • Doctor of Divinity • *Med.* Duchenne dystrophy • *postcode for* Dundee

D/D demand draft • dock dues

DDA Dangerous Drugs Act

D-Day Day Day (the specified day, i.e. 6 June 1944, for the Allied invasion of Europe)

DDC Dewey Decimal Classification (of library books) • *Med.* dideoxycytidine (Aids treatment) • *Computing* direct digital control

DDD deadline delivery date

DDE dynamic data exchange

DDGAMS Deputy Director-General, Army Medical Services

DDI (*or* **ddI**) *Med.* dideoxyinosine (Aids treatment)

DDL *Computing* data description language(s) • Deputy Director of Labour

DDM Diploma in Dermatological Medicine

DDME Deputy Director of Mechanical Engineering

DDMI Deputy Director of Military Intelligence

DDMOI Deputy Director of Military Operations and Intelligence

DDMS Deputy Director of Medical Services

DDMT Deputy Director of Military Training

DDNI Deputy Director of Naval Intelligence

DDO Diploma in Dental Orthopaedics • District Dental Officer

DDPH Diploma in Dental Public Health

DDPR Deputy Director of Public Relations

DDPS Deputy Director of Personal Services

DDR Deutsche Demokratische Republik (German Democratic Republic *or* East Germany; now part of Germany) • Diploma in Diagnostic Radiology

DDRA Deputy Director, Royal Artillery

DDRD Deputy Directorate of Research and Development

dd/s delivered sound

DDS Dewey Decimal System (library-book classification) • Director of Dental Services • (*or* **DDSc**) Doctor of Dental Science • Doctor of Dental Surgery

DDSD Deputy Director of Staff Duties

DDSM (USA) Defense Distinguished Service Medal

DDST Deputy Director of Supplies and Transport

DDT dichlorodiphenyl-trichloroethane (insecticide)

DDVP dimethyldichloro-vinyl phosphate (dichlorvos; insecticide)

DDWE&M Deputy Director of Works, Electrical and Mechanical

d.e. *Book-keeping* double entry

DE *US postcode for* Delaware • Department of Employment • *postcode for* Derby • Doctor of Engineering

Dea. Deacon

DEA Department of Economic Affairs (former UK government department)

deb. *Finance* debenture • debit

dec. deceased • declaration • *Grammar* declension • decrease • *Music* decrescendo (Italian; decrease loudness)

Dec. (*or* Dec) December

decd deceased

decl. *Grammar* declension

DEconSc Doctor of Economic Science

decresc. *Music* decrescendo (Italian; decrease loudness)

ded. dedicate(d) • dedication

DEd Doctor of Education

def. defective • defence • defendant • deferred • definite • definition

DEFCON ('def,kɒn) *Military* defence readiness condition

deft. defendant

deg. degree

DEHA di-2-ethylhexyl adipate (plasticizer in clingfilm)

DEI Dutch East Indies (former name for Indonesia)

del. delegate • delete

Del. Delaware

deld. delivered

deleg. delegate

dem. demand • demurrage

Dem. (USA) Democrat(ic)

DEME Directorate of Electrical and Mechanical Engineering

DEMS defensively equipped merchant ships

DemU (Northern Ireland) Democratic Unionist

den. denier

Den. Denmark

DEn (*or* **D.En.**) Department of Energy

DEN District Enrolled Nurse

DEng (*or* **DEngg**) Doctor of Engineering

DEngS Doctor of Engineering Science

denom. *Religion* denomination

dent. dental • dentist(ry)

DEOVR Duke of Edinburgh's Own Volunteer Rifles

dep. depart(s) • departure • deponent • depose(d) • deposit • depot • (*or* **Dep.**) deputy

DEP Department of Employment and Productivity

dept department

dept. deputy

der. derivation • derivative

Derby. Derbyshire

deriv. derivation • derivative • derive(d)

DERL derived emergency reference level (of radiation)

Des. Designer

DES *Computing* data encryption standard • Department of Education and Science

desc. descendant

DesRCA Designer of the Royal College of Art

destn destination

det. detach • detachment •

detail • determine • *Med.* detur (Latin: let it be given)

Det Detective (as in **Det Con**, Detective Constable; **Det Insp**, Detective Inspector; **Det Sgt**, Detective Sergeant; **Det Supt**, Detective Superintendent)

DET diethyltryptamine (hallucinogenic drug)

Deut. *Bible* Deuteronomy

DEW (dju:) *Military* distant early-warning (as in **DEW line**; network of radar stations)

df. draft

d.f. *Commerce* dead freight

DF Defender of the Faith • (*or* **D/F**) *Telecom.* direction finder (*or* finding) • *symbol for* Djibouti franc (monetary unit) • Doctor of Forestry

DFA Doctor of Fine Arts

DFC Distinguished Flying Cross

DFHom Diploma of the Faculty of Homeopathy

DFLS Day Fighter Leaders' School

DFM Distinguished Flying Medal

dft defendant • draft

dg *symbol for* decigram(s)

DG Deo gratias (Latin:

thanks be to God) • Director-General • Dragoon Guards • *postcode for* Dumfries

DGAA Distressed Gentlefolks Aid Association

DGAMS Director-General, Army Medical Services

DGEME Director-General, Electrical and Mechanical Engineering

DGMS Director-General of Medical Services

DGMT Director-General of Military Training

DGMW Director-General of Military Works

DGNPS Director-General of Naval Personal Services

DGO Diploma in Gynaecology and Obstetrics

DGP Director-General of Personnel

DGPS Director-General of Personal Services

DGS Diploma in Graduate Studies

Dh *symbol for* dirham (monetary unit of United Arab Emirates)

DH *Sport* dead heat • Department of Health • *symbol for* dirham (Moroccan monetary unit) • Doctor of Hu-

manities • *postcode for* Durham

DHA District Health Authority

Dhc Doctor honoris causa (honorary doctorate)

DHL Doctor of Hebrew Letters (*or Literature*) • Doctor of Humane Letters

DHMSA Diploma in the History of Medicine (Society of Apothecaries)

DHQ district (*or divisional*) headquarters

DHSS Department of Health and Social Security (former government department, now split into the DoH and DSS)

DHumLit Doctor of Humane Letters

DHyg Doctor of Hygiene

di. diameter

Di *Chem., symbol for* didymium

DI Department of the Interior • Detective Inspector • *Med.* donor insemination

dia. diameter

diag. diagram

dial. dialect(al)

diam. diameter

DIANE (dar'æn) Direct Information Access Network for Europe

DIAS Dublin Institute of Advanced Sciences

DIC Diploma of Membership of the Imperial College of Science and Technology (London)

dict. dictation • dictator • dictionary

dicta. dictaphone

DICTA Diploma of Imperial College of Tropical Agriculture

diff. differ • difference • different • differential

dig. digest (book or summary) • digit(al)

DIG Deputy Inspector-General

DIH Diploma in Industrial Health

dil. dilute(d)

DIL *Electronics* dual in-line (as in **DIL switch**)

dim. dimension • *Music* diminuendo • diminutive

Din *symbol for* dinar (Yugoslavian monetary unit)

DIN Deutsches Institut für Normung (German national standards organization; as in **DIN connector**, etc.)

DIng Doctor of Engineering (Latin *Doctor Ingeniariae*)

dinky (*or* **Dink, DINK**) ('dɪŋkɪ *or* dɪŋk) *Colloquial* double (*or* dual) income, no kids (used of couples)

dio. diocese

dioc. diocesan • diocese

dip. diploma

Dip (dɪp) Diploma (in degrees and qualifications)

DIP (dɪp) *Electronics* dual in-line package

DipAD Diploma in Art and Design

DipAe Diploma in Aeronautics

DipASE Diploma in Advanced Study of Education, College of Preceptors

DipAvMed Diploma of Aviation Medicine, Royal College of Physicians

DipBA Diploma in Business Administration

DipBS Diploma in Fine Art, Byam Shaw School

DipCAM Diploma in Communication, Advertising, and Marketing of CAM Foundation

DipCD Diploma in Child Development • Diploma in Civic Design

DipCE Diploma in Civil Engineering

DipChemEng Diploma in Chemical Engineering

DipCom Diploma in Commerce

DipEcon Diploma in Economics

DipEd Diploma in Education

DipEl Diploma in Electronics

DipESL Diploma in English as a Second Language

DipEth Diploma in Ethnology

DipFD Diploma in Funeral Directing

DipFE Diploma in Further Education

DipGSM Diploma in Music, Guildhall School of Music and Drama

DipHA Diploma in Hospital Administration

DipHE Diploma in Higher Education

DipHum Diploma in Humanities

dipl. diploma · diplomat(ic)

DipLA Diploma in Landscape Architecture

DipLib Diploma of Librarianship

DipM Diploma in Marketing

DipMet Diploma in Metallurgy

DipN Diploma in Nursing

DipNEd Diploma in Nursery School Education

DipPharmMed Diploma in Pharmaceutical Medicine

DipREM Diploma in Rural Estate Management

DipSoc Diploma in Sociology

DipTA Diploma in Tropical Agriculture

DipT&CP Diploma in Town and Country Planning

DipTech Diploma in Technology

DipTh Diploma in Theology

DipTP Diploma in Town Planning

DipTPT Diploma in Theory and Practice of Teaching

dir. direct(ed) · direction · *Currency* dirham (*see also under* Dh; DH)

DIR *Photog.* developer inhibitor release

dis. discharge · discount

disb. disbursement

disc. discount · discover(ed)

dismac ('dɪs,mæk) *Military* digital scene-matching area correlation sensors

dist. distant • distinguish(ed) • district

distr. distribution • distributor

DistTP Distinction in Town Planning

DIT double income tax (in **DIT relief**)

div (dɪv) *Maths.* divergence

div. divide(d) • dividend • division • divorce(d)

DIY (*or* **d.i.y.**) do-it-yourself ;

DJ (*or* **d.j.**) dinner jacket • (*or* **d.j.**) disc jockey • Doctor of Law (Latin *Doctor Juris*)

DJAG Deputy Judge Advocate-General

DJI *Finance* (USA) Dow Jones Index

DJIA *Finance* (USA) Dow Jones Industrial Average

DJS Doctor of Juridical Science

DJT Doctor of Jewish Theology

DJur Doctor of Law (Latin *Doctor Juris*)

dk dark • deck • dock

DK *international vehicle registration for* Denmark

Dkr *symbol for* krone (monetary unit of Denmark and Greenland)

dkyd dockyard

dl (*or* **dL**) *symbol for* decilitre(s)

DL *postcode for* Darlington • Deputy Lieutenant • diesel • *Theatre* down left (of stage)

D/L demand loan

DLC Diploma of Loughborough College • *Theatre* down left centre (of stage)

dld. delivered

DLES Doctor of Letters in Economic Studies

DLI Durham Light Infantry

DLit Doctor of Literature

DLitt Doctor of Letters (Latin *Doctor Litterarum*)

DLittS Doctor of Sacred Letters

DLJ Dame of Justice of the Order of St Lazarus of Jerusalem

DLO dead letter office (*see under* RLO) • Diploma in Laryngology and Otology (*or* Otorhinolaryngology) • (*or* **d.l.o.**) dispatch (money payable) loading only

dlr dealer

DLR Docklands Light Railway

DLS (*or* **DLSc**) Doctor of Library Science

dly daily

dm *symbol for* decimetre(s)

DM (ital.) Daily Mail • *symbol for* Deutschmark (German monetary unit) • direct mail • Doctor of Medicine

DMA Diploma in Municipal Administration • *Computing* direct memory access

DMAC *Television* duobinary multiplexed analogue component

D-mark Deutschmark

DMC district medical committee

DMD Doctor of Medical Dentistry (*or* Dental Medicine) • *Med.* Duchenne muscular dystrophy

DME Diploma in Mechanical Engineering

DMet Doctor of Metallurgy

DMI Director of Military Intelligence

DMin Doctor of Ministry

DMJ Diploma in Medical Jurisprudence

DMJ(Path) Diploma in Medical Jurisprudence (Pathology)

DML Doctor of Modern Languages

DMLJ Dame of Merit of the Order of St Lazarus of Jerusalem

DMO Director of Military Operations • district medical officer

DMR Diploma in Medical Radiology

DMRD Diploma in Medical Radiological Diagnosis

DMRE (*or* **DMR&E**) Diploma in Medical Radiology and Electrology

DMRT Diploma in Medical Radiotherapy

DMS Diploma in Management Studies • Director of Medical Services • Doctor of Medical Science • Doctor of Medicine and Surgery

DMSO *Med.* dimethylsulphoxide (used in ointments)

DMSSB Direct Mail Services Standard Board

DMT dimethyltryptamine (hallucinogenic drug) • Director of Military Training

DMU *Commerce* decision-making unit (within an organization) • directly managed unit (of NHS hospitals)

DMus Doctor of Music

DMZ demilitarized zone

DN (or **D/N**) debit note • de novo (Latin: from the beginning) • Diploma in Nursing • *postcode for* Doncaster

DNA *Genetics* deoxyribonucleic acid • District Nursing Association

DNB (ital.) Dictionary of National Biography

DNC *Computing* distributed numerical control

DNE Diploma in Nursing Education • Director of Naval Equipment

DNF (or **dnf**) did not finish (of competitors in a race)

DNI Director of Naval Intelligence

DNOC dinitro-*o*-cresol (pesticide)

DNR *Med.* do not resuscitate

DNS Department for National Savings

do. ditto

DO *Finance* deferred ordinary (shares) • (or **d/o**) *Commerce* delivery order • Diploma in Ophthalmology • Diploma in Osteopathy • (or **d.o.**) *Grammar* direct object • (or **D/O**) *Commerce* direct order • dissolved oxygen • Doctor of Optometry • Doctor of Osteopathy

DOA *Med.* dead on arrival

DOAE Defence Operational Analysis Establishment (of the Ministry of Defence)

d.o.b. (or **DOB**) date of birth

DObstRCOG Diploma of the Royal College of Obstetricians and Gynaecologists

doc. document(s)

Doc. Doctor

DOC Denominazione di Origine Controllata (Italian: name of origin controlled; Italian wine classification) • District Officer Commanding

DocEng Doctor of Engineering

DOCG Denominazione di Origine Controllata Garantita (Italian: name of origin guaranteed controlled; Italian wine classification)

DOE (or **DoE**) Department of the Environment • (or **d.o.e.**) depends on experience (referring to salary in job advertisements) • (or **DoE**) Director of Education

DoH (or **DOH**) Department of Health

DOHC double (*or* dual) overhead camshaft

DOI (*or* **DoI**) Department of Industry

dol. *Music* dolce (Italian: sweetly; i.e. gently) • dollar

DOL Doctor of Oriental Learning

dom. domain • domestic • dominant • dominion

Dom. Dominica • *RC Church* Dominican • Dominus (Latin: Lord)

DOM Deo Optimo Maximo (Latin: to God, the best, the greatest) • *Colloquial* dirty old man • *international vehicle registration for* Dominican Republic

DOMS Diploma in Ophthalmic Medicine and Surgery

DON Diploma in Orthopaedic Nursing

DORA ('dɔːrə) Defence of the Realm Act (1914)

Dors. Dorset

DOrth Diploma in Orthodontics

DOS Director of Ordnance Services • (dɒs) *Computing* disk operating system • Doctor of Ocular Science

DoT Department of Transport

dow. (*or* **Dow.**) dowager

DOW (*or* **d.o.w.**) died of wounds

doz. dozen

d.p. *Med.* directione propria (Latin: with proper direction; in prescriptions) • direct port

DP data processing • delivery point • disabled person • displaced person • duty paid

D/P *Commerce* documents against payment (*or* presentation)

DPA Diploma in Public Administration • discharged prisoners' aid

DPB *Finance* deposit pass book

DPCM *Telecom.* differential pulse code modulation

DPD Data Protection Directive • Diploma in Public Dentistry

DPEc Doctor of Political Economy

DPed Doctor of Pedagogy

DPh Doctor of Philosophy

DPH Diploma in Public Health • Director of Public Health

DPhil ('di: 'fɪl) Doctor of Philosophy

DPhysMed Diploma in Physical Medicine

dpi *Computing* dots per inch

dpl. (*or* **DPL**) diplomat

DPM data-processing manager • Diploma in Psychological Medicine

DPMI *Computing* DOS Protected Mode Interface

DPP *Insurance* deferred payment plan • Director of Public Prosecutions

DPR Data Protection Register • Director of Public Relations

DPS Director of Personal Services • Director of Postal Services • dividend per share • Doctor of Public Service

dpt department • deposit • depot

DPT diphtheria, pertussis (whooping cough), tetanus (in **DPT vaccine**)

DPW Department of Public Works

dr debtor • *symbol for* dram

dr. debit • drachm • drachma (*see also under* Dr) • draw(n) • (*or* **Dr.**) drawer

Dr Director • Doctor • sym-

bol for drachma (Greek monetary unit) • Drive (in street names)

DR (USA) Daughters of the Revolution • *Navigation* dead reckoning • dining room • Diploma in Radiology • *Theatre* down right (of stage) • dry riser (pipe with attachment for fireman's hose)

D/R deposit receipt

DRAC Director, Royal Armoured Corps

DRAM (dræm) *Computing* dynamic random-access memory

DRAW (drɔ:) *Computing* direct read after write

DRC Diploma of the Royal College of Science and Technology, Glasgow • *Theatre* down right centre (of stage)

DRCOG Diploma of the Royal College of Obstetricians and Gynaecologists

DRCPath Diploma of the Royal College of Pathologists

DRD Diploma in Restorative Dentistry

DRDW *Computing* direct read during write

DRE Director of Religious Education • (*or* **DRelEd**)

Dr ing Doctor of Religious Education

Dr ing Doctor of Engineering

Dr jur Doctor of Laws

DRM Diploma in Radiation Medicine

DRO disablement resettlement officer

DrOecPol Doctor of Political Economics (Latin *Doctor Oeconomiae Politicae*)

DRP dividend reinvestment plan

Dr rer. nat. Doctor of Natural Science

DRS Diploma in Religious Studies

DRSAMD Diploma of the Royal Scottish Academy of Music and Drama

DRSE *Med.* drug-related side effects

d.s. date of service · daylight saving · days after sight · day's sight · document signed

DS *Music* dal segno (Italian: (repeat) from the sign) · *Finance* debenture stock · Detective Sergeant · Directing Staff · Doctor of Science · Doctor of Surgery · Down's syndrome · driver seated (in **DS vehicle**)

DSA Diploma in Social Administration

DSAC Defence Scientific Advisory Council

DSAO Diplomatic Service Administration Office

DSc Doctor of Science

DSC *Military* Distinguished Service Cross · Doctor of Surgical Chiropody

DSCHE Diploma of the Scottish Council for Health Education

DScMil Doctor of Military Science

DSD Director of Staff Duties

DSDP Deep-Sea Drilling Project

DSL Doctor of Sacred Letters

DSM *Military* Distinguished Service Medal · Doctor of Sacred Music

DSO *Military* (Companion of the) Distinguished Service Order

DSocSc Doctor of Social Science(s)

d.s.p. decessit sine prole (Latin: died without issue)

d.s.p.l. decessit sine prole legitima (Latin: died without legitimate issue)

DSR *Commerce* debt service ratio • *Med.* dynamic spatial reconstructor

Dss Deaconess

DSS Department of Social Security • Director of Social Services • Doctor of Holy (*or* Sacred) Scripture (Latin *Doctor Sacrae Scripturae*) • Doctor of Social Science

DSSc Diploma in Sanitary Science

DSSL document style specification language

DST Daylight Saving Time • deep-sleep therapy • Director of Supplies and Transport • Doctor of Sacred Theology • Double Summer Time

DStJ Dame of Justice (*or* of Grace) of the Order of St John of Jerusalem

dstn destination

D. Surg. Dental Surgeon

DSW Doctor of Social Welfare (*or* Work)

DT (ital.) Daily Telegraph • *Colloquial* (USA) detective • *postcode for* Dorchester (Dorset)

DTA Diploma in Tropical Agriculture

d.t.b.a. *Commerce* date to be advised

DTCD Diploma in Tuberculosis and Chest Diseases

d.t.d. *Med. detur talis dosis* (Latin: let such a dose be given)

DTD Diploma in Tuberculous Diseases • *Computing* document type definition

DTE *Computing* data terminal equipment

DTech Doctor of Technology

DTh (*or* **DTheol**) Doctor of Theology

DTH Diploma in Tropical Hygiene

DTI Department of Trade and Industry

DTIC dacarbazine (anticancer drug)

DTL *Electronics* diode-transistor logic • down the line (in shooting)

DTM Diploma in Tropical Medicine

DTMH (*or* **DTM&H**) Diploma in Tropical Medicine and Hygiene

DTp Department of Transport

DTP desktop publishing

DTPA *Med.* diethylene-triaminepentaacetic acid (diagnostic aid)

DTPH Diploma in Tropical Public Health

DTR double taxation relief

DT's (ˌdiːˈtiːz) *Colloquial* delirium tremens

Du. Duke • Dutch

DU Doctor of the University • *Med.* duodenal ulcer

Dunelm. Dunelmensis (Latin: (Bishop) of Durham)

DUniv Doctor of the University

dup. duplicate

DUP (Northern Ireland) Democratic Unionist Party

Dur. Durham

DUV damaging ultraviolet (radiation)

DV Deo volente (Latin: God willing) • Douay Version (of the Bible)

DVA Diploma of Veterinary Anaesthesia

DV&D Diploma in Venereology and Dermatology

DVH Diploma in Veterinary Hygiene

DVLA Driver and Vehicle Licensing Authority

DVLC Driver and Vehicle Licensing Centre (Swansea)

DVM Doctor of Veterinary Medicine

DVMS Doctor of Veterinary Medicine and Surgery

DVR Diploma in Veterinary Radiology

DVS Doctor of Veterinary Surgery

DVSc (*or* **DVSci**) Doctor of Veterinary Science

d.w. dead weight

DW (*or* **D/W**) *Commerce* dock warrant

DWA driving without awareness

d.w.c. deadweight capacity

dwr drawer

dwt pennyweight

d.w.t. (*or* **DWT**) deadweight tonnage

DX *Photog.* daylight exposure (indicating that the speed of a film can be set automatically in a suitably equipped camera) • *Telecom.* long-distance (*or* -distant)

dy. delivery

Dy *Chem., symbol for* dysprosium

DY *international vehicle registration for* Benin (formerly Dahomey) • dockyard • *postcode for* Dudley

Dyd. Dockyard

dz. dozen

DZ *international vehicle registration for* Algeria • *Military* drop zone

E

e (*or* **e.**) electromotive • (*or* **e⁻**) *Physics*, symbol for electron • (ital.) *Physics*, symbol for electron (or proton) charge • *Physics*, symbol for positron (in **e⁺**) • *Maths.*, symbol for the transcendental number 2.718 282... • indicating the fifth vertical row of squares from the left on a chessboard

e. eldest • engineer(ing) • *Telephony*, symbol for Erlang (unit of traffic intensity)

E earth (indicating the terminal in an electrical circuit) • east(ern) • *postcode for east London* • *Colloquial* Ecstasy (hallucinogenic drug) • (ital.) *Physics*, symbol for electric field strength (light ital. in nonvector equations; bold ital. in vector equations) • (ital.) *Physics*, symbol for electromotive force • symbol for emalangeni (sing. lilangeni; monetary unit of Swaziland) • (ital.) *Physics*, symbol for energy • E-number (EC-

approved code number of a food additive, as in **E200**) • symbol for exa- (prefix indicating 10¹⁸, as in **EJ**, exajoule) • (ital.; *or* **Eᵥ**) *Physics*, symbol for illuminance • (ital.; *or* **Eₑ**) *Physics*, symbol for irradiance • international vehicle registration for Spain • (ital.) *Physics*, symbol for Young modulus • indicating casual workers (occupational grade) • indicating a musical note or key • *Logic*, indicating a universal negative categorical proposition

E. (*or* **E**) Earl • Egypt(ian) • England • English

ea. each

EA East Anglia • enterprise allowance

EAA Edinburgh Architectural Association

EAC East African Community

EACSO (iːˈɑːksəʊ) East African Common Services Organization

EAGGF European Agricultural Guidance and Guarantee Fund (in the EC)

EAK *international vehicle registration for* (East Africa) Kenya

EAN *Computing* European Academic Network

e. & e. each and every

E & OE errors and omissions excepted (on invoice forms)

e.a.o.n. except as otherwise noted

EAP East Africa Protectorate • English for academic purposes

EARN (ɜːn) *Computing* European Academic and Research Network

EAROM ('ɪərɒm) *Computing* electrically alterable read-only memory

EAS *Aeronautics* equivalent air speed

EAT *international vehicle registration for* (East Africa) Tanzania (*see also* EAZ)

EAU *international vehicle registration for* (East Africa) Uganda

EAW Electrical Association for Women

EAZ *international vehicle registration for* (East Africa)

Tanzania (Zanzibar; *see also under* EAT)

EB electricity board • (ital.) Encyclopaedia Britannica

EBC English Benedictine Congregation

EBCDIC ('ɛpsɪˌdɪk) *Computing* extended binary-coded decimal-interchange code

e-beam electron beam

EBM *Med.* expressed breast milk

EbN east by north

EBNF *Computing* extended BNF (Backus normal form)

E-boat Enemy War Motorboat (German torpedo boat in World War II)

Ebor. ('iːbɔː) Eboracensis (Latin: (Archbishop) of York)

EBR electron-beam recording

EBRD European Bank for Reconstruction and Development

EbS east by south

EBU English Bridge Union • European Broadcasting Union

EBV *Med.* Epstein–Barr virus

EC East Caribbean •

postcode for East Central London • east coast • *international vehicle registration for* Ecuador • emergency commission • Engineering Corps • Established Church • (Canada) Etoile du Courage (French: Star of Courage) • European Community (now often used in place of EEC)

ECA Economic Commission for Africa (UN agency) • Educational Centres Association

ECAFE Economic Commission for Asia and the Far East (*see* ESCAP)

eccl. (*or* **eccles.**) ecclesiastic(al)

Eccles. (*or* **Eccl.**) *Bible* Ecclesiastes

ecclesiast. ecclesiastical

Ecclus. *Bible* Ecclesiasticus

ECD estimated completion date

ECE Economic Commission for Europe (UN agency)

ECFMG Educational Council for Foreign Medical Graduates

ECG *Med.* electrocardiogram (*or* electrocardiograph)

ECGD Export Credits Guarantee Department

ECLAC Economic Commission for Latin America and the Caribbean (UN agency)

ECM *Military* electronic countermeasure(s) (for jamming enemy signals, destroying guided missiles, etc.)

ECMA ('ɛkmə) European Computer Manufacturers' Association (Geneva)

ecol. ecological • ecology

econ. economical • economics • economy

ECOSOC ('ɛkəʊ,sɒk) Economic and Social Council (of the UN)

ECOVAST ('ɛkəʊ,væst) European Council for the Village and Small Town

ECOWAS (ɛ'kəʊəs) Economic Community of West African States

ECP *Finance* Euro-commercial paper

ECPA Electric Consumers Protection Act (1986)

ECR electronic cash register

ECS European Communications Satellite

ECSC European Coal and Steel Community

ECT *Med.* electroconvulsive therapy • *Med.* emission-computerized (or -computed) tomography

ecu (or **ECU**) ('eɪkjuː or 'ɛkjuː) European Currency Unit (in the EC)

ECU English Church Union

Ecua. Ecuador

ed. edited • edition • editor • education

Ed. Editor

ED *Pharmacol.* effective dose (as in **ED₅₀**, mean effective dose) • Efficiency Decoration • *Physics* equivalent dose (of radiation) • European Democrat • *Finance* ex dividend

EdB Bachelor of Education

EDB ethene dibromide (antiknock agent and soil fumigant)

EDC Economic Development Committee • Engineering Design Centre • European Defence Community • *Obstetrics* expected date of confinement

EdD Doctor of Education

EDE *Physics* effective dose equivalent (of radiation)

EDF European Development Fund

EDG European Democratic Group

Edin. Edinburgh

edit. edited • edition • editor

EdM Master of Education

EDM *Surveying* electronic distance measurement

edn edition

EDP (or **e.d.p.**) electronic data processing

EDR (Japanese) Electronic Dictionary Research

EdS Education Specialist

EDS Electronic Data Systems Corporation

EDT (USA, Canada) Eastern Daylight Time

educ. educated • (or **educn**) education • educational

EDV *Med.* end-diastolic volume

EE Early English • Eastern Electricity • electrical engineer(ing) • (or **e.e.**) errors excepted

EEA European Economic Area

EE & MP Envoy Extraordinary and Minister Plenipotentiary

EEB European Environmental Bureau

EEC European Economic Community (*see also under* EC)

EEF Egyptian Expeditionary Force • Engineering Employers' Federation

EEG electroencephalogram (*or* electroencephalograph)

EEIBA Electrical and Electronic Industries Benevolent Association

EEMS *Computing* enhanced expanded memory specification

EENT *Med.* eye, ear, nose, and throat

EEO equal employment opportunity

EER energy–efficiency ratio

EEROM ('ɪərɒm) *Computing* electrically erasable read-only memory

EET Eastern European Time

EETPU Electrical, Electronic, Telecommunications, and Plumbing Union (*see* AEEU)

EETS Early English Text Society

EEZ exclusive economic zone

EF *Genetics* elongation factor

EFA European Fighter Aircraft

EFCE European Federation of Chemical Engineering

EFI electronic fuel injection (of car engines)

EFIS *Aeronautics* electronic flight-information system

EFL English as a foreign language • external financial limit

EFM *Med.* electronic fetal monitor

EFT electronic funds-transfer

EFTA ('ɛftə) European Free Trade Association

EFTPOS ('ɛftpɒs) electronic funds-transfer at point of sale

EFTS electronic funds-transfer system

e.g. exempli gratia (Latin: for example)

Eg. Egypt(ian) • Egyptology

EGA *Computing* enhanced graphics adapter

EGF *Med.* epidermal growth factor

EGM extraordinary general meeting

EGmbH (Germany)
Eingetragene Gesellschaft
mit beschränkter Haftung
(registered limited company)

EGR *Finance* earned
growth rate • exhaust gas
recirculation (as in **EGR
valve**)

Egypt. Egyptian

eh. ehrenhalber (German:
honorary)

EH *postcode for* Edinburgh

EHF *Radio* extremely high
frequency

EHO Environmental
Health Officer

EHT (*or* **e.h.t.**) *Electronics*
extra-high tension

EHV extra-high voltage

EI East Indian • East Indies • *Photog.* exposure index

EIA Engineering Industries
Association • environmental
impact analysis (*or* assessment) • Environmental Investigation Agency • *Med.*
exercise-induced asthma

EIB European Investment
Bank

EICS East India
Company's Service

EIEE *Med.* early infantile
epileptic encephalopathy

E-in-C Engineer-in-Chief

EIS Educational Institute
of Scotland • environmental
impact statement • *Computing* executive information
system

EISA *Computing* extended
industry standard architecture

EIU Economist Intelligence Unit

ELA electronic learning aid

ELBS English Language
Book Society

ELDO ('ɛldəʊ) *Astronautics* European Launcher Development Organization
(now part of ESA)

elec. (*or* **elect.**) electric(al) • electricity • electronic

elem. element(s) • elementary

elev. elevation

ELF *Radio* extremely low
frequency

ELISA (ɪ'laɪzə) *Med.*
enzyme-linked immunosorbent assay

Eliz. Elizabethan

ELR exceptional leave to
remain (for four years in
the UK; granted to asylumseekers)

ELT English language

teaching (for foreign students)

ELV expendable launch vehicle

e.m. (or **em**) electromagnetic

EM Earl Marshal · Edward Medal · electromagnetic · electromotive · electronic mail · electron microscope (or microscopy) · Engineer of Mines · enlisted man

EMA European Monetary Agreement

email (or **e-mail, E-mail**) ('iːmeɪl) electronic mail

EMBO European Molecular Biology Organization

embryol. embryology

EMCOF ('ɛmkɒf) European Monetary Cooperation Fund

EME East Midlands Electricity

EMet Engineer of Metallurgy

emf (or **e.m.f.**) *Physics* electromotive force

EMG *Med.* electromyogram (or electromyograph)

EMI Electric and Musical Industries

Emp. Emperor · Empire · Empress

EMP electromagnetic pulse

EMR (or **emr**) electromagnetic radiation

EMS emergency medical service · European Monetary System · *Computing* expanded memory specification

emu (or **e.m.u.**) *Physics* electromagnetic unit

EMU economic and monetary union (within the EC) · *Astronautics* extravehicular mobility unit

en *Chem.* ethylenediamine (used in formulae)

EN *postcode for* Enfield · Enrolled Nurse

ENB English National Ballet

enc. enclosed · enclosure

Enc. Brit. (or **Ency. Brit., Encyc. Brit.**) Encyclopaedia Britannica

encl. enclosed · enclosure

ency. (or **encyc., encycl.**) encyclopedia

ENE east-northeast

ENEA European Nuclear Energy Agency

eng. engine · engineer(ing) · engraved · engraver · engraving

Eng. England · English

ENG electronic news gathering (in TV broadcasting)

EN(G) Enrolled Nurse (General) (formerly SEN)

Eng. hn *Music* English horn

engin. engineer(ing)

engr engineer • engraver

engr. engrave(d) • engraving

ENIAC ('ɛnɪæk) Electronic Numerical Integrator and Calculator (first electronic calculator)

enl. enlarge(d) • enlargement • enlisted

EN(M) Enrolled Nurse (Mental)

EN(MH) Enrolled Nurse (Mental Handicap)

ENO English National Opera

Ens. (*or* ens.) *Music* ensemble • Ensign

ENSA ('ɛnsə) Entertainments National Service Association (in World War II)

ENT *Med.* ear, nose, and throat

entom. (*or* entomol.) entomological • entomology

Ent. Sta. Hall entered (registered) at Stationers' Hall (requirement to secure copyright on books before 1924)

env. envelope • environs

e.o. ex officio

EO Equal Opportunities • Executive Officer • executive order

EOB *Computing* end of block • Executive Office Building

EOC end of cycle • Equal Opportunities Commission

EOD end of data (computing code) • *Military* explosive ordnance disposal (*or* demolition)

EOE equal opportunity employer • errors and omissions excepted (on invoice forms) • European Options Exchange

EOF *Computing* end of file

EOJ *Computing* end of job

e.o.m. *Commerce* end of the month

EOPH Examined Officer of Public Health

EOQC European Organization for Quality Control

EOR *Computing* end of record

EORTC European Organization for Research on Treatment of Cancer

EOT *Computing* end of

tape (as in **EOT marker**) • *Computing* end of transmission

e.p. *Chess* en passant

Ep. *Bible* Epistle

EP *Navigation* estimated position • extended-play (gramophone record)

EPA *Med.* eicosapentaenoic acid (cholesterol-reducing fatty acid)

EPC easy-processing channel (in **EPC black**, filler in rubber compounding) • European Patent Convention

EPCOT Experimental Prototype Community of Tomorrow (Florida)

EPG *Med.* electropalatogram (or electropalatology) • Eminent Persons Group

Eph. (or **Ephes.**) *Bible* Ephesians

EPI Eysenck Personality Test

EPIC (or **Epic**) ('ɛpɪk) European Prospective Investigation into Cancer

Epiph. Epiphany

EPIRB *Navigation* emergency position indicator radio beacon

Epis. (or **Episc.**) Episco-

pal(ian) • (or **Epist.**) *Bible* Epistle

EPM (or **EPMA**) electron-probe microanalysis

EPNdB effective perceived noise decibels

EPNS electroplated nickel silver

EPO *Med.* erythropoietin • European Patent Office

EPOS ('iːpɒs) *Commerce* electronic point of sale (as in **EPOS terminal**, **EPOS system**)

EPP European People's Party • executive pension plan

EPR electron paramagnetic resonance (as in **EPR spectroscopy**)

EPROM ('iːprɒm) *Computing* erasable programmable read-only memory

e.p.s. earnings per share

EPT *Med.* early pregnancy test • excess profits tax

EPU European Payments Union

eq. equal • equation • equivalent

EQ educational quotient • *Electronics* equivalence (as in **EQ gate**)

EQC external quality control

eqn equation

eqpt equipment

equiv. equivalent

er elder

Er *Chem., symbol for* erbium

ER Eastern Region (British Rail) • Eduardus Rex (Latin: King Edward) • efficiency report • Elizabeth Regina (Latin: Queen Elizabeth) • *Med.* emergency room

ERA Electrical Research Association • (USA) Equal Rights Amendment

ERC Economic Research Council • Electronics Research Council

ERCP *Med.* endoscopic retrograde cholangiopancreatography

ERD Emergency Reserve Decoration

ERDF European Regional Development Fund

Erf (ɜːf) *Chem.* electrorheological fluid

ERG electrical resistance gauge • *Med.* electroretinogram

ERI (*or* **ER(I), ER et I**) Edwardus Rex et Imperator (Latin: Edward King and Emperor)

ERM *Finance* Exchange Rate Mechanism

Ernie (*or* **ERNIE**) (ˈɜːnɪ) electronic random number indicating equipment (premium-bond computer)

ERP European Recovery Programme

ERS earnings-related supplement • emergency radio service • emergency response system

ERT excess retention tax

ERTS Earth Resources Technology Satellite

ERV English Revised Version (of the Bible)

ERW enhanced radiation weapon

Es *Chem., symbol for* einsteinium

ES Education Specialist • *international vehicle registration for* El Salvador

ESA European Space Agency

ESB electrical stimulation of the brain

Esc *Computing* escape key • *symbol for* escudo (Portuguese monetary unit)

ESCAP Economic and Social Commission for Asia and the Pacific (UN agency; formerly ECAFE)

Esd. *Bible* Esdras

Esda ('ɛzdə) electrostatic deposition (*or* document) analysis (as in **Esda test**)

ESE east-southeast

ESF European Science Foundation

ESG Education Support Grant • *Engineering* English Standard Gauge

ESL English as a second language

ESN educationally subnormal

ESNS educationally subnormal, serious

ESOL ('iːsɒl) English for speakers of other languages

ESOP ('iːsɒp) employee share-ownership plan

esp. especially • *Music* espressivo (Italian: expressively)

ESP English for specific (*or* special) purposes • extra-sensory perception

ESPRIT ('ɛsprɪt) European strategic programme for research and development in information technology

Esq. esquire (in correspondence)

ESR *Med.* erythrocyte sedimentation rate

ESRC Economic and Social Research Council (formerly SSRC) • Electricity Supply Research Council

ESRIN ('ɛzrɪn) European Space Research Institute (Italy)

ESRO ('ɛzrəʊ) European Space Research Organization (now part of ESA)

Ess. Essex

Esso ('ɛsəʊ) Standard Oil (phonetic spelling of SO)

est. establish(ed) • *Law* estate • estimate(d) • estimation • estuary

Est. Established

EST (USA, Canada) Eastern Standard Time • electroshock therapy (*or* electric-shock treatment)

estab. establish(ed) • establishment

Esth. *Bible* Esther

esu (*or* **e.s.u.**) *Physics* electrostatic unit

ESU English-Speaking Union

Et *Chem.*, symbol for ethyl (used in formulae)

ET (USA) Eastern Time • *international vehicle registration for* (Arab Republic of) Egypt • Employment Training (for the unemployed) •

ephemeris time • extraterrestrial

ETA estimated time of arrival • (or **Eta**; ˈɛtə) Euzkadi ta Askatsuna (Basque: Basque Nation and Liberty; nationalist organization)

et al. et alibi (Latin: and elsewhere) • et alii (Latin: and others)

etc. et cetera (Latin: and other things)

ETD estimated time of departure • *Telecom.* extension trunk dialling

ETF *Banking* electronic transfer of funds

Eth. Ethiopia(n) • Ethiopic

ETH *international vehicle registration for* Ethiopia

ethnol. ethnology

ETI estimated time of interception • extraterrestrial intelligence

ETR estimated time of return

et seq. et sequens (Latin: and the following)

ETSU Energy Technology Support Unit (of the Department of Energy)

ETUC European Trade Union Confederation

et ux. et uxor (Latin: and wife)

ETV educational television

ety. (or **etym.**, **etymol.**) etymological • etymologist • etymology

Eu *Chem., symbol for* europium

EUA *Finance* European unit of account

EUDISED (ˈjuːdɪˌsɛd) European Documentation and Information Service for Education

Eur. Europe(an)

Euratom (juəˈrætəm) European Atomic Energy Community

Eur Ing European Engineer

EUROM (ˈjuərɒm) European Federation for Optics and Precision Mechanics

EUV *Physics* extreme ultraviolet

EUW European Union of Women

eV eingetragener Verein (German: registered society) • *Physics, symbol for* electronvolt

EV English Version (of the Bible) • *Image technol.* exposure value

EVA *Chem.* ethene and

vinyl acetate (copolymers) • *Astronautics* extravehicular activity

evan. (*or* **evang.**) evangelical • evangelist

e.w. each way (betting)

EW electronic warfare

EWO Educational Welfare Officer • European Women's Orchestra

ex. examination • examine(d) • example • except(ed) • exception • exchange • excluding • excursion • execute(d) • executive • express • extra

Ex. *Bible* Exodus

EX *postcode for* Exeter

exam. examination

ex aq. *Med.* ex aqua (Latin: from water)

ex b. *Finance* ex bonus (without bonus)

exc. excellent • except • excepted • exception • excursion

Exc. Excellency

ex cap. *Finance* ex capitalization (without capitalization)

exch. exchange • (*or* **Exch.**) exchequer

excl. (*or* **exclam.**) exclamation • (*or* **exclam.**) exclamatory • excluding • exclusive

ex cp. *Finance* ex coupon (without the interest on the coupon)

exd examined

ex div. *Finance* ex dividend (without dividend)

exec. executive • executor

exes expenses

ex int. *Banking* ex interest (without interest)

ex lib. ex libris (Latin: from the books (*or* library) of)

ex n. *Stock exchange* ex new (of shares)

EXNOR (ˈɛksnɔː) *Computing, Electronics* exclusive-NOR (as in **EXNOR gate**)

Exod. *Bible* Exodus

ex off. ex officio (Latin: by right of office)

exor executor

EXOR (ˈɛksɔː) *Computing, Electronics* exclusive-OR (as in **EXOR gate**)

exp *Maths., symbol for* exponential

exp. expenses • experiment(al) • expire(d) • export(ed) • exporter • express

expt experiment

exptl experimental

exr executor

exrx executrix

exs expenses

ext. extension • extent • external(ly) • (*or* **ext**) extinct • extra • (*or* **ext**) extract

EXTEND (ɪkˈstend) Exercise Training for the Elderly and/or Disabled

exx examples • executrix

Ez. *Bible* Ezra

EZ easy

Ezek. *Bible* Ezekiel

Ezr. *Bible* Ezra.

F

f *Music* fah (in tonic sol-fa) • *symbol for* femto- (prefix indicating 10^{-15}, as in **fm**, femtometre) • (*or* **f/**, **f:**) *Photog.* f-number (ratio of the focal length of a lens to its aperture, as in **f8**) • (ital.) *Physics, symbol for* focal length • (ital.) *Music* forte (Italian; loudly) • (ital.) *Physics, symbol for* frequency • (ital.) *Physical chem., symbol for* fugacity • (ital.) *Maths., symbol for* function (as in $f(x)$) • *indicating* the sixth vertical row of squares from the left on a chessboard

f. fathom(s) • female • *Grammar* feminine • *Horse racing* filly • *Metallurgy* fine • folio • following (page) • foot • *Sport* foul • franc(s) • *symbol for* guilder (monetary unit of the Netherlands)

F Fahrenheit (in °F, degree Fahrenheit) • *Logic, Maths.* false • *symbol for* farad(s) • (ital.) *Physics, symbol for* Faraday constant • fast (on a clock or watch regulator) • (USA) fighter (specifying a type of military aircraft, as in **F-106**) • *Genetics, symbol for* filial generation (as in F_1, first generation) • *Chem., symbol for* fluorine • (*or* **F/**, **F:**) *Photog.* f-number (as in **F4**; *see* *under* f) • (*ital.*) *Physics, symbol for* force • *symbol for* franc (monetary unit of various countries) • *international vehicle registration for* France • (*ital.*) *Thermodynamics, symbol for* Helmholtz function • *indicating* a musical note or key • *Astronomy, indicating* a spectral type

F. (*or* **F**) fathom(s) • Federation • Fellow • female • *Grammar* feminine • *Horse racing* filly • *Metallurgy* fine • folio • *Sport* foul

f.a. *Slang* fanny adams (*or* fuck all) • *Commerce* free alongside • freight agent

FA Faculty of Actuaries • *Slang* fanny adams (*or* fuck all) • *Military* field artillery • Football Association

f.a.a. *Marine insurance* free of all averages

FAA Fellow of the Australian Academy (of Science) • Film Artists' Association • Fleet Air Arm

FAAV Fellow of the Central Association of Agricultural Valuers

FAB fuel-air bomb

fac. facsimile • factor • factory • (*or* **Fac.**) faculty

f.a.c. (as) fast as can (be)

FACE Fellow of the Australian College of Education • (fes) field artillery computer equipments

FACOM Fellow of the Australian College of Occupational Medicine

FACRM Fellow of the Australian College of Reproductive Medicine

facs. facsimile

FAD *Biochem.* flavin adenine dinucleotide

FAE *Military* fuel-air explosive(s)

FAGO Fellowship in Australia in Obstetrics and Gynaecology

Fah. (*or* **Fahr.**) Fahrenheit

FAHA Fellow of the Australian Academy of the Humanities

FAI Fédération aéronautique internationale (French: International Aeronautical Federation) • Football Association of Ireland

FAIAS Fellow of the Australian Institute of Agricultural Science

FAIB Fellow of the Australian Institute of Builders

FAIBiol Fellow of the Australian Institute of Biology

FAIE Fellow of the Australian Institute of Energy

FAIEx Fellow of the Australian Institute of Export

FAIFST Fellow of the Australian Institute of Food Science and Technology

FAII Fellow of the Australian Insurance Institute

FAIM Fellow of the Australian Institute of Management

FAIP Fellow of the Australian Institute of Physics

fam. familiar • family

FAM Free and Accepted Masons

FAMA Fellow of the Australian Medical Association

FAMEME Fellow of the Association of Mining Electrical and Mechanical Engineers

FAMI Fellow of the Australian Marketing Institute

FAMS Fellow of the Ancient Monuments Society

F & AP *Insurance* fire and allied perils

f & d (*or* **F & D**) freight and demurrage

f & f fixtures and fittings

F and Gs (*or* **F&Gs**) *Bookbinding* folded and gathered pages

f & t (*or* **F & T**) *Insurance* fire and theft

FANY (*or* **Fany, Fanny**) ('fænɪ) First Aid Nursing Yeomanry

f.a.o. finish all over • for the attention of

FAO Food and Agriculture Organization (of the UN)

FAP *Ethology* fixed action pattern

f.a.q. *Commerce* fair average quality • *Commerce* free alongside quay

FAR *Insurance* free (of claim) for accident reported

FArborA Fellow of the Arboricultural Association

FARE Federation of Alcoholic Rehabilitation Establishments

FARELF Far East Land Forces

f.a.s. *Commerce* free alongside ship

FAS Fellow of the Anthropological Society • Fellow of the Antiquarian Society • *Med.* fetal alcohol syndrome • *Commerce* free alongside ship

FASI Fellow of the Architects' and Surveyors' Institute

FASSA Fellow of the

Academy of Social Sciences in Australia

fath. fathom

FAusIMM Fellow of the Australasian Institute of Mining and Metallurgy

fax (or **FAX**) (fæx) facsimile transmission

FB *Med.* foreign body

FBA Federation of British Artists • Fellow of the British Academy • fluorescent brightening agent (used in detergents)

FBCO Fellow of the British College of Ophthalmic Opticians (or Optometrists)

FBCS Fellow of the British Computer Society

FBEC(S) Fellow of the Business Education Council (Scotland)

FBHI Fellow of the British Horological Institute

FBHS Fellow of the British Horse Society

FBI (USA) Federal Bureau of Investigation

FBIBA Fellow of the British Insurance Brokers' Association

FBID Fellow of the British Institute of Interior Design

FBIM Fellow of the British Institute of Management

FBINZ Fellow of the Bankers' Institute of New Zealand

FBIPP Fellow of the British Institute of Professional Photography

FBIS Fellow of the British Interplanetary Society

FBL flight-by-light (aircraft control system)

FBO (or **f.b.o.**) for the benefit of

FBOA Fellow of the British Optical Association

FBOU Fellow of the British Ornithologists' Union

FBPsS Fellow of the British Psychological Society

FBSM Fellow of the Birmingham School of Music

FBT fringe benefit tax

FBu *symbol for* Burundi franc (monetary unit)

FBU Fire Brigades Union

FBW *Aeronautics* fly-by-wire

f.c. *Printing* follow copy

FC (Australia) Federal Cabinet • fieri curavit (Latin: the donor directed this to be done; on gravestones and other monuments) • Football Club

FCA Fellow of the Institute of Chartered Accountants

FCAI Fellow of the New Zealand Institute of Cost Accountants

FCAnaes Fellow of the College of Anaesthetists

fcap (*or* **f/cap, f'cap**) foolscap

FCAR *Insurance* free of claim for accident reported

FCB *Computing* file control block

FCBSI Fellow of the Chartered Building Societies Institute

f.c.c. *Crystallog.* face-centred cubic

FCCA Fellow of the Chartered Association of Certified Accountants

FCCEA Fellow of the Commonwealth Council for Educational Administration

FCCS Fellow of the Corporation of Secretaries (formerly Certified Secretaries)

FCD First Chief Directorate (of the KGB)

FCEC Federation of Civil Engineering Contractors

FCFI Fellow of the Clothing and Footwear Institute

FCGI Fellow of the City and Guilds London Institute

FChS Fellow of the Society of Chiropodists

FCI Fellow of the Institute of Commerce

FCIA Fellow of the Corporation of Insurance Agents • Foreign Credit Insurance Association

FCIArb Fellow of the Chartered Institute of Arbitrators

FCIB Fellow of the Chartered Institute of Bankers • Fellow of the Corporation of Insurance Brokers

FCIBSE Fellow of the Chartered Institution of Building Services Engineers

FCII Fellow of the Chartered Insurance Institute

FCILA Fellow of the Chartered Institute of Loss Adjusters

FCIM Fellow of the Chartered Institute of Marketing

FCIOB Fellow of the Chartered Institute of Building

FCIS Fellow of the Institute of Chartered Secretaries and Administrators (formerly Chartered Institute of Secretaries)

FCISA Fellow of the Chartered Institute of Secretar-

FCIT Fellow of the Chartered Institute of Transport

FCMA Fellow of the Institute of Cost and Management Accountants

FCMS Fellow of the College of Medicine and Surgery

FCNA Fellow of the College of Nursing, Australia

f. co. *Printing* fair copy

FCO Foreign and Commonwealth Office

FCollP Fellow of the College of Preceptors

FCOphth Fellow of the College of Ophthalmologists

FCOT Fellow of the College of Occupational Therapists

fcp. foolscap

FCP Fellow of the College of Clinical Pharmacology • Fellow of the College of Preceptors

FCPS Fellow of the College of Physicians and Surgeons

fcs (*or* **Fcs**) francs

FCS Federation of Conservative Students • Fellow of the Chemical Society (now

part of the Royal Society of Chemistry; *see under* FRSC)

FCSD Fellow of the Chartered Society of Designers

FCSP Fellow of the Chartered Society of Physiotherapy

FCST Fellow of the College of Speech Therapists

FCT Fellow of the Association of Corporate Treasurers

FCTB Fellow of the College of Teachers of the Blind

FCU fighter control unit

f.d. focal distance • (*or* **f/d**) free delivery

FD Fidei Defensor (Latin: Defender of the Faith (Henry VIII); e.g. on British coins) • (*or* **f/d**) free-delivered (at docks)

FDF Food and Drink Federation

FDM *Telecom.* frequency-division multiplexing

FDO *Taxation* for declaration (purposes) only

FDP (Germany) Freie Demokratische Partei (Free Democratic Party)

FDR Franklin Delano Roosevelt (1882–1945, US president 1933–45)

FDS Fellow in Dental Surgery

FDSRCPSGlas Fellow in Dental Surgery of the Royal College of Physicians and Surgeons of Glasgow

FDSRCS Fellow in Dental Surgery of the Royal College of Surgeons of England

FDSRCSE Fellow in Dental Surgery of the Royal College of Surgeons of Edinburgh

Fe *Chem.*, symbol *for* iron (Latin *ferrum*)

FE Far East • further education

FEAF Far East Air Force

Feb February

fec. fecit (Latin: (he or she) made it; on works of art next to the artist's name)

FEC Foreign Exchange Certificate (tourist currency used in China; *compare* RMB)

FECI Fellow of the Institute of Employment Consultants

Fed. (*or* **fed.**) Federal(ist) • Federated • Federation

FED Federal Reserve System

FEER *Banking* fundamental equilibrium exchange rate

FEIDCT Fellow of the Educational Institute of Design Craft and Technology

FEIS Fellow of the Educational Institute of Scotland

FEL free-electron laser

fem. female • feminine

FEM *Maths.* finite-element method

FEng Fellow of the Fellowship of Engineering

FEP fluorinated ethene propene (a plastic)

FES Fellow of the Entomological Society • Fellow of the Ethnological Society

FET ('ɛf 'iː 'tiː *or* fɛt) field-effect transistor

ff (*or* **ff.**) fecerunt (Latin: (they) made it; on works of art next to the artists' names) • folios • following (pages, lines, etc.) • (ital.) *Music* fortissimo (Italian; very loudly)

f.f. fixed focus

FF Fianna Fáil (Irish Gaelic: warriors of Ireland; Irish political party) • *Military* field force

f.f.a. *Commerce* free from alongside (ship)

FFA (Scotland) Fellow of the Faculty of Actuaries •

Fellow of the Institute of Financial Accountants

FFARACS Fellow of the Faculty of Anaesthetists of the Royal Australasian College of Surgeons

FFARCS Fellow of the Faculty of Anaesthetists of the Royal College of Surgeons of England

FFARCSI Fellow of the Faculty of Anaesthetists of the Royal College of Surgeons in Ireland

FFB Fellow of the Faculty of Building

FFC Foreign Funds Control

FFCMI Fellow of the Faculty of Community Medicine of Ireland

FFD Fellow of the Faculty of Dental Surgeons

FFDRCSI Fellow of the Faculty of Dentistry of the Royal College of Surgeons in Ireland

fff (ital.) *Music* fortississimo (Italian; as loudly as possible)

FFF Free French Forces

FFHC Freedom from Hunger Campaign

FFHom Fellow of the Faculty of Homoeopathy

FFI Finance for Industry • French Forces of the Interior

FFOM Fellow of the Faculty of Occupational Medicine

FFOMI Fellow of the Faculty of Occupational Medicine of Ireland

FFPath, RCPI Fellow of the Faculty of Pathologists of the Royal College of Physicians of Ireland

FFPHM Fellow of the Faculty of Public Health Medicine

FFPM Fellow of the Faculty of Pharmaceutical Medicine

FFPS Fauna and Flora Preservation Society

FFr (*or* **Ffr**) French franc

f.f.s.s. full-frequency stereophonic sound

ffy faithfully

f.g. *Commerce* fully good

FG Fine Gael (Irish Gaelic: tribe of the Gaels; Irish political party)

FGA Fellow of the Gemmological Association • (*or* **f.g.a.**) foreign general average

FGCM Fellow of the Guild of Church Musicians

f.g.f. *Commerce* fully good, fair

FGI Fellow of the Institute of Certified Grocers

FGS Fellow of the Geological Society

FGSM Fellow of the Guildhall School of Music and Drama

FH *Med.* fetal heart • *Med.* family history

FHAS Fellow of the Highland and Agricultural Society of Scotland

FHB (or **f.h.b.**) *Colloquial* family hold back

FHCIMA Fellow of the Hotel Catering and Institutional Management Association

FHH *Med.* fetal heart heard

FHNH *Med.* fetal heart not heard

FHR *Med.* fetal heart rate

FHS Fellow of the Heraldry Society

FHSM Fellow of the Institute of Health Services Management

FI Falkland Islands • *Engineering* flow injection

FIA Fellow of the Institute of Actuaries • (or **f.i.a.**) *Commerce* full interest admitted

FIAA Fellow of the Institute of Actuaries of Australia

FIAA&S Fellow of the Incorporated Association of Architects and Surveyors

FIAAS Fellow of the Institute of Australian Agricultural Science

FIAgrE Fellow of the Institution of Agricultural Engineers

FIAL Fellow of the International Institute of Arts and Letters

FIAM Fellow of the Institute of Administrative Management • Fellow of the International Academy of Management

FIAP Fellow of the Institution of Analysts and Programmers

FIArbA Fellow of the Institute of Arbitrators of Australia

Fiat (or **FIAT**) ('fiːət, -æt) Fabbrica Italiana Automobili Torino (Italian Motor Works in Turin)

fib. *Med.* fibula

f.i.b. free into barge • free into bunker

FIBD Fellow of the Institute of British Decorators

FIBiol Fellow of the Institute of Biology

FIBOR Frankfurt Inter-Bank Offered Rate

FIBP Fellow of the Institute of British Photographers

FIBScot Fellow of the Institute of Bankers in Scotland

FIC Fellow of Imperial College, London

FICA Fellow of the Commonwealth Institute of Accountants

FICAI Fellow of the Institute of Chartered Accountants in Ireland

FICD Fellow of the Institute of Civil Defence

FICE Fellow of the Institution of Civil Engineers

FICeram Fellow of the Institute of Ceramics

FICFor Fellow of the Institute of Chartered Foresters

FIChemE Fellow of the Institution of Chemical Engineers

FICI Fellow of the Institute of Chemistry of Ireland

FICM Fellow of the Institute of Credit Management

FICMA Fellow of the Institute of Cost and Management Accountants

FICS Fellow of the Institute of Chartered Shipbrokers • Fellow of the International College of Surgeons

FICT Fellow of the Institute of Concrete Technologists

FICW Fellow of the Institute of Clerks of Works of Great Britain

FIDA Fellow of the Institute of Directors, Australia

Fid. Def. (*or* **FID DEF**) Fidei Defensor (*see under* FD)

FIDE Fédération internationale des échecs (French: International Chess Federation) • Fellow of the Institute of Design Engineers

FIE Fellow of the Institute of Engineers and Technicians

FIE(Aust) Fellow of the Institution of Engineers, Australia

FIED Fellow of the Institution of Engineering Designers

FIEE Fellow of the Institution of Electrical Engineers

FIEI Fellow of the Institution of Engineers in Ireland

FIElecIE Fellow of the Institution of Electronic Incorporated Engineers

FIEx Fellow of the Institute of Export

fi. fa. *Law* fieri facias (writ of execution; Latin: have it done)

FIFA ('fiːfə) Fédération internationale de football association (French: International Federation of Association Football)

FIFF Fellow of the Institute of Freight Forwarders

FIFireE Fellow of the Institution of Fire Engineers

FIFO (*or* **fifo**) ('faɪfəʊ) *Computing, Accounting* first in first out

FIFST Fellow of the Institute of Food Science and Technology

fig. figurative(ly) • (*or* **Fig.**) figure(s)

FIGasE Fellow of the Institution of Gas Engineers

FIGCM Fellow of the Incorporated Guild of Church Musicians

FIH Fellow of the Institute of Housing

FIHE Fellow of the Institution of Health Education

FIHort Fellow of the Institute of Horticulture

FIHospE Fellow of the Institute of Hospital Engineering

FIHT Fellow of the Institution of Highways and Transportation

FIIA Fellow of the Institute of Internal Auditors

FIIC Fellow of the International Institute for Conservation of Historic and Artistic Works

FIIM Fellow of the Institution of Industrial Managers

FIInfSc Fellow of the Institute of Information Scientists

FIInst Fellow of the Imperial Institute

FILDM Fellow of the Institute of Logistics and Distribution Management

FILO first in last out

FIM Fellow of the Institute of Metals

FIMA Fellow of the Institute of Mathematics and its Applications

FIMarE Fellow of the Institute of Marine Engineers

FIMBRA ('fɪmbrə) Financial Intermediaries, Managers, and Brokers Regulatory Association

FIMC Fellow of the Insti-

FIMechE Fellow of the
Institution of Mechanical
Engineers

FIMGTechE Fellow of
the Institution of Mechanical and General Technician
Engineers

FIMH Fellow of the Institute of Military History

FIMI Fellow of the Institute of the Motor Industry

FIMinE Fellow of the Institution of Mining Engineers

FIMIT Fellow of the Institute of Musical Instrument
Technology

FIMLS Fellow of the Institute of Medical Laboratory
Sciences (formerly Technology, FIMLT)

FIMM Fellow of the Institute of Mining and Metallurgy

FIMS Fellow of the Institute of Mathematical Statistics

fin. finance · financial ·
finis (Latin: the end) · finish

Fin. Finland · Finnish

FInstAM Fellow of the Institute of Administrative
Management

FInstB Fellow of the Institution of Buyers

FInstCh Fellow of the Institute of Chiropodists

FInstD Fellow of the Institute of Directors

FInstE Fellow of the Institute of Energy

FInstFF Fellow of the Institute of Freight Forwarders

FInstLEx Fellow of the
Institute of Legal Executives

FInstMC Fellow of the Institute of Measurement and
Control

FInstP Fellow of the Institute of Physics

FInstPet Fellow of the Institute of Petroleum

FInstPI Fellow of the Institute of Patentees and Inventors

FInstPS Fellow of the Institute of Purchasing and
Supply

FInstSMM Fellow of the
Institute of Sales and Marketing Management

FINucE Fellow of the Institution of Nuclear Engineers

f.i.o. for information only

FIOA Fellow of the Institute of Acoustics

FIOP Fellow of the Institute of Plumbing • Fellow of the Institute of Printing

FIPA Fellow of the Institute of Practitioners in Advertising

FIPENZ Fellow of the Institution of Professional Engineers, New Zealand

FIPG Fellow of the Institute of Professional Goldsmiths

FIPM Fellow of the Institute of Personnel Management

FIPR Fellow of the Institute of Public Relations

FIProdE Fellow of the Institution of Production Engineers

FIQ Fellow of the Institute of Quarrying

FIQA Fellow of the Institute of Quality Assurance

FIQS Fellow of the Institute of Quantity Surveyors

fir. firkin

FIRA Furniture Industry Research Association

FIREE(Aust) Fellow of the Institute of Radio and Electronics Engineers (Australia)

FIRTE Fellow of the Institute of Road Transport Engineers

FIRSE Fellow of the Institute of Railway Signalling Engineers

FIS Family Income Supplement • Fellow of the Institute of Statisticians • (*or* **f.i.s.**) free into store

FISA Fellow of the Incorporated Secretaries Association

FISE Fellow of the Institution of Sales Engineers • Fellow of the Institution of Sanitary Engineers

FIST Fellow of the Institute of Science Technology

FISTC Fellow of the Institute of Scientific and Technical Communicators

FIStructE Fellow of the Institution of Structural Engineers

FISVA Fellow of the Incorporated Society of Valuers and Auctioneers

FISW Fellow of the Institute of Social Work

f.i.t. free of income tax

FITD Fellow of the Institute of Training and Development

FITE Fellow of the Institution of Electrical and Electronics Technician Engineers

FIWEM Fellow of the Institution of Water and Environmental Management

FIWSc Fellow of the Institute of Wood Science

FJI Fellow of the Institute of Journalists • *international vehicle registration for* Fiji

FK *postcode for* Falkirk

FKC Fellow of King's College (London)

FKCHMS Fellow of King's College Hospital Medical School

Fkr *symbol for* Faroese krone (monetary unit)

fl. floor • *Med.* flores (Latin: flowers; powdered form of a drug) • floruit (Latin: flourished; indicates the period of greatest activity of a person whose birth and death dates are not known) • fluid • *Music* flute • (Netherlands) guilder (from its former name *florin*)

Fl. Flanders • Flemish

FL Flight Lieutenant • *US postcode for* Florida • *international vehicle registration for* Liechtenstein

Fla. Florida

FLA Fellow of the Library Association

FLAI Fellow of the Library Association of Ireland

FLCM Fellow of the London College of Music

FLCO Fellow of the London College of Osteopathy

fld field

fl. dr. fluid dram

Flem. Flemish

FLHS Fellow of the London Historical Society

FLI Fellow of the Landscape Institute

FLIA Fellow of the Life Insurance Association

FLN (Algeria) Front de Libération Nationale (French: National Liberation Front)

flops (*or* **FLOPS**) (flops) *Computing* floating-point operations per second (a measure of computer power, as in **Mflops**, megaflops)

flor. floruit (*see under* fl.)

fl oz *symbol for* fluid ounce

fl. pl. *Botany* flore pleno (Latin: with double flowers)

FLQ (Canada) Front de Liberation du Québec (French: Quebec Liberation Front)

FLS Fellow of the Linnean Society

flst. flautist

Flt *Air force* Flight

F/Lt (*or* **F.Lt**) Flight Lieutenant

Flt Cmdr Flight Commander

Flt Lt Flight Lieutenant

Flt Off. Flight Officer

Flt Sgt Flight Sergeant

fm fathom(s) • *Physics, symbol for* femtometre(s) • from

f.m. *Radio* frequency modulation

Fm *Chem., symbol for* fermium

FM *Computing* facilities management • Field Marshal • *Radio* frequency modulation

FMA Fellow of the Museums Association

FMANZ Fellow of the Medical Association of New Zealand

FMB Federation of Master Builders

FMC Fellow of the Medical Council

FMCG fast-moving consumer goods

FMD foot and mouth disease

FMES Fellow of the Minerals Engineering Society

FMG *symbol for* franc (monetary unit of Madagascar)

Fmk (*or* **FMk**) *symbol for* markka (Finnish monetary unit)

fml formal

FMN *Biochem.* flavin mononucleotide

FMS Fellow of the Institute of Management Studies • Fellow of the Medical Society • *Aeronautics* flight-management systems

FNAEA Fellow of the National Association of Estate Agents

FNCO Fleet Naval Constructor Officer

FNECInst Fellow of the North East Coast Institution of Engineers and Shipbuilders

FNI Fellow of the Nautical Institute

FNZEI Fellow of the New Zealand Educational Institute

FNZIA Fellow of the New Zealand Institute of Architects

FNZIAS Fellow of the New Zealand Institute of Agricultural Science

FNZIC Fellow of the New Zealand Institute of Chemistry

FNZIE Fellow of the New

Zealand Institution of Engineers

FNZIM Fellow of the New Zealand Institute of Management

FNZPsS Fellow of the New Zealand Psychological Society

fo. folio

f/o *Commerce* for orders

FO *Army* Field Officer • *Air force* Flying Officer • Foreign Office (now part of the FCO) • *Military* forward observer

FOB (*or* **f.o.b.**) *Commerce* free on board

FoC father of the (trade-union) chapel

FOC (*or* **f.o.c.**) *Commerce* free of charge • free of claims

FOD (*or* **f.o.d.**) free of damage

FODA Fellow of the Overseas Doctors' Association

FOE (*or* **FoE**) Friends of the Earth

FOFA follow-on forces attack

FOH *Theatre* front of house

FOIA (USA) Freedom of Information Act

FOIC Flag Officer in charge

fol. folio • follow(ed) • following

folg. following

foll. followed • following

FONA Flag Officer, Naval Aviation

FONAC Flag Officer, Naval Air Command

FOQ (*or* **f.o.q.**) *Commerce* free on quay

for. foreign(er) • forestry

FOR Fellowship of Operational Research • (*or* **f.o.r.**) free on rail

Ford (fɔːd) (Kenya) Forum for the Restoration of Democracy (political party)

FOREST (ˈfɒrɪst) Freedom Organization for the Right to Enjoy Smoking Tobacco

fort. fortification • fortified

Fortran (*or* **FORTRAN**) (ˈfɔːtræn) *Computing* formula translation (a programming language)

f.o.s. *Commerce* free on ship (*or* steamer) • *Commerce* free on station

f.o.t. (*or* **FOT**) *Commerce* free of tax

f.o.w. *Commerce* first open water • *Commerce* free on wagon

FOX (fɒks) *Commerce* Futures and Options Exchange (in **London FOX**)

fp (ital.) *Music* forte-piano (Italian; loud (then) soft) • freezing point

f.p. fine paper • *Chem.* flash point • freezing point • fully paid (of shares)

FP *Insurance* fire policy • *Insurance* floating policy • freezing point • fully paid (of shares)

FPA Family Planning Association • *Marine insurance* free of particular average

FPC Family Practitioner Committee • fish protein concentrate

FPEA Fellow of the Physical Education Association

FPhS Fellow of the Philosophical Society of England

FPhyS Fellow of the Physical Society

FPIA Fellow of the Plastics Institute of Australia

FPMI Fellow of the Pensions Management Institute

FPO field post office

FPRI Fellow of the Plastics and Rubber Institute

fps (*or* **f.p.s.**) feet per second (as in **fps** units) • *Physgot.* frames per second

fr. fragment • franc(s) • from

f.r. folio recto (Latin: on the right-hand page)

Fr *RC Church* Brother (Latin *Frater*) • *Christianity* Father • *Chem.*, symbol for francium

Fr. France • Frau (German: Mrs) • Friday

FR *international vehicle registration for* Faroe Islands • Federal Republic • freight release

F/R folio reference

Fra (frɑː) *RC Church* Brother (Italian *frate*)

FRA *Finance* forward rate agreement

FRACDS Fellow of the Royal Australian College of Dental Surgeons

FRACGP Fellow of the Royal Australian College of General Practitioners

FRACI Fellow of the Royal Australian Chemical Institute

FRACMA Fellow of the Royal Australian College of Medical Administrators

FRACO Fellow of the

Royal Australian College of Ophthalmologists

FRACOG Fellow of the Royal Australian College of Obstetricians and Gynaecologists

FRACP Fellow of the Royal Australasian College of Physicians

FRACR Fellow of the Royal Australasian College of Radiologists

FRACS Fellow of the Royal Australasian College of Surgeons

FRAD Fellow of the Royal Academy of Dancing

FRAeS Fellow of the Royal Aeronautical Society

FRAgSs Fellow of the Royal Agricultural Societies

FRAHS Fellow of the Royal Australian Historical Society

FRAI Fellow of the Royal Anthropological Institute

FRAIA Fellow of the Royal Australian Institute of Architects

FRAIC Fellow of the Royal Architectural Institute of Canada

FRAIPA Fellow of the Royal Australian Institute of Public Administration

FRAM Fellow of the Royal Academy of Music

FRAME (freim) Fund for the Replacement of Animals in Medical Experiments

FRANZCP Fellow of the Royal Australian and New Zealand College of Psychiatrists

FRAPI Fellow of the Royal Australian Planning Institute

FRAS Fellow of the Royal Asiatic Society • Fellow of the Royal Astronomical Society

FRASE Fellow of the Royal Agricultural Society of England

FRBS Fellow of the Royal Botanic Society • Fellow of the Royal Society of British Sculptors

FRC Financial Reporting Council

FRCD *Banking* floating-rate certificate of deposit

FRCM Fellow of the Royal College of Music

FRcn Fellow of the Royal College of Nursing

FRCO Fellow of the Royal College of Organists

FRCO(CHM) Fellow of the Royal College of Organists with Diploma in Choir Training

FRCOG Fellow of the Royal College of Obstetricians and Gynaecologists

FRCP Fellow of the Royal College of Physicians

FRCPA Fellow of the Royal College of Pathologists of Australasia

FRCPath Fellow of the Royal College of Pathologists

FRCPE (or **FRCPEd**) Fellow of the Royal College of Physicians of Edinburgh

FRCPGlas Fellow of the Royal College of Physicians and Surgeons of Glasgow

FRCPI Fellow of the Royal College of Physicians of Ireland

FRCPsych Fellow of the Royal College of Psychiatrists

FRCR Fellow of the Royal College of Radiologists

FRCS Fellow of the Royal College of Surgeons

FRCScI Fellow of the Royal College of Science, Ireland

FRCSE (or **FRCSEd**) Fellow of the Royal College of Surgeons of Edinburgh

FRCSGlas Fellow of the Royal College of Physicians and Surgeons of Glasgow

FRCSI Fellow of the Royal College of Surgeons of Ireland

FRCSoc Fellow of the Royal Commonwealth Society

FRCVS Fellow of the Royal College of Veterinary Surgeons

FREconS Fellow of the Royal Economic Society

FREI Fellow of the Real Estate Institute (Australia)

freq. frequent(ly) • *Grammar* frequentative

FRES Federation of Recruitment and Employment Services

FRG Federal Republic of Germany

FRGS Fellow of the Royal Geographical Society

FRGSA Fellow of the Royal Geographical Society of Australasia

FRHistS Fellow of the Royal Historical Society

FRHS Fellow of the Royal Horticultural Society

Fri. Friday

FRIAS Fellow of the Royal Incorporation of

Architects in Scotland • Fellow of the Royal Institute for the Advancement of Science

FRIBA Fellow of the Royal Institute of British Architects

FRIC Fellow of the Royal Institute of Chemistry (now part of the Royal Society of Chemistry; *see under* FRSC)

FRICS Fellow of the Royal Institution of Chartered Surveyors

FRIH (New Zealand) Fellow of the Royal Institute of Horticulture

FRIN Fellow of the Royal Institute of Navigation

FRINA Fellow of the Royal Institution of Naval Architects

FRIPA Fellow of the Royal Institute of Public Administration

FRIPHH Fellow of the Royal Institute of Public Health and Hygiene

Fris. Frisian

Frl. Fräulein (German: Miss)

FRMCM Fellow of the Royal Manchester College of Music

FRMedSoc Fellow of the Royal Medical Society

FRMetS Fellow of the Royal Meteorological Society

FRMS Fellow of the Royal Microscopical Society

FRN *Finance* floating-rate note

FRNCM Fellow of the Royal Northern College of Music

FRNS Fellow of the Royal Numismatic Society

FRO *Insurance* fire risk only

front. (*or* **frontis.**) frontispiece

FRPharmS Fellow of the Royal Pharmaceutical Society

FRPS Fellow of the Royal Photographic Society

FRPSL Fellow of the Royal Philatelic Society, London

Frs. Frisian

FRS (USA) Federal Reserve System • Fellow of the Royal Society

FRSA Fellow of the Royal Society of Arts

FRSAI Fellow of the Royal Society of Antiquaries of Ireland

FRSAMD Fellow of the Royal Scottish Academy of Music and Drama

FRSC Fellow of the Royal Society of Chemistry (formerly FCS; FRIC)

FRSCM Fellow of the Royal School of Church Music

FRSE Fellow of the Royal Society of Edinburgh

FRSGS Fellow of the Royal Scottish Geographical Society

FRSH Fellow of the Royal Society for the Promotion of Health

FRSL Fellow of the Royal Society of Literature

FRSM Fellow of the Royal Society of Medicine

FRSNZ Fellow of the Royal Society of New Zealand

FRST Fellow of the Royal Society of Teachers

FRSTM&H Fellow of the Royal Society of Tropical Medicine and Hygiene

frt (or **Frt**) freight

FRTPI Fellow of the Royal Town Planning Institute

FRTS Fellow of the Royal Television Society

FRVC Fellow of the Royal Veterinary College

FRVIA Fellow of the Royal Victorian Institute of Architects

FRZSScot Fellow of the Royal Zoological Society of Scotland

FS field security

FSA Fellow of the Society of Antiquaries

FSAA Fellow of the Society of Incorporated Accountants and Auditors

FSAE Fellow of the Society of Art Education • Fellow of the Society of Automotive Engineers

FSAI Fellow of the Society of Architectural Illustrators

FSAM Fellow of the Society of Art Masters

FSAScot (or **FSAS**) Fellow of the Society of Antiquaries of Scotland

FSASM Fellow of the South Australian School of Mines

FSBI Fellow of the Savings Bank Institute

FSCA Fellow of the Society of Company and Commercial Accountants

FSDC Fellow of the Society of Dyers and Colourists

FSE Fellow of the Society of Engineers

FSF Fellow of the Institute

of Shipping and Forwarding Agents

FSG Fellow of the Society of Genealogists

FSGT Fellow of the Society of Glass Technology

FSH *Biochem.* follicle-stimulating hormone

FSLAET Fellow of the Society of Licensed Aircraft Engineers and Technologists

FSLTC Fellow of the Society of Leather Technologists and Chemists

FSMC Freeman of the Spectacle-Makers' Company

FSME Fellow of the Society of Manufacturing Engineers

FSO Foreign Service Officer

FSR Field Service Regulations

FSRP Fellow of the Society for Radiological Protection

FSS Fellow of the Royal Statistical Society

FSTD Fellow of the Society of Typographic Designers

FSVA Fellow of the Incorporated Society of Valuers and Auctioneers

ft feint • *Med.* fiat (Latin: let there be made) • *symbol for* foot (*or* feet) • fort

ft. fortification

Ft *symbol for* forint (Hungarian monetary unit) • Fort

FT Financial Times

FTA (Index) Financial Times Actuaries Share Index

FTAM *Computing* file transfer, access, and management

FTASI Financial Times Actuaries All-Share Index

FTAT Furniture, Timber, and Allied Trades Union

FTC flying training command • Full Technological Certificate (of City and Guilds Institute)

FTCD Fellow of Trinity College, Dublin

FTCL Fellow of Trinity College of Music, London

fth. (*or* **fthm**) fathom

FTI Fellow of the Textile Institute

FTII Fellow of the Institute of Taxation

FT (Index) Financial Times Ordinary Share Index

ft-lb foot-pound

FT Ord Financial Times

(Industrial) Ordinary Share Index

FTP Fellow of Thames Polytechnic

FTPA Fellow of the Town and Country Planning Association

ft/s feet (or foot) per second

FTS Fellow of the Australian Academy of Technological Sciences and Engineering • Fellow of the Tourism Society • flying training school

FTSE 100 (or **FT-SE 100**) Financial Times Stock Exchange 100 Index (or Footsie)

FTZ free-trade zone

FUMIST Fellow of the University of Manchester Institute of Science and Technology

fur. furlong(s)

fut. future • Finance futures

f.v. fishing vessel • (or **fv**)

folio verso (Latin: on the reverse (i.e. left-hand) page)

FVP flash vacuum pyrolysis

FVRDE Fighting Vehicle Research and Development Establishment

FWA Fellow of the World Academy of Arts and Sciences

FWCC Friends' World Committee for Consultation

fwd forward

f.w.d. four-wheel drive • front-wheel drive

FWeldI Fellow of the Welding Institute

f.w.t. (or **FWT**) fair wear and tear

FY postcode for Blackpool

FYC Family and Youth Concern

FYI (or **f.y.i.**) for your information

FZS Fellow of the Zoological Society

G

g *Physics, symbol for* acceleration of free fall • gallon(s) • *Chem.* gaseous (as in **H₂O(g)**) • *Physics, symbol for* gluon • *symbol for* gram(s) • *Physics, symbol for* grav • *indicating* the seventh row of vertical squares from the left on a chessboard

g. geographical (as in **g. mile**) • guilder(s) • guinea(s)

G (ital.) *Physics, symbol for* conductance • *Magnetism, symbol for* gauss • *Films* (Australia, USA) general exhibition (certification) • *symbol for* giga- (prefix indicating 10⁹, as in **GHz** (gigahertz), *or* (in computing) 2³⁰) • *postcode for* Glasgow • *symbol for* gourde (Haitian monetary unit) • *Slang* grand (1000 pounds or dollars) • (ital.) *Physics, symbol for* gravitational constant • *Biochem., symbol for* guanine • *Biochem., symbol for* guanosine • *symbol for* guarani (Paraguayan monetary

unit) • (ital.) *Physics, symbol for* shear modulus • *indicating* a musical note or key

G. (*or* **G**) German(y) • good • Gulf (on maps, etc.)

G3 Group of Three (most powerful western economies)

G5 *Finance* Group of Five (nations that agreed to exchange-rate stabilization)

G7 (*or* **G-7**) Group of Seven (leading industrial nations)

G10 *Finance* Group of Ten (nations lending money to the IMF)

G24 Group of Twenty Four (industrialized nations)

G77 Group of Seventy Seven (developing countries)

g.a. *Marine insurance* general average

Ga *Chem., symbol for* gallium

Ga. Georgia

GA Gaelic Athletic (Club) • Gamblers Anonymous • general agent • *Linguistics*

General American • General Assembly (of the UN) • (or **G/A**) *Marine insurance* general average • Geographical Association • Geologists' Association • *US postcode for* Georgia • *Sport* goal attack

GAA (Ireland) Gaelic Athletic Association

GAB general arrangements to borrow (in the IMF)

GABA ('gæbə) *Biochem.* gamma-aminobutyric acid (a neurotransmitter)

GAFTA ('gæftə) Grain and Free Trade Association

GAI Guild of Architectural Ironmongers

gal (*or* **gal.**) gallon(s)

Gal. *Bible* Galatians

gall. gallon

galv. galvanic • galvanize(d)

G&AE *Accounting* general and administrative expense

G and O *Med.* gas and oxygen (in anaesthetic)

G & S Gilbert and Sullivan

G & T (*or* **g and t**) gin and tonic

GAR Grand Army of the Republic (in the American Civil War)

GATT (*or* **Gatt**) (gæt)

General Agreement on Tariffs and Trade

gaz. gazette • gazetteer

Gb *Magnetism, symbol for* gilbert

GB Great Britain (abbrev. *or* IVR)

GBA *international vehicle registration for* Alderney

GBE (Knight *or* Dame) Grand Cross of the Order of the British Empire

GBG *international vehicle registration for* Guernsey

GBH grievous bodily harm

GBJ *international vehicle registration for* Jersey

GBM *international vehicle registration for* Isle of Man

g.b.o. goods in bad order

GBS George Bernard Shaw (1856–1950, Irish-born dramatist and critic)

GBZ *international vehicle registration for* Gibraltar

GC George Cross

GCA Girls' Clubs of America • *Aeronautics* ground-controlled approach • *international vehicle registration for* Guatemala

GCB (Knight *or* Dame) Grand Cross of the Order of the Bath

GCBS General Council of British Shipping

GCC Gas Consumers Council • Gulf Cooperation Council

GCD (or **g.c.d.**) *Maths.* greatest common divisor

GCE General Certificate of Education

GCF (or **g.c.f.**) *Maths.* greatest common factor

GCH (Knight) Grand Cross of the Hanoverian Order

GCHQ Government Communications Headquarters

GCI *Aeronautics* ground-controlled interception

GCIE (Knight) Grand Commander of the Order of the Indian Empire

GCLJ Grand Cross of St Lazarus of Jerusalem

GCLH Grand Cross of the Legion of Honour

GCM Good Conduct Medal • (or **g.c.m.**) *Statistics* greatest common measure • (or **g.c.m.**) *Maths.* greatest common multiple

GCMG (Knight or Dame) Grand Cross of the Order of St Michael and St George

GCON Grand Cross of the Order of the Niger

GCSE General Certificate of Secondary Education

GCSG (Knight) Grand Cross of the Order of St Gregory the Great

GCSI (Knight) Grand Commander of the Order of the Star of India

GCSJ (Knight) Grand Cross of Justice of the Order of St John of Jerusalem

GCStJ (Bailiff or Dame) Grand Cross of the Most Venerable Order of the Hospital of St John of Jerusalem

GCVO (Knight or Dame) Grand Cross of the Royal Victorian Order

gd good • (or **g.d.**) granddaughter • ground

Gd *Chem., symbol for* gadolinium

GD *Netball* goal defence • Grand Duke (or Duchess or Duchy)

GDBA Guide Dogs for the Blind Association

GDC General Dental Council

Gdns Gardens

GDP (or **gdp**) gross domestic product

GDR German Democratic

Republic (East Germany; now part of Germany)

gds goods

Ge *Chem., symbol for* germanium

GEC (UK) General Electric Company

GED general educational development

GEF Global Environment Facility (of the World Bank)

gen. gender • genealogy • general(ly) • generic • genitive • *Biology* genus

Gen. General • *Bible* Genesis • Geneva

geneal. genealogy

genit. genitive

Genl General

geod. geodesy • geodetic

geog. geographer • geographic(al) • geography

geol. geologic(al) • geologist • geology

geom. geometric(al) • geometry

ger. gerund(ive)

Ger. German(y)

Gerbil ('dʒɜ:bɪl) Great Education Reform Bill (1988)

Ges. Gesellschaft (German: company *or* society)

Gestapo (ge'stɑːpəʊ) Geheime Staatspolizei (German: secret state police; in Nazi Germany)

gds goods

Ge *Chem., symbol for* germanium

GeV *Physics, symbol for* gigaelectronvolt(s)

GF *symbol for* Guinean franc

GFOFs *Stock exchange* geared futures and options and funds

GFR German Federal Republic

GFS Girls' Friendly Society

GG Girl Guides • Governor General

gge garage

g.gr. great gross (144 dozen)

GH *international vehicle registration for* Ghana • *Biochem.* growth hormone

GHOST (gəʊst) global horizontal sounding technique (for collecting atmospheric data)

GHQ *Military* General Headquarters

GHz *symbol for* gigahertz

gi. gill (unit of measure)

Gi *Magnetism, symbol for* gilbert

GI (*or* **g.i.**) galvanized iron • (*or* **g.i.**) gastrointestinal • generic issue • (Royal) Glasgow Institute (of the Fine Arts) • (USA) government (*or* general) issue (hence, a US serviceman)

Gib. Gibraltar

GIFT (gɪft) *Med.* gamete intrafallopian transfer (for assisting conception)

GIGO (*or* **gigo**) ('gaɪgəʊ) *Computing* garbage in, garbage out

GIMechE Graduate of the Institution of Mechanical Engineers

GINO ('dʒiːnəʊ) graphical input output (for computer graphics)

GIP (*or* **g.i.p.**) glazed imitation parchment (a type of paper)

Gk Greek

GK goalkeeper

GKC G(ilbert) K(eith) Chesterton (1874–1936, British journalist and author)

gl. gill (unit of measure) • glass • gloss

g/l grams per litre

GL *postcode for* Gloucester • Grand Luxe (of a car)

4GL *Computing* fourth-generation language

GLAB Greater London Arts Board

glam (glæm) *Colloquial* greying, leisured, affluent, married

Glam. Glamorgan

Glas. Glasgow

GLC *Chem.* gas–liquid chromatography, • Greater London Council (abolished 1986) • ground-level concentration (of radioactive material)

GLCM ground-launched cruise missile

gld. guilder

Gln (*or* **gln**) *Biochem.* glutamine

Glos Gloucestershire

gloss. glossary

glt *Bookbinding* gilt

Glu (*or* **glu**) *Biochem.* glutamic acid

Gly (*or* **gly**) *Biochem.* glycine

gm gram

g m *symbol for* gram metre

GM *Physics* Geiger–Müller (as in **GM counter**) • general manager • General Motors Corporation • geometric mean • George Medal • *Education* grant maintained

G-man (USA) Government man (an FBI agent)

g.m.b. good merchantable brand

GMB General, Municipal,

Boilermakers (trade union; formerly GMBATU; GMWU) • Grand Master (of the Order) of the Bath

GMBE Grand Master of the Order of the British Empire

GmbH (Germany) Gesellschaft mit beschränkter Haftung (private limited company; Ltd)

Gmc Germanic

GMC general management committee • General Medical Council • Guild of Memorial Craftsmen

GMIE Grand Master of the Order of the Indian Empire

GMKP Grand Master of the Knights of St Patrick

GMMG Grand Master of the Order of St Michael and St George

GMP Grand Master of the Order of St Patrick

g.m.q. good merchantable quality

GMS *Education* grant-maintained status

GMSI Grand Master of the Order of the Star of India

GMST *Astronomy* Greenwich Mean Sidereal Time

GMT Greenwich Mean Time

GMW gram-molecular weight

gn. guinea

GNC General Nursing Council (replaced by UKCC)

gnd ground

GNP gross national product

Gnr *Military* Gunner

gns guineas

GNVQ General National Vocational Qualification

GO General Office(r) • *Military* general order

g.o.b. good ordinary brand

GOC General Officer Commanding

GOC-in-C General Officer Commanding-in-Chief

GOE General Ordination Examination

GOM Grand Old Man

GOP (USA) Grand Old Party (the Republican Party)

Gosplan ('gɒs,plæn) Gos-(udarstvennaya) Plan(ovaya Comissiya) (Russian: State Planning Commission)

GOT *Biochem., Med.* glutamatic oxaloacetic transaminase (renamed aspartate aminotransferase, AST)

Goth. Gothic

Gov. (or **gov.**) government • governor

Govt (or **govt**) government

gox (or **GOX**) (goks) *Chem.* gaseous oxygen

gp (or **Gp**) group

GP Gallup Poll • *Music* general pause • general practitioner • general purpose • Gloria Patri (Latin: glory be to the Father) • graduated pension • Grand Prix

GPALS Global Protection Against Limited Strikes (reduced SDI programme)

Gp Capt Group Captain

gpd gallons per day

gph (or **GPH**) gallons per hour

GPI *Med.* general paralysis of the insane

GPM (or **gpm**) gallons per minute

GPMU Graphical, Paper, and Media Union (formed by merger of NGA and SOGAT)

GPO General Post Office

GPR ground-penetrating radar

GPS (or **gps**) gallons per second • (Australia) Great Public Schools (indicating a group of mainly nonstate schools, and of sporting competitions between them)

GPT *Biochem., Med.* glutamic pyruvic transaminase (renamed alanine aminotransferase, ALT) • Guild of Professional Toastmasters

GPU General Postal Union (*see* UPU) • Gosudarstvennoye Politicheskoye Upravlenie (Russian: State Political Administration; Soviet state security system, 1922–23)

GQ *Military* general quarters

gr. grade • (or **gr**) grain (the unit) • gram • gross

Gr. Grecian • Greece • Greek

GR *Science* gamma ray • *Physics* general relativity • Georgius Rex (Latin: King George) • *international vehicle registration for* Greece • Gulielmus Rex (Latin: King William)

grad. graduate(d)

gram. grammar(ian) • grammatical

GRC General Research Corporation

GRE Guardian Royal Exchange Assurance Group

gro. gross (unit of quantity)

grp group

grs grains · gross

gr. t. gross ton

GRU Glavnoye Razvedyvatelnoye Upravleniye (Russian: Central Intelligence Office)

gr. wt. gross weight

gs. guineas

g.s. (*or* **gs**) grandson

GS General Secretary · general service · *Military* General Staff · *Netball* goal shooter · grammar school

GSA Girls' Schools Association · Glasgow School of Art

GSC *Chem.* gas–solid chromatography

g.s.m. *Commerce* good sound merchantable (quality)

GSM general sales manager · (*or* **GSMD**) (Member of the) Guildhall School of Music and Drama

GSO General Staff Officer

GSP *Chem.* glass–fibre strengthened polyester · Good Service Pension

GSR galvanic skin reflex (*or* response)

GSS Government Statistical Service

GST *Astronomy* Greenwich Sidereal Time

g-st *Knitting* garter-stitch

gt *Bookbinding* gilt · great

gt. *Med.* gutta (Latin: a drop)

GT gas turbine · *Physics* gauge theory · Gran Turismo (Italian: grand touring; sports car)

Gt Brit. (*or* **Gt Br.**) Great Britain

GTC (Scotland) General Teaching Council · (*or* **g.t.c.**) *Commerce* good till cancelled (*or* countermanded)

gtd guaranteed

GTI Gran Turismo Injection (sports car)

GTO Gran Turismo Omologata (Italian: certified for grand touring; of sports cars)

GTS gas turbine ship

GU (*or* **g.u.**) genitourinary · US postcode for Guam · postcode for Guildford

guar. guarantee(d)

Guat. Guatemala

gui. *Music* guitar

GUI Golfing Union of Ireland • ('guːɪ) *Computing* graphic user interface

Guin. Guinea

Gulag ('guːlæg) Glavnoye Upravleniye Lagerei (Soviet prison and labour camp system)

GUM (gʌm) (Russia) Gosudarstvenni Universalni Magazin (Universal State Store)

GUT (gʌt) *Physics* grand unified theory

GUY *international vehicle registration for* Guyana

g.v. gravimetric volume

GV (France) grande vitesse (fast goods train)

gvt (*or* **Gvt**) government

GVW gross vehicle weight

GW *symbol for* gigawatt(s) • guided weapons (as in **GW cruiser**)

GWR Great Western Railway

Gy *Physics, symbol for* gray

gyn. (*or* **GYN, gynaecol.**) gynaecological • gynaecology

H

h (ital.) *Physics, symbol for* heat transfer coefficient • *symbol for* hecto- (prefix indicating 100, as in **hm**, hectometre) • (ital.) *symbol for* height • *symbol for* hour • (ital.) *Physics, symbol for* Planck constant • (ital.) *Thermodynamics, symbol for* specific enthalpy • (ital.) *Maths.*, indicating a small increment • *indicating the*

eighth vertical row of squares from the left on a chessboard

h. harbour • hard(ness) • height • high • horizontal • *Music* horn • hour • hundred • husband

H (ital.) *Thermodynamics, symbol for* enthalpy • hard (indicating the degree of hardness of lead in a pencil; also in **HB**, hard black;

HH (or **2H**), double hard; etc.) • *Physics, symbol for* henry(s) • *Slang* heroin • *Med., Pharmacol.* histamine receptor (in **H₁, H₂**; used in specifying types of antihistamines) • *international vehicle registration for* Hungary • *Chem., symbol for* hydrogen • (bold ital.) *Physics, symbol for* magnetic field strength

H. (or **H**) *Advertising* halfpage • Harbour • hardness • *Cards* hearts • herbaceous • hospital • hydrant

ha *symbol for* hectare

h.a. hoc anno (Latin: in this year)

Ha *Chem., symbol for* hahnium (element 105)

HA *Horticulture* hardy annual • *postcode for* Harrow • Health Authority • heavy artillery • Highway(s) Act • Historical Association

HAA heavy anti-aircraft • *Immunol.* hepatitis-associated antigen

HA & M (ital.) Hymns Ancient and Modern

Hab. *Bible* Habakkuk

HAC Honourable Artillery Company

HAF Hellenic Air Force

Hag. *Bible* Haggai

HAI hospital-acquired infection

H. & B. *Botany* Humboldt and Bonpland (indicating the authors of a species, etc.)

h & c (or **H & C**) hot and cold (water)

Hants Hampshire

h. app. heir apparent

HARCVS Honorary Associate of the Royal College of Veterinary Surgeons

HART (hɑːt) (New Zealand) Halt All Racist Tours (antiracist sports organization)

Harv. (USA) Harvard University

HAT housing action (or association) trust

HB hard-black (on pencils; indicating medium-hard lead) • *Horticulture* hardy biennial

H.B. & K. *Botany* Humboldt, Bonpland, and Kunth (indicating the authors of a species, etc.)

HBC *Electrical engineering* high breaking capacity • Hudson's Bay Company

HBIG hepatitis B immunoglobulin

HBLV *Med.* human B-lymphotropic virus

HBM Her (*or* His) Britannic Majesty (*or* Majesty's)

H-bomb hydrogen bomb

HBP high blood pressure

HBV hepatitis B virus

h.c. (*or* **hc**) honoris causa (Latin: for the sake of honour; honorary) • hot and cold (water)

h/c *Insurance* held covered

HC Heralds' College • High Church • Highway Code • Holy Communion • House of Commons

H/C *Insurance* held covered

HCAAS Homeless Children's Aid and Adoption Society

hcap (*or* **h'cap**) handicap

HCBA Hotel and Catering Benevolent Association

HCF (*or* **h.c.f.**) *Maths.* highest common factor • Honorary Chaplain to the Forces

HCFC *Chem.* hydrochlorofluorocarbon

HCH hexachlorocyclohexane (an insecticide)

HCI human–computer interface (*or* interaction)

HCIMA Hotel Catering and Institutional Management Association

HCM His (*or* Her) Catholic Majesty

hcp handicap

h.c.p. *Crystallog.* hexagonal close-packed

HCSA Hospital Consultants and Specialists Association

hd hand • head

h.d. heavy duty • *Med.* hora decubitus (Latin: at bedtime)

HD Hodgkin's disease • *postcode for* Huddersfield • *Chem.* hydrogen-deuterium

HDA (Australia) Hawkesbury Diploma in Agriculture

hdbk handbook

HDD *Aeronautics, Computing* head-down display • Higher Dental Diploma

HDipEd Higher Diploma in Education

hdkf handkerchief

HDL *Biochem., Med.* high-density lipoprotein

HDLC *Computing* high-level data link control (a communications protocol)

hdlg handling

HDP (*or* **HDPE**) *Chem.*

high-density polyethylene (*or* polyethene)

hdqrs headquarters

HDR hot dry rock (in **HDR energy**)

HDTV high-definition television

hdwd hardwood • headword

He *Chem., symbol for* helium

HE higher education • high explosive • His Eminence • His (*or* Her) Excellency • horizontal equivalent

HEAO High Energy Astronomy (*or* Astrophysical) Observatory

Heb. Hebrew (language) • *Bible* Hebrews

HEC (école des) hautes études commerciales (French: (college of) higher commercial studies) • Higher Education Corporation

HEH His (*or* Her) Exalted Highness

HEIC Honourable East India Company

HEICS Honourable East India Company's Service

heir app. heir apparent

heir pres. heir presumptive

HEO Higher Executive Officer • highly elliptic-inclined orbit (as in **HEO satellite**)

HEOS high-elliptic-inclined-orbit satellite

HEP *Statistics* human error probability

her. heraldic • heraldry

herp. (*or* **herpet.**, **herpetol.**) herpetologist • herpetology

Herts Hertfordshire

hex (hɛks) *Computing* hexadecimal (notation)

hex. hexachord • hexagonal

hf half

Hf *Chem., symbol for* hafnium

HF hard firm (on pencils; indicating hard lead) • *Radio, etc.* high frequency

HFA *Chem.* hydrofluoroalkane

HFARA Honorary Foreign Associate of the Royal Academy

hf. bd. *Bookbinding* half binding (*or* bound)

HFC *Electricity* high-frequency current • *Chem.* hydrofluorocarbon

HFRA Honorary Foreign Member of the Royal Academy

hg *symbol for* hectogram(s)

Hg *Chem., symbol for* mercury (Latin *hydrargyrum*)

HG *postcode for* Harrogate • High German • His (*or* Her) Grace • Home Guard • Horse Guards

HGG *Med.* hypogammaglobulinaemia

hGH (*or* **HGH**) *Biochem.* human growth hormone

hgt height

HGTAC Home Grown Timber Advisory Committee

HGV heavy goods vehicle

HGW heat-generating waste

hh hands (height measurement for horses)

HH (*or* **2H**) double hard (on pencils; indicating very hard lead) • *Astronomy* Herbig–Haro (in **HH object**) • (Member of the Hesketh Hubbard Art Society) • His (*or* Her) Highness • His Holiness (title of the Pope)

HHA *Horticulture* half-hardy annual • Historic Houses Association

HHB *Horticulture* half-hardy biennial

hhd hogshead

HHH (*or* **3H**) treble hard (on pencils; indicating very hard lead)

HHNK *Med.* hyperglycaemic hyperosmolar nonketoacidotic coma (in diabetes)

H-Hour Hour Hour (i.e. the specified time at which an operation is to begin)

HHP *Horticulture* half-hardy perennial

HHS (USA) Department of Health and Human Services (replaced HEW)

HI *US postcode for* Hawaii • Hawaiian Islands • hearing impaired • hic iacet (Latin: here lies; on gravestones)

HIDB Highlands and Islands Development Board

hi-fi ('haɪˌfaɪ) high fidelity

HIH His (*or* Her) Imperial Highness

hilac (*or* **HILAC**) ('haɪlæk) *Nuclear physics* heavy-ion linear accelerator

HILAT ('haɪlæt) high-latitude (in **HILAT satellite**)

HIM His (*or* Her) Imperial Majesty

Hind. Hindi • Hindu • Hindustan(i)

His (*or* **his**) *Biochem.* histidine

HIS hic iacet sepultus *or*

sepulta (Latin: here lies buried; on gravestones)

hist. (or **histol.**) histology • history

HIV human immunodeficiency virus (the cause of AIDS)

HJ hic jacet (Latin: here lies; on gravestones) • Hilal-e-Jurat (Pakistani honour)

HJS hic jacet sepultus or sepulta (Latin: here lies buried; on gravestones)

HK Hong Kong (abbrev. or IVR) • House of Keys (Manx Parliament)

HKJ international vehicle registration for (Hashemite Kingdom of) Jordan

hl (or **hL**) symbol for hectolitre(s)

HL House of Lords

HLA Immunol. human lymphocyte antigen (as in **HLA system**)

HLD Doctor of Humane Letters

HLI Highland Light Infantry

HLW high-level (radioactive) waste

hm symbol for hectometre(s)

HM Chem. hazardous material • headmaster (or head-mistress) • Her (or His) Majesty

HMA Head Masters' Association • Computing high-memory area

HMAS Her (or His) Majesty's Australian Ship

HMC Headmasters' Conference • Hospital Management Committee • Household Mortgage Corporation

HMCA Hospital and Medical Care Association

HMCIC Her (or His) Majesty's Chief Inspector of Constabulary

HMCN Her (or His) Majesty's Canadian Navy

HMCS Her (or His) Majesty's Canadian Ship

HMF Her (or His) Majesty's Forces

HMG Her (or His) Majesty's Government

HMHS Her (or His) Majesty's Hospital Ship

HMI Her (or His) Majesty's Inspector (of schools) • Computing human–machine interface

HMIED Honorary Member of the Institute of Engineering Designers

HMIP Her (or His)

Majesty's Inspectorate of Pollution

HMNZS Her (*or* His) Majesty's New Zealand Ship

HMOCS Her (*or* His) Majesty's Overseas Civil Service

HMP hoc monumentum posuit (Latin: (he *or* she) erected this monument)

HMS Her (*or* His) Majesty's Service • Her (*or* His) Majesty's Ship

HMSO Her (*or* His) Majesty's Stationery Office

HMV His Master's Voice (gramophone-record company)

hn *Music* horn

HNC *Education* Higher National Certificate

HND *Education* Higher National Diploma

ho. house

Ho *Chem.*, symbol for holmium

HO *Law* habitual offender • head office • Home Office

HoC House of Commons

HoD head of department

H of C House of Commons

H of K House of Keys

H of L House of Lords

H of R (USA) House of Representatives

Hol *Geology* Holocene

HOLLAND hope our love lasts (*or* lives) and never dies

hon. honorary • honourable

Hon (*or* **Hon.**) Honorary (in titles, as in **HonFInstP**, Honorary Fellow of the Institute of Physics) • Honorary Member (in titles, as in **HonRCM**, Honorary Member of the Royal College of Music) • Honourable (title)

Hond. Honduras

hons honours

Hon. Sec. Honorary Secretary

HOOD (hŏŏd) *Computing* hierarchical object-oriented design

Hook. *Botany* (Sir William) Hooker (indicating the author of a species, etc.)

Hook. fil. *Botany* Hooker fils (Sir Joseph Hooker, son of Sir William Hooker; indicating the author of a species, etc.)

hor. horizon • horizontal

horol. horology

hort. horticultural • horticulture

Hos. *Bible* Hosea

hosp. hospital

hp *symbol for* horsepower

h.p. hire purchase

HP *Horticulture* hardy perennial • *postcode for* Hemel Hempstead • (USA) Hewlett–Packard (electronics and computing manufacturer) • high performance • *Electricity* high power • hire purchase • house physician • Houses of Parliament

hpch. (*or* **hpd**) harpsichord

HPk Hilal-e-Pakistan (Pakistani honour)

HPP *Chem.* high-pressure polyethylene (*or* polyethene)

HPV *Med.* human papilloma virus

HQ (*or* **h.q.**) headquarters

HQA Hilal-i-Quaid-i-Azam (Pakistani honour)

hr hour

Hr Herr (German: Mr, Sir)

HR *Med.* heart rate • *postcode for* Hereford • Home Rule(r) • (USA) House of Representatives

HRCA Honorary Royal Cambrian Academician

HRE Holy Roman Emperor (*or* Empire)

HRGI Honorary Member of the Royal Glasgow Institute of the Fine Arts

HRH Her (*or* His) Royal Highness

HRHA Honorary Member of the Royal Hibernian Academy

HRI Honorary Member of the Royal Institute of Painters in Water Colours

HRIP hic requiescit in pace (Latin: here rests in peace; on gravestones)

Hrn Herr(e)n (German: Messrs, Sirs)

HROI Honorary Member of the Royal Institute of Oil Painters

HRP *Military* human remains pouch

hrs hours

HRSA Honorary Member of the Royal Scottish Academy

HRSW Honorary Member of the Royal Scottish Water Colour Society

HRT *Med.* hormone replacement therapy

h.s. hoc sensu (Latin: in this sense) • *Med.* hora somni (Latin: at bedtime)

HS hic sepultus *or* sepulta (Latin: here is buried; on gravestones) • high school • Home Secretary

HSA *Med.* human serum albumin

HSC Health and Safety Commission • Higher School Certificate (replaced by GCE A level)

HSDU hospital sterilization and disinfection unit

HSE Health and Safety Executive • hic sepultus (*or* sepulta) est (Latin: here lies buried; on gravestones)

HSH Her (*or* His) Serene Highness

HSI *Computing* human–system interface (*or* interaction)

HSM Her (*or* His) Serene Majesty

HSS Fellow of the Historical Society (Latin *Historicae Societatis Socius*)

HSSU hospital sterile supply unit

HST Hawaii Standard Time • high-speed train • Hubble Space Telescope

HSV herpes simplex virus

ht height

HT *Sport* half time • Hawaii Time

5-HT *Biochem.* 5-hydroxytryptamine

HTLV *Med.* human T-cell lymphotropic virus

Hts Heights (in place names)

HTV Harlech Television

HU *postcode for* Hull

HUAC ('hjuːæk) House (of Representatives) Un-American Activities Committee

HUD *Aeronautics, Computing* head-up display

Hugo ('hjuːgəʊ) Human Genome Organization

hum. human • (*or* **Hum.**) humanities (classics) • humorous

HUMINT (*or* **humint**) ('hjuːmɪnt) *Military* human intelligence (espionage activities)

HUMV ('hʌm,viː) *Military* human light vehicle

Hung. Hungarian • Hungary

Husat ('hjuːsæt) Human Science and Advanced Technology Research Institute

h.v. high velocity

HV health visitor • high velocity • high voltage

HVA Health Visitors' Association (trade union; now a section of the MFS)

HVAC heating, ventilation, air conditioning • high-voltage alternating current

HVCert Health Visitor's Certificate

HVDC high-voltage direct current

HVP hydrolysed vegetable protein

h.w. *Cricket* hit wicket

h/w herewith

HW hazardous waste • high water • hot water

HWM high-water mark

HX *postcode for* Halifax

hy heavy

hyg. hygiene

hyp. *Maths.* hypotenuse • (*or* **hypoth.**) hypothesis • (*or* **hypoth.**) hypothetical

Hz *Physics, symbol for* hertz

---

i *symbol for* the imaginary number √−1

i. incisor (tooth) • *Banking* interest • *Grammar* intransitive

I (ital.) *Physics, symbol for* electric current • *symbol for* inti (Peruvian monetary unit) • *Chem., symbol for* iodine • (ital.) *Physics, symbol for* isospin quantum number • *international vehicle registration for* Italy • (ital.; *or* **I**ᵥ) *Physics, symbol for* luminous intensity • *Roman numeral for* one • (ital.; *or* **I**ₑ) *Physics, symbol* *for* radiant intensity • *Logic, indicating* a particular affirmative categorial statement

I. (*or* **I**) Iesus (Latin: Jesus) • Imperator (Latin: Emperor) • Imperatrix (Latin: Empress) • Independence • Independent • Infidelis (Latin: unbeliever, infidel) • Institute • International • Ireland • Island (*or* Isle)

i.a. in absentia (Latin: while absent)

Ia. Iowa

IA Indian Army • information anxiety • Institute of

Actuaries • *US postcode for Iowa*

IA5 *Computing* International Alphabet, Number 5

IAA indoleacetic acid (plant hormone) • International Advertising Association

IAAF International Amateur Athletic Federation

IAAS Incorporated Association of Architects and Surveyors

IAC Institute of Amateur Cinematographers

IACP International Association of Chiefs of Police

IACS International Annealed Copper Standard

IADR International Association for Dental Research

IAEA International Atomic Energy Agency

IAF Indian Air Force • Indian Auxiliary Force

IAGB & I Ileostomy Association of Great Britain and Ireland

IAHM Incorporated Association of Headmasters

IALA International Association of Lighthouse Authorities

IAM Institute of Administrative Management • Institute of Advanced Motorists • Institute of Aviation Medicine

IAMC Indian Army Medical Corps

IAO Incorporated Association of Organists

IAOC Indian Army Ordnance Corps

IAPS Incorporated Association of Preparatory Schools

IAPSO International Association for the Physical Sciences of the Oceans

IARF International Association for Religious Freedom

IARO Indian Army Reserve of Officers

IARU International Amateur Radio Union

IAS *Computing* immediate access store • Indian Administrative (formerly Civil) Service • (*or* **i.a.s.**) *Aeronautics* indicated air speed

IASS International Association for Scandinavian Studies

IAT International Atomic Time

IATA (aɪˈɑːtə, iːˈɑːtə) International Air Transport Association

IATUL International Association of Technological University Libraries

IAU International Association of Universities • International Astronomical Union

IAWPRC International Association on Water Pollution Research and Control

ib. ibidem (*see* ibid.)

IB in bond • International Bank (for Reconstruction and Development) • invoice book

IBA Independent Broadcasting Authority • *Horticulture* indole 3-butyric acid (rooting compound) • International Bar Association

IBB Invest in Britain Bureau

IBBR *Finance* interbank bid rate

IBD *Med.* inflammatory bowel disease

IBEL *Finance* interest-bearing eligible liability

IBF International Badminton Federation • International Boxing Federation

IBG Institute of British Geographers

IBI (*or* **i.b.i.**) Book-keeping invoice book inwards

ibid. ibidem (Latin: in the

same place; indicating a previously cited reference to a book, etc.)

IBiol Institute of Biology

IBM International Business Machines (Corporation; computer manufacturer)

IBMBR *Finance* interbank market bid rate

IBO (*or* **i.b.o.**) Book-keeping invoice book outwards

IBRD International Bank for Reconstruction and Development (the World Bank)

IBRO International Bank Research Organization • International Brain Research Organization

IBS (*or* **IB(Scot)**) Institute of Bankers in Scotland

IBTE Institution of British Telecommunications Engineers

i/c in charge (of) • in command

IC identity card • Iesus Christus (Latin: Jesus Christ) • *Grammar* immediate constituent • *Astrology* Imum Coeli (the lowest point on the ecliptic below the horizon) • *Electronics* integrated circuit • *Engineering* internal-combustion (engine)

ICA ignition control additive (for motor vehicles) • Institute of Chartered Accountants in England and Wales • Institute of Contemporary Arts • International Coffee Agreement • International Colour Authority • International Cooperation Administration • International Council on Archives • International Cyclist Association

ICAA Invalid Children's Aid Association

ICAEW Institute of Chartered Accountants in England and Wales

ICAI Institute of Chartered Accountants in Ireland

ICAO International Civil Aviation Organization

ICAS Institute of Chartered Accountants of Scotland

ICBM intercontinental ballistic missile

ICBN International Code of Botanical Nomenclature

ICBP International Council for Bird Preservation

ICC International Chamber of Commerce • International Convention Centre (Birmingham) • International (formerly Imperial) Cricket Conference

ICCA International Cocoa Agreement

ICCH International Commodities Clearing House

ICCPR International Covenant on Civil and Political Rights (of the UN)

ICCROM International Centre for Conservation at Rome

ICD International Classification of Diseases (WHO publication)

Ice. Iceland(ic)

ICE *Med.* ice, compress, elevation (treatment for limb bruises) • Institution of Civil Engineers • internal-combustion engine

ICED International Council for Educational Development

ICEF International Federation of Chemical, Energy, and General Workers' Unions

Icel. Iceland(ic)

IC engine internal-combustion engine

ICER Industry Council for Electronic Equipment Recycling

ICES International Council for the Exploration of the Sea

ICF *Nuclear engineering* inertial-confinement fusion • International Canoe Federation

ICFTU International Confederation of Free Trade Unions

ICHCA International Cargo Handling Co-ordination Association

IChemE Institution of Chemical Engineers

ichth. (*or* **ichthyol.**) ichthyology

ICI Imperial Chemical Industries • International Commission on Illumination

ICIDH International Classification of Impairments, Disabilities, and Handicaps (WHO publication)

ICJ International Commission of Jurists • International Court of Justice

ICL International Computers Ltd

ICM Institute for Complementary Medicine • Institute of Credit Management • International Confederation of Midwives

ICMS International Centre for Mathematical Sciences (Edinburgh)

ICN Infection Control Nurse • International Council of Nurses

ICNA Infection Control Nurses' Association

ICNB International Code of Nomenclature of Bacteria

ICNCP International Code of Nomenclature of Cultivated Plants

ICNV International Code of Nomenclature of Viruses

ICO Islamic Conference Organization

ICOM International Council of Museums

ICOMOS International Council of Monuments and Sites

ICorrST Institution of Corrosion Science and Technology

ICP *Med.* intracranial pressure

ICPO International Criminal Police Organization (Interpol)

ICR *Computing* intelligent character recognition

ICRC International Committee of the Red Cross

ICRF Imperial Cancer Research Fund

ICRP International Commission on Radiological Protection

ICRU International Commission on Radiation Units (and Measurements)

ICS Indian Civil Service (*see under* IAS) • Institute of Chartered Shipbrokers • International Chamber of Shipping • *Finance* investors' compensation scheme

ICSA Institute of Chartered Secretaries and Administrators

ICSH *Biochem.* interstitial-cell-stimulating hormone

ICSID International Council of Societies of Industrial Design

ICSLS International Convention for Safety of Life at Sea

ICSU International Council of Scientific Unions (in UNESCO)

ICU *Med.* intensive care unit

ICW Institute of Clerks of Works of Great Britain • International Congress of Women • *Telecom.* interrupted continuous waves

ICWA Institute of Cost and Works Accountants

ICZN International Code of Zoological Nomenclature

id. idem (Latin: the same)

Id. Idaho

ID *US postcode for* Idaho • identification • (*or* **i.d.**) inside diameter • Intelligence Department • (*or* **i.d.**) *Med.* intradermal • *symbol for* Iraqi dinar (monetary unit)

IDA International Development Association • Islamic Democratic Association

IDB illicit diamond buying (*or* buyer) • Internal Drainage Board

IDC industrial development certificate

IDD insulin-dependent diabetes • international direct dialling

IDDD *Telecom.* international direct distance dial(ling)

IDDM insulin-dependent diabetes mellitus

IDF International Dental Federation

IDMS *Computing* integrated data-management system

IDN in Dei nomine (Latin: in God's name)

IDP *Computing* integrated

data processing • International Driving Permit

IDRC International Development Research Centre

IDS Income Data Services • Industry Department for Scotland • Institute of Development Studies

IDV International Distillers and Vintners

i.e. id est (Latin: that is) • inside edge

IE Indo-European (languages)

IEA Institute of Economic Affairs • (*or* **IE(Aust)**) Institution of Engineers, Australia • International Energy Agency

IEC industrial energy conservation • International Electrotechnical Commission

IED improvised explosive device

IEDD improvised explosive device disposal (type of bomb disposal)

IEE Institution of Electrical Engineers

IEEIE Institution of Electrical and Electronics Incorporated Engineers

IEHO Institution of Environmental Health Officers

IEI Institution of Engineers of Ireland

IEME Inspectorate of Electrical and Mechanical Engineering

IEng Incorporated Engineer

IERE Institution of Electronic and Radio Engineers

IES Indian Educational Service • Institution of Engineers and Shipbuilders in Scotland

IET interest equalization tax

IExpE Institute of Explosives Engineers

IF *Genetics* initiation factor • *Med.* interferon • *Electronics* intermediate frequency

IFA independent financial adviser

IFAC International Federation of Automatic Control

IFAD International Fund for Agricultural Development (of the UN)

IFALPA International Federation of Air Line Pilots' Associations

IFAW International Fund for Animal Welfare

IFC International Finance Corporation • (USA and Canada) International Fisheries Commission

IFCTU International Federation of Christian Trade Unions (now called World Confederation of Labour, WCL)

IFE *Computing* intelligent front end

iff *Logic, Maths.* if and only if

IFF Identification, Friend or Foe (radar identification system)

IFGO International Federation of Gynaecology and Obstetrics

IFIP International Federation for Information Processing

IFL International Friendship League

IFLA International Federation of Library Associations

IFMC International Folk Music Council

IFORS International Federation of Operational Research Societies

IFP (South Africa) Inkatha Freedom Party

IFPI International Federation of the Phonographic Industry

IFR *Aeronautics* instrument flying regulations

IFRB International Frequency Registration Board

IFS Indian Forest Service • International Federation of Surveyors • Irish Free State

Ig *Immunol.* immunoglobulin (as in **IgA, IgE, IgG**)

IG *postcode for* Ilford • Indo-Germanic (languages) • Inspector General • Instructor in Gunnery

IGasE Institution of Gas Engineers

IGD illicit gold dealer

IGF *Med.* insulin-like growth factor

IGFA International Game Fish Association

IGM *Chess* International Grandmaster

ign. ignite(s) • ignition • ignotus (Latin: unknown)

IGS independent grammar school

IGU International Gas Union • International Geographical Union

IGY International Geophysical Year (1.7.57 to 31.12.58)

IH iacet hic (Latin: here lies; on gravestones)

IHC (New Zealand) intellectually handicapped child

IHD International Hydrological Decade (1965–74) • ischaemic heart disease

IHF International Hospitals Federation

IHospE Institute of Hospital Engineering

ihp indicated horsepower

IHS Jesus (Greek IHΣΟΥΣ)

IHSM Institute of Health Services Management

IHT Institution of Highways and Transportation

IIAC Industrial Injuries Advisory Council

IIAS International Institute of Administrative Sciences

IIB Institut international des brevets (French: International Patent Institute)

iid *Statistics* independent identically distributed (of random variables)

IID insulin-independent diabetes

IIEP International Institute of Educational Planning

3i Investors in Industry

IIL (*or* I²L) *Electronics* integrated injection logic

IIM Institution of Industrial Managers

IInfSc Institute of Information Scientists

IIP International Ice Patrol

IIR *Chem.* isobutylene-isoprene rubber

IIS International Institute of Sociology

IISS International Institute of Strategic Studies

IIT Indian Institute of Technology

IKBS *Computing* intelligent knowledge-based system

IL *US postcode for* Illinois • Institute of Linguists • *Immunol.* interleukin (as in **IL-1, IL-2**) • *international vehicle registration for* Israel

ILA International Law Association • International Longshoremen's Association

ILC International Law Commission (of the UN)

ILEA ('ɪlɪə) Inner London Education Authority

ILEC Inner London Education Committee

ill. illustrate(d) • illustration

Ill. Illinois

illus. (*or* **illust.**) illustrate(d) • illustration • illustrator

ILN (ital.) Illustrated London News

ILO International Labour Organization (of the UN)

ILP Independent Labour Party

ILR independent local radio

ILS *Aeronautics* instrument landing system

ILTF International Lawn Tennis Federation

ILU Institute of London Underwriters

ILW *Nuclear engineering* intermediate-level waste

IM Indian Marines • *Chess* International Master • (*or* **i.m.**) *Med.* intramuscular

IMA Institute of Mathematics and its Applications • International Music Association • Irish Medical Association

IMarE Institute of Marine Engineers

IMARSAT (*or* **Imarsat**) ('ɪmɑːˌsæt) International Maritime Satellite Organization

IMC Institute of Management Consultants • Institute of Measurement and Control • *Aeronautics* instrument meteorological conditions

IMCO Intergovernmental Maritime Consultative Organization (of the UN)

IMEA Incorporated Municipal Electrical Association

IMechE Institution of Mechanical Engineers

IMINT (*or* **Imint**) ('ɪmɪnt) *Military* image intelligence (gained from aerial photography)

IMF International Monetary Fund

IMG International Management Group

IMGTechE Institution of Mechanical and General Technician Engineers

IMinE Institution of Mining Engineers

IMINT (*or* **Imint**) ('ɪmɪnt) *Military* image intelligence (gained from aerial photography)

imit. imitate • imitation • imitative

IMM Institution of Mining and Metallurgy

IMMTS Indian Mercantile Marine Training Ship

IMO International Maritime Organization • International Meteorological Organization • International Miners' Organization

imp. imperative • imperfect • imperial • impersonal • import(ed) • important • importer • impression • imprimatur • imprint

Imp. Imperator (Latin: Emperor) • Imperatrix (Latin: Empress) • Imperial

IMP (imp) *Bridge* International Match Point

imper. imperative

imperf. imperfect • imperforate (of stamps)

impers. impersonal

impf. (*or* **impft**) imperfect

impv. imperative

IMRO ('ɪmrəʊ) Investment Management Regulatory Organization

IMS Indian Medical Service • *Computing, trademark* Information Management System • Institute of Management Services • International Musicological Society

IMT International Military Tribunal

IMU International Mathematical Union

IMunE Institution of Municipal Engineers (now part of the Institution of Civil Engineers)

IMW Institute of Masters of Wine

in *symbol for* inch(es)

in. inch(es)

In *Chem., symbol for* indium

IN *US postcode for* Indiana • Indian Navy

INAO (France) Institut national des appellations d'origine des vins et eaux-de-vie (body controlling wine production)

inbd inboard (on an aircraft, boat, etc.)

Inbucon ('ɪnbjuː,kɒn) International Business Consultants

inc. include(d) • including • inclusive • income • incomplete • incorporate(d) • increase

Inc. Incorporated (after names of business organizations; US equivalent of Ltd)

INCA International Newspaper Colour Association

incl. include(s) • included • including • inclusive

incog. incognito

incorp. (*or* **incor.**) incorporated • incorporation

INCPEN ('ɪŋk,pɛn) Industry Committee for Packaging and the Environment

incr. increase(d) • increasing

in d. *Med.* in dies (Latin: daily)

ind. independence • independent • index • indicative • indirect(ly) • industrial • industry

Ind. *Politics* Independent • India(n) • Indiana • Indies

IND *international vehicle registration for* India • in nomine Dei (Latin: in God's name)

indef. indefinite

indic. indicating • indicative • indicator

indiv. (*or* **individ.**) individual

induc. induction

ined. ineditus (Latin: unpublished)

inf. (*or* **Inf.**) infantry • inferior • infinitive • influence • information • infra (Latin: below)

INF intermediate-range nuclear forces (as in **INF treaty**)

infin. infinitive

infl. influence(d)

INH *Med.* isonicotinic acid hydrazide (isoniazid; antituberculosis drug)

init. initial(ly) • initio (Latin: in the beginning)

INLA Irish National Liberation Army

in lim. in limine (Latin: at the outset)

in loc. in loco (Latin: in place of)

in loc. cit. in loco citato

(Latin: in the place cited (in text))

in mem. in memoriam (Latin: to the memory (of))

inorg. inorganic

in pr. in principio (Latin: in the beginning)

INR independent national radio (as in **INR licence**) • Index of Nursing Research

INRI Iesus Nazarenus Rex Iudaeorum (Latin: Jesus of Nazareth, King of the Jews)

ins. inches • inspector • insulate(d) • insulation • insurance

INS International News Service

INSA Indian National Science Academy

INSEA International Society for Education through Art

INSEAD (*or* **Insead**) Institut européen d'administration des affaires (French: European Institute of Administrative Affairs)

INSET (*or* **Inset**) ('ɪnsɛt) *Education* in-service training

insol. insoluble

insp. inspect(ed) • inspection • (*or* **Insp.**) inspector

inst. instant (this month) •

instantaneous • (*or* **Inst.**) institute • (*or* **Inst.**) institution • instrument(al)

InstAct Institute of Actuaries

InstBE Institution of British Engineers

InstE Institute of Energy

instl. installation

InstMM Institution of Mining and Metallurgy

instn (*or* **Instn**) institution

InstP Institute of Physics

InstPet Institute of Petroleum

InstPI Institute of Patentees and Inventors

instr. instructor • instrument(al)

InstR Institute of Refrigeration

InstSMM Institute of Sales and Marketing Management

InstT Institute of Transport

int. (military) intelligence • interest • interim • interior • internal • (*or* **Int.**) international • interpret(er) • *Music* introit

int. al. inter alia (Latin: among other things)

Intelsat (*or* **INTELSAT**) ('ɪntɛl,sæt) International Telecommunications Satellite Consortium

intens. intensifier • intensive

inter. intermediate

interj. interjection

internat. international

Interpol ('ɪntə,pɒl) International Criminal Police Organization

interrog. interrogate • interrogation • interrogative

intl international

intr. (*or* **intrans.**) intransitive

intro. (*or* **introd.**) introduce • introduction • introductory

INTUC ('ɪntʌk) Indian National Trade Union Congress

INucE Institution of Nuclear Engineers

inv. invent(ed) • invention • inventor • invoice

invt. (*or* **invty**) inventory

IO intelligence officer

I/O *Computing* input/output

IOB (*or* **IoB**) Institute of Bankers (renamed Chartered Institute of Bankers, CIB) • Institute of Building (renamed Chartered Institute of Building, CIOB)

IOC International Olympic Committee

IOCU International Organization of Consumers' Unions

IoD Institute of Directors

IODE (Canada) Imperial Order of Daughters of the Empire

IOF Independent Order of Foresters

I of E Institute of Export

I of M Isle of Man

IOGT International Order of Good Templars

IoJ Institute of Journalists

IOM Indian Order of Merit • Isle of Man

IOOF Independent Order of Oddfellows

IOP *Computing* input/output processor • Institute of Painters in Oil Colours

IoS (ital.) The Independent on Sunday

IOSCO (*or* **Iosco**) (aɪˈɒskəʊ) International Organization of Securities Commissions

IOU I owe you

IOW (*or* **IoW**) Isle of Wight

IP *Med.* in-patient • *postcode for* Ipswich

IPA Institute of Practitioners in Advertising • International Phonetic Alphabet • International Phonetic Association • International Publishers' Association

IPC International Polar Commission • International Publishing Corporation

IPCC Intergovernmental Panel on Climatic Change (of the UN)

IPCS Institution of Professional Civil Servants

IPD *Law* (Scotland) in praesentia dominorum (Latin: in the presence of the Lords (of Session))

IPE Institution of Plant Engineers • Institution of Production Engineers • International Petroleum Exchange

IPFA (Member or Associate of the Chartered) Institute of Public Finance and Accountancy

IPHE Institution of Public Health Engineers (*see* IWEM)

IPI Institute of Patentees and Inventors • International Press Institute

IPlantE Institution of Plant Engineers

IPM Institute of Personnel Management

IPP *Med.* intermittent positive pressure (ventilation)

IPPA Independent Programme Producers' Association

IPPF International Planned Parenthood Federation

IPPR Institute for Public Policy Research

IPPS Institute of Physics and the Physical Society

IPPV *Med.* intermittent positive-pressure ventilation

IPR Institute of Public Relations

IProdE Institution of Production Engineers

ips inches per second • *Computing* instructions per second

IPS inches per second • Indian Police Service • Indian Political Service • Institute of Purchasing and Supply

IPT Institute of Petroleum Technologists

IPTS *Physics* International Practical Temperature Scale

IPU Inter-Parliamentary Union

i.q. idem quod (Latin: the same as)

IQ intelligence quotient

IQA Institute of Quality Assurance

IQS Institute of Quantity Surveyors

i.r. inside radius

Ir *Chem., symbol for* iridium

Ir. Ireland • Irish

IR information retrieval • infrared (radiation) • Inland Revenue • international registration • *international vehicle registration for* Iran • Iranian rial (monetary unit) • *Chem.* isoprene rubber

IRA Irish Republican Army

IRAD Institute for Research on Animal Diseases

Iran. Iranian

IRBM intermediate-range ballistic missile

IRC Industrial Reorganization Corporation

IRCert Industrial Relations Certificate

Ire. Ireland

IREE(Aust) Institution of Radio and Electronics Engineers (Australia)

IRF International Rowing Federation

IRFB International Rugby Football Board

Iris ('aɪrɪs) infrared intruder system

IRIS International Research and Information Service

IRL *international vehicle registration for* Republic of Ireland

IRM *Ethology* innate releasing mechanism

IRN Independent Radio News

IRO Inland Revenue Office • International Refugee Organization

IRPA International Radiation Protection Association

IRQ *Computing* interrupt request • *international vehicle registration for* Iraq

IRR *Finance* internal rate of return

irreg. irregular(ly)

IRRI International Rice Research Institute

IRRV Institute of Revenues, Rating, and Valuation

IRTE Institute of Road Transport Engineers

Is. *Bible* Isaiah • Island(s) • Isle(s)

IS *international vehicle registration for* Iceland • International Society of Sculptors, Painters, and Gravers

Isa. *Bible* Isaiah

ISA industry standard architecture • International Sociological Association • *Aeronautics* International Standard Atmosphere (formerly Interim Standard Atmosphere)

ISAM *Computing* indexed sequential access method

ISBA Incorporated Society of British Advertisers

ISBN International Standard Book Number

ISC Imperial Service College (Haileybury) • Indian Staff Corps • *Med.* intermittent self-catheterization

ISCE International Society of Christian Endeavour

ISCh Incorporated Society of Chiropodists

ISCM International Society for Contemporary Music

ISCO Independent Schools Careers Organization

ISD international subscriber dialling

ISDN *Computing, Telecom.* Integrated Services Digital Network

ISE Indian Service of Engineers • Institution of Structural Engineers • International Stock Exchange of the UK and the Republic of Ireland Ltd

ISF International Shipping Federation

ISI International Statistical Institute • Iron and Steel Institute

ISIS (*or* **Isis**) ('aɪsɪs) Independent Schools Information Service

ISJC Independent Schools Joint Council

ISK *symbol for* króna (Icelandic monetary unit)

isl. (*or* **Isl.**) island • isle

ISM Incorporated Society of Musicians

ISME International Society for Musical Education

ISMRC Inter-Services Metallurgical Research Council

ISO Imperial Service Order • International Standards Organization (International Organization for Standardization)

ISP Institute of Sales Promotion • International Study Programme

ISPEMA Industrial Safety (Personal Equipment) Manufacturers' Association

ISQ *Med.* in statu quo (Latin: in the same state; unchanged)

ISR information storage and retrieval

ISRO International Securities Regulatory Organization

iss. issue

ISSN International Standard Serial Number

IST Indian Standard Time • Institute of Science Technology

ISTC Institute of Scientific and Technical Communicators • Iron and Steel Trades' Confederation

ISTD Imperial Society of Teachers of Dancing

isth. (*or* **Isth.**) isthmus

IStructE Institution of Structural Engineers

ISU International Seamen's Union

ISV International Scientific Vocabulary • independent software vendor

ISVA Incorporated Society of Valuers and Auctioneers

ISWG *Engineering* Imperial Standard Wire Gauge

It. Italian • Italy

IT ignition temperature • information technology • *Physics* International Table (in **IT calorie**)

i t a (*or* **ITA**) initial teaching alphabet

ITA Independent Television

Authority (superseded by the IBA)

ITAI Institution of Technical Authors and Illustrators

ital. italic

Ital. Italian

ITALY I trust and love you

ITB Industry Training Board • International Time Bureau

ITC Independent Television Commission • International Tin Council • International Trade Centre

ITE Institute of Terrestrial Ecology

ITEME Institution of Technician Engineers in Mechanical Engineering

ITF International Tennis Federation • International Trade Federations • International Transport Workers' Federation

ITI Institute of Translation and Interpreting

ITMA Institute of Trade Mark Agents • ('ɪtmə) It's That Man Again (BBC radio series)

ITN Independent Television News

ITO International Trade Organization

ITS Industrial Training Service • International Trade Secretariat

ITT International Telephone and Telegraph Corporation

ITTF International Table Tennis Federation

ITU *Med.* intensive therapy unit • International Telecommunication Union (of the UN) • International Typographical Union

ITV Independent Television

IU immunizing unit • *Pharmacol.* international unit(s)

IUA International Union of Architects

IUB International Union of Biochemistry

IUCD *Med.* intrauterine contraceptive device

IUCN International Union for the Conservation of Nature and Natural Resources

IUCW International Union for Child Welfare

IUD *Med.* intrauterine death • *Med.* intrauterine (contraceptive) device

IUGG International Union of Geodesy and Geophysics

IUGR *Med.* intrauterine growth retardation

IUGS International Union of Geological Sciences

IUHPS International Union of the History and Philosophy of Science

IULA International Union of Local Authorities

IUMI International Union of Marine Insurance

IUPAC ('juːpæk) International Union of Pure and Applied Chemistry

IUPAP ('juːpæp) International Union of Pure and Applied Physics

IUPS International Union of Physiological Sciences

IUTAM International Union of Theoretical and Applied Mechanics

i.v. increased value • *Med.* intravenous(ly) • invoice value

IV *Med.* intravenous(ly) • *postcode for* Inverness • invoice value

IVA individual voluntary arrangement (in bankruptcy proceedings)

IVB invalidity benefit

IVC *Med.* inferior vena cava

IVF *Med.* in vitro fertilization

IVP *Med.* intravenous pyelogram

IVR international vehicle registration

IVS International Voluntary Service

IWA Inland Waterways Association

IWC International Whaling Commission

IWEM Institution of Water and Environmental Management (formerly IPHE; IWPC)

IWGC Imperial War Graves Commission (now Commonwealth War Graves Commission)

IWPC Institute of Water Pollution Control (*see* IWEM)

IWW Industrial Workers of the World • International Workers of the World

IY Imperial Yeomanry

IYRU International Yacht Racing Union

IZ I Zingari (cricket club)

IZS *Med.* insulin zinc suspension (diabetes treatment).

J

j (*ital.*) *Physics*, symbol for current density

J (*bold ital.*) *Physics*, symbol for angular momentum • (*ital.*) *Physics*, symbol for current density • *Cards* jack • international vehicle registration for Japan • *Science*, symbol for joule(s) • (*bold ital.*) *Physics*, symbol for magnetic polarization • (*ital.*) *Physics*, obsolete symbol for mechanical equivalent of heat

J. (*or* **J**) Jacobean • January • Jesus • Journal • Judge • July • June • Justice

Ja. January

JA international vehicle registration for Jamaica • (*or* **J/A**) *Banking* joint account • Judge Advocate • Justice of Appeal

Jaat *Military* joint air attack team

Jac. Jacobean

JACT Joint Association of Classical Teachers

Jafo (dʒæfəʊ) *Military slang* just another fucking observer

JAG Judge Advocate General

JAL Japan Airlines

Jam. Jamaica • *Bible* James

Jan (*or* **Jan.**) January

j. & w.o. *Insurance* jettisoning and washing overboard

JANET ('dʒænɪt) *Computing* Joint Academic Network

Jap. Japan(ese)

JAP (dʒæp) *Colloquial* (USA) Jewish American Princess

Jas. *Bible* James

JAT Jugoslovenski Aero-Transport (Yugoslav Airlines)

JATO (*or* **jato**) ('dʒeɪtəʊ) *Aeronautics* jet-assisted take-off

Jav. Java(nese) • (*or* **jav.**) *Athletics* javelin

JBCNS Joint Board of Clinical Nursing Studies

JC (*or* **J.C.**) Jesus Christ • (*or* **J.C.**) Julius Caesar •

Law jurisconsult (legal adviser; jurist)

JCB Bachelor of Canon Law (Latin *Juris Canonici Baccalaureus*) • Bachelor of Civil Law (Latin *Juris Civilis Baccalaureus*) • Joseph Cyril Bamford (excavating machine; named after its manufacturer)

JCC Junior Chamber of Commerce

JCD Doctor of Canon Law (Latin *Juris Canonici Doctor*) • Doctor of Civil Law (Latin *Juris Civilis Doctor*)

JCI Junior Chamber International

JCL *Computing* job-control language • Licentiate in Canon Law (Latin *Juris Canonici Licentiatus*) • Licentiate in Civil Law (Latin *Juris Civilis Licentiatus*)

JCP Japan Communist Party

JCR junior common room (in certain universities)

JCS Joint Chiefs of Staff • (ital.) Journal of the Chemical Society

jct. (*or* **jctn**) junction

JCWI Joint Council for the Welfare of Immigrants

jd joined

JD Doctor of Laws *or* Juris-prudence (Latin *Jurum Doctor*) • *symbol for* Jordan dinar (monetary unit) • *Astronomy* Julian date • juvenile delinquent

JDipMA Joint Diploma in Management Accounting Services

Jer. *Bible* Jeremiah

JESSI Joint European Submicron Silicon Initiative

JET (dʒet) *Nuclear engineering* Joint European Torus (Culham, Oxfordshire)

JETP (ital.) Journal of Experimental and Theoretical Physics

J/F *Book-keeping* journal folio

JFET ('dʒeɪfet) *Electronics* junction field-effect transistor

JFK John Fitzgerald Kennedy (US president (1961–63) *or* airport)

j.g. junior grade

JHS Jesus Hominum Salvator (Latin: Jesus Saviour of Men)

jic just in case

JICTAR ('dʒɪktaː) Joint Industry Committee for Television Advertising Research

JIT (*or* **jit**) just-in-time (manufacturing method)

JJ (*or* **JJ.**) Judges • Justices

Jl. (*or* **jl.**) journal • July

JLP Jamaica Labour Party

JMB Joint Matriculation Board

jn join • (*or* **Jn**) junction • (*or* **Jn**) junior

jnc. (*or* **Jnc.**) junction

j.n.d. just noticeable difference

jnl (*or* **Jnl**) journal

jnlst journalist

jnr (*or* **Jnr**) junior

JNR Japanese National Railways

jnt joint

JNTO Japan National Tourist Organization

jnt stk joint stock

JO job order • (ital.) *Journal Officiel* (French: Official Gazette) • junior officer

Jon. *Bible* Jonah

Josh. *Bible* Joshua

jour. journeyman

JOVIAL ('dʒəʊvɪəl) *Computing* Jules' own version of international algorithmic language (named after Jules Schwarz, computer scientist)

JP (*or* **j.p.**) jet propulsion (*or* jet-propelled) • Justice of the Peace

JPS jet-propulsion system(s)

Jr (*or* **jr**) Junior

JR Jacobus Rex (Latin: King James)

JRC Junior Red Cross

JSB joint-stock bank

JSD Doctor of Juristic Science

JSDC Joint Service Defence College

JSLS Joint Services Liaison Staff

JSP Japan Socialist Party

JSPS Japan Society for the Promotion of Science

JSSC Joint Services Staff College

J-stars ('dʒeɪˌstɑːz) joint surveillance and targeting acquisition radar system

jt joint

Jt Ed. Joint Editor

JTIDS Joint Tactical Information Distribution Systems

jtly jointly

Jud. (*or* **Judg.**) *Bible* Judges • *Bible* Judith

JUD Doctor of Canon and Civil Law (Latin *Juris Utriusque Doctor*)

judgt judgment

JUGFET ('dʒʌgfɛt) *Electronics* junction-gate field-effect transistor

Jul. July

Jun. June • (*or* **jun.**) junior

junc. (*or* **Junc.**) junction

Junr (*or* **junr**) junior

JurD Doctor of Law (Latin *Juris Doctor*)

jurisd. jurisdiction

jurisp. jurisprudence

jus. (*or* **just.**) justice

JV *Commerce* joint venture

jwlr jeweller

j.w.o. *Insurance* jettisoning and washing overboard

JWV Jewish War Veterans

Jy July

K

k (ital.) *Physics, symbol for* Boltzmann constant • *symbol for* kilo- (prefix indicating 1000, as in **km**, kilometre; *or* (in computing) 1024, as in **kbyte**, kilobyte) • (ital.) *Physics, symbol for* thermal conductivity • (bold ital.) *Maths., symbol for* a unit coordinate vector

k. (USA) karat • king • knit

K (ital.) *Physics, symbol for* bulk modulus • *international vehicle registration for* Cambodia • (ital.) *Ecology, symbol for* carrying capacity (as in **K-strategist**) • (ital.)

Chem., symbol for equilibrium constant • *Physics, symbol for* kaon • *Science, symbol for* kelvin(s) • *Computing, symbol for* kilo- (*see under* k) • *symbol for* kina (monetary unit of Papua New Guinea) • *Chess, symbol for* king • kip (Laotian monetary unit; *see also under* KN) • *Music* Kirkpatrick (preceding a number in Ralph Kirkpatrick's catalogue of Domenico Scarlatti's works) • *Music* Köchel (preceding a number in Ludwig von Köchel's catalogue of Mozart's works) • *symbol for* (Zambian) kwacha (monetary unit; *see also under* MK) • *symbol for* kyat (Burmese monetary unit) • *Chem., symbol for* potassium (Latin *kalium*) • *indicating* one thousand

K. (*or* **K**) King (*or* King's) • knit

K9 *Military* canine (K9 dogs; army dogs)

KA *postcode for* Kilmarnock • Knight of St Andrew, Order of Barbados

Kan. (*or* **Kans.**) Kansas

k & b kitchen and bathroom

KANU ('kɑːnuː) Kenya African National Union

KAR King's African Rifles

kb *Physics, symbol for* kilobar(s) • *Genetics, symbol for* kilobase(s)

KB *Computing* kilobyte • King's Bench • *Chess* king's bishop • Knight Bachelor • *Knitting* knit into back of stitch • *Computing* knowledge base

kbd keyboard

KBE Knight Commander of the Order of the British Empire

kbp *Genetics, symbol for* kilobase pair

KBP *Chess* king's bishop's pawn

KBS Knight of the Blessed Sacrament • *Computing* knowledge-based system

kbyte *Computing* kilobyte

kc *Physics* kilocycle

KC Kansas City • Kennel Club • King's College • King's Counsel • Knight Commander • *RC Church* Knights of Columbus

kcal *symbol for* kilocalorie(s)

KCB Knight Commander of the Order of the Bath

KCC (Knight) Commander of the Order of the Crown, Belgium and the Congo Free State

K cell *Immunol.* killer cell

KCH King's College Hospital (London) • Knight Commander of the Hanoverian Order

KCHS Knight Commander of the Order of the Holy Sepulchre

KCIE Knight Commander of the Order of the Indian Empire

KCLJ Knight Commander of the Order of St Lazarus of Jerusalem

KCMG Knight Commander of the Order of St Michael and St George

kcs (or **kc/s**) kilocycles per second

Kčs symbol for koruna (monetary unit of the Czech Republic and Slovakia)

KCSA Knight Commander of the Military Order of the Collar of St Agatha of Paterna

KCSG Knight Commander of the Order of St Gregory the Great

KCSI Knight Commander of the Order of the Star of India

KCSJ Knight Commander of the Order of St John of Jerusalem (Knights Hospitaller)

KCSS Knight Commander of the Order of St Silvester

KCVO Knight Commander of the Royal Victorian Order

KD kiln dried • (or **k.d.**) knock down (at an auction sale) • (or **k.d.**) Commerce knocked down (of goods for sale) • symbol for Kuwaiti dinar (monetary unit)

KDC (or **k.d.c.**) Commerce

knocked-down condition (of goods)

KDG King's Dragoon Guards

KE kinetic energy

KEAS (or **k.e.a.s.**) Aeronautics knots equivalent airspeed

KEH King Edward's Horse

Ken. Kentucky

KEO King Edward's Own

keV Physics, symbol for kiloelectronvolt(s)

kg keg • symbol for kilogram(s)

KG Knight of the Order of the Garter

KGB Komitet Gosudarstvennoi Bezopasnosti (Russian: Committee of State Security)

KGCB Knight Grand Cross of the Bath

Kgs Bible Kings

KH Knight of the Hanoverian Order

KHC Honorary Chaplain to the King

KHDS Honorary Dental Surgeon to the King

KHNS Honorary Nursing Sister to the King

KHP Honorary Physician to the King

KHS Honorary Surgeon to

the King • Knight of the Order of the Holy Sepulchre

kHz *symbol for* kilohertz

KIA killed in action

KIAS (*or* **k.i.a.s.**) *Aeronautics* knots indicated airspeed

K-i-H Kaisar-i-Hind (Emperor of India; medal)

KIO Kuwait Investment Office

kJ *symbol for* kilojoule(s)

KJ *Med.* knee jerk

KJV King James Version (of the Bible)

KKK Ku Klux Klan

KKt *Chess* king's knight

KKtP *Chess* king's knight's pawn

KL Kuala Lumpur

KLH Knight of the Legion of Honour

KLJ Knight of the Order of St Lazarus of Jerusalem

KLM Koninklijke Luchtvaart Maatschappij (Royal Dutch Airlines)

KLSE Kuala Lumpur Stock Exchange

km *symbol for* kilometre(s)

KM Knight of Malta

KMT Kuomintang (Chinese Nationalist Party)

kn *Nautical, symbol for* knot • krona (Swedish monetary unit; *see also* SKr) • krone (Danish or Norwegian monetary unit; *see also* Dkr; NKr)

KN *Chess* king's knight • *symbol for* kip (Laotian monetary unit)

KNP *Chess* king's knight's pawn

Knt Knight

KO (*or* **k.o.**) *Colloquial* knock out (*or* knockout)

KOC Kuwait Oil Company

K of C *RC Church* Knights of Columbus

Komintern ('kɒmɪn‚tɜːn) Communist International (Russian *Kom(munisticheskiĭ) Intern(atsional)*)

KORR King's Own Royal Regiment

KOSB King's Own Scottish Borderers

KOYLI King's Own Yorkshire Light Infantry

KP *Chess* king's pawn • Knight of the Order of St Patrick

KPD Kommunistische Partei Deutschlands (German Communist Party)

kph kilometres per hour

KPM King's Police Medal

KPNLF Khmer People's National Liberation Front

KPU Kenya People's Union

kr. krona (Swedish monetary unit; *see also* SKr) • króna (Icelandic monetary unit; *see also* ISK) • krone (Danish or Norwegian monetary unit; *see also* Dkr; NKr)

Kr *Chem., symbol for* krypton

KR King's Regiment • *Military* King's Regulations • *Chess* king's rook

KRL *Computing* knowledge representation language (in artificial intelligence)

KRP *Chess* king's rook's pawn

KRRC King's Royal Rifle Corps

KS *US postcode for* Kansas • *Med.* Kaposi's sarcoma • King's Scholar

KSC Knight of St Columba

KSG Knight of the Order of St Gregory the Great

KSh *symbol for* Kenya shilling (monetary unit)

KSJ Knight of the Order of St John of Jerusalem (Knights Hospitaller)

KSLI King's Shropshire Light Infantry

KSS Knight of the Order of St Silvester

KSSU KLM, SAS, Swissair, UTA (international airline organization)

KStJ Knight of the Order of St John of Jerusalem (Knights Hospitaller)

kt (USA) karat • *symbol for* kilotonne(s) • *Nautical* knot

Kt knight

KT *postcode for* Kingston-upon-Thames • Knight (of the Order) of the Thistle • Knight Templar

Kt Bach. Knight Bachelor

Ku *Chem., symbol for* kurchatovium (element 104)

kV *symbol for* kilovolt(s)

KV *Music* Köchel Verzeichnis (German: Köchel catalogue; *see under* K)

kVAr *Electrical engineering, symbol for* kilovar(s)

kVp kilovolts, peak (applied across an X-ray tube)

kW *symbol for* kilowatt(s)

KW *postcode for* Kirkwall, Orkney

kWh (*or* **kW h**) *symbol for* kilowatt hour(s)

KWIC (kwɪk) key word in context (as in **KWIC index**)

KWOC (kwɒk) key word out of context (as in **KWOC index**)

KWP Korean Workers' Party

KWT *international vehicle registration for* Kuwait

ky. kyat (Burmese monetary unit; *see also under* K)

Ky. Kentucky

KY *US postcode for* Kentucky • *postcode for* Kirkaldy • Kol Yisrael (Israeli broadcasting station)

KZ *Military* killing zone.

L

l (ital.) *Chem.* laevorotatory (as in **l-tartaric acid**) • *Music* lah (in tonic sol-fa) • (ital.) *symbol for* length • *Meteorol.* lightning • *Chem.* liquid (as in **H₂O(l)**) • *symbol for* litre(s)

l. lake • law • leaf • league • left • length • line (of written matter) • link • low • *Currency* pound (Latin *libra*; symbol: £)

L (bold ital.) *Physics, symbol for* angular momentum • (ital.) *Chem., symbol for* Avogadro constant • *Roman numeral for* fifty • *Electrical engineering, symbol for* inductor • *Linguistics* language (as in **L₁**, first language; **L₂**, second language) • (ital.) *Phys-*ics, symbol for latent heat • learner (driver; on British motor vehicles) • *symbol for* lempira (Honduran monetary unit) • (ital.) *symbol for* length • *Aeronautics* lift • *Immunol.* light (in **L-chain** of an immunoglobulin molecule) • *symbol for* litre(s) • live (on electric plugs) • *postcode for* Liverpool • (ital.) *Geography, symbol for* longitude • (ital.; *or* **L_v**) *Physics, symbol for* luminance • *international vehicle registration for* Luxembourg • (ital., *or* **L_e**) *Physics, symbol for* radiance • (small cap.) *Chem., indicating* an optically active compound having a configuration related to laevorotatory glyceraldehyde (as in **L-lactic acid**)

L. (or **L**) Lady • Lake • large • Latin • law • League • left or (in the theatre) stage left • lethal • liber (Latin: book) • Politics Liberal • Licentiate (in degrees, etc.) • Lieutenant • line (of written matter) • link • Biology Linnaeus (indicating the author of a species, etc.) • lira or (pl.) lire (Italian monetary unit; see also Lit) • Loch • locus (Latin: place) • Lodge (fraternal) • London • Lough • low • Currency pound (Latin libra; symbol: £)

La Chem., symbol for lanthanum

La. Lane • Louisiana

LA postcode for Lancaster • Photog. large aperture • Latin America(n) • law agent • Legislative Assembly • Library Association • Literate in Arts • Liverpool Academy • local agent • local authority • Los Angeles • US postcode for Louisiana

LAA light anti-aircraft

lab. laboratory • labourer

Lab. Politics Labour • Labrador

LAC leading aircraftman • Licentiate of the Apothecaries' Company • London Athletic Club

LACSA Lineas Aéreas Costarricenses (Costa Rican Airlines)

LACSAB Local Authorities' Conditions of Service Advisory Board

LACW leading aircraftwoman

LAD Linguistics language acquisition device

ladar ('leɪdɑː) laser detection and ranging

L. Adv. Lord Advocate

LAFTA ('læftə) Latin American Free Trade Association (see LAIA)

LAH Licentiate of the Apothecaries' Hall (Dublin)

LAI Botany leaf area index

LAIA Latin American Integration Association (formerly LAFTA)

LAK (læk) Med. lymphokine-activated killer (in **LAK cell**; used in cancer treatment)

lam. laminate(d)

Lam. Botany Lamarck (indicating the author of a species, etc.) • *Bible* Lamentations

LAMDA ('læmdə) London Academy of Music and Dramatic Art

LAMSAC Local Authorities' Management Services and Computer Committee

LAN (*or* **Lan**) (læn) Linea Aérea Nacional (de Chile) (Chilean national airlines; Lan Chile) • *Computing* local-area network

Lancs Lancashire

L & NWR London and North-Western Railway

L & SWR London and South-Western Railway

L & YR Lancashire and Yorkshire Railway

lang. language

Lantirn ('læntən) *Military* low-altitude navigation and targeting infrared system

LAO *international vehicle registration for* Laos • Licentiate in the Art of Obstetrics

Lap. Lapland

LAPT London Association for the Protection of Trade

LAR *international vehicle registration for* Libya

LARSP Language Assess-

ment, Remediation, and Screening Procedure

LAS London Archaeological Service

laser ('leɪzə) light amplification by stimulated emission of radiation

LASER London and South Eastern Library Region

LASH (læʃ) *Commerce* lighter aboard ship

lat. (*or* **lat**) *Geography* latitude

Lat. Latin

LATS (læts) *Med.* long-acting thyroid stimulator

LAUTRO (*or* **Lautro**) ('lɔːtrəʊ) Life Assurance and Unit Trust Regulatory Organization

LAV light armoured vehicle • Lineas Aéreas Venezolanas (Venezuelan Airlines) • lymphadenopathy-associated virus (original name for the Aids virus, HIV)

LAX Los Angeles international airport

lb (*or* **lb.**) pound(s) (weight; Latin *libra*)

l.b. landing barge • *Cricket* leg bye

LB *international vehicle regis-*

tration for Liberia • light bomber • local board

LBA late booking agent (euphemism for ticket tout)

LB & SCR London, Brighton, and South Coast Railway

LBC London Broadcasting Company

L/Bdr (*or* **LBdr**) Lance-Bombardier

lbf *Physics, symbol for* pound-force

LBJ Lyndon Baines Johnson (1908–73, US president 1963–69)

LBO *Commerce* leveraged buyout

LBS London Business School

LBV Late Bottled Vintage (of port wine)

lbw *Cricket* leg before wicket

l.c. left centre • (*or* **lc, l/c**) letter of credit • loco citato (Latin: in the place cited; textual annotation) • (*or* **lc**) *Printing* lower case

LC Cross of Leo • landing craft • Legislative Council • (*or* **L/C**) letter of credit • (USA) Library of Congress • *Military slang* line crosser (a defector) • Lord

Chamberlain • Lord Chancellor

LCAD London Certificate in Art and Design

LCB *Theatre* left centre back (of stage) • London Convention Bureau • Lord Chief Baron

LCC *Electronics* leadless chip carrier • *Accounting, Computing* life-cycle cost(ing) • London Chamber of Commerce • London County Council (superseded by the Greater London Council, GLC)

LCD *Electronics* liquid-crystal display • (*or* **l.c.d.**) *Maths.* lowest common denominator

LCDT London Contemporary Dance Theatre

LCE London Commodity Exchange

LCF (*or* **l.c.f.**) *Maths.* lowest common factor

LCh Licentiate in Surgery (Latin *Licentiatus Chirurgiae*)

LCJ Lord Chief Justice

LCL *Commerce* less-than-container load • Licentiate in Canon Law

LCM London College of Music • (*or* **l.c.m.**) *Maths.*

lowest (*or* least) common multiple

LCN *Aeronautics* load classification number

L-Col Lieutenant-Colonel

L-Corp. Lance-Corporal

LCP Licentiate of the College of Preceptors • *Chem.* liquid-crystal polymer • London College of Printing

L/Cpl Lance-Corporal

LCPS Licentiate of the College of Physicians and Surgeons

LCSP London and Counties Society of Physiologists

LCST Licentiate of the College of Speech Therapists

LCT landing craft tank

LCV Licentiate of the College of Violinists

ld *Printing* lead • load

l.d. legal dose

Ld Limited (company) • Lord (title)

LD Lady Day • Laus Deo (Latin: Praise be to God) • *Education, Psychol.* learning-disabled • *Pharmacol.* lethal dose (as in **LD₅₀**, median lethal dose) • Liberal and Democratic • *symbol for* Libyan dinar (monetary unit) • Licentiate in Divin-

ity • *postcode for* Llandrindod Wells • London Docks • Low Dutch

LDC less-developed country

LDDC London Docklands' Development Corporation

ldg landing • loading

Ldg *Navy* Leading (rank)

Ldge Lodge

L.d'H. Légion d'Honneur

LDiv Licentiate in Divinity

LDL *Biochem.* low-density lipoprotein

LDN less-developed nation

Ldp Lordship

LDP (Japan) Liberal-Democratic Party • *Finance* London daily price

LDPE *Chem.* low-density polyethylene (used in packaging materials)

ldr leader

lds loads

LDS Latter-day Saints • laus Deo semper (Latin: praise be to God for ever) • Licentiate in Dental Surgery

LDSc Licentiate in Dental Science

LDV Local Defence Volunteers (Home Guard)

Le *symbol for* leone (monetary unit of Sierra Leone)

LE (or **£E**) *symbol for* Egyptian pound (monetary unit) • *postcode for* Leicester • London Electricity • *Med.* lupus erythematosus

lea. league • leather • leave

LEA Local Education Authority

LEAP (liːp) Life Education for the Autistic Person

LEB London Electricity Board

LEC Local Enterprise Company

lect. lecture(r)

LED *Electronics* light-emitting diode

leg. legal • legate • (or **Leg.**) legation • *Music* legato (Italian: bound; i.e. smoothly) • (or **legis.**) legislation • (or **legis.**) legislative • (or **legis.**) legislature

Leics Leicestershire

Leip. Leipzig

LEM (lɛm) *Astronautics* lunar excursion module

LEPRA ('lɛprə) Leprosy Relief Association

LES Liverpool Engineering Society

LETS Local Employment and Trade System

Leu (or **leu**) *Biochem.* leucine

Lev. (or **Levit.**) *Bible* Leviticus

lex. lexicon

lexicog. lexicographer • lexicographical • lexicography

lf *Printing* light face

l.f. ledger folio

Lf limit of flocculation (in toxicology)

LF *Radio* low frequency

LFBC London Federation of Boys' Clubs

LFCDA London Fire and Civil Defence Authority

lg long

lg. large

LG Lady Companion of the Order of the Garter • Life Guards • Low German

lge large

LGer Low German

LGk Late Greek

LGM Little Green Men

LGr Late Greek

LGSM Licentiate of the Guildhall School of Music

LGTB Local Government Training Board

lgth length

lg tn long ton

LGU Ladies' Golf Union

l.h. left half • left hand(ed)

LH left hand(ed) • *Military*

Light Horse • *Biochem.* luteinizing hormone

LHA Lord High Admiral

lhb *Sport* left halfback

LHC Lord High Chancellor

l.h.d. left-hand drive

LHD Doctor of Humanities *or* of Literature (Latin *Litterarum Humaniorum Doctor*)

LHeb Late Hebrew

LH-RH *Biochem., Med.* luteinizing-hormone-releasing hormone

LHS left hand side

LHSM Licentiate of the Institute of Health Services Management

LHT Lord High Treasurer

Li *Chem., symbol for* lithium

LI Light Infantry • Long Island (New York)

LIAB Licentiate of the International Association of Book-Keepers

lib. liber (Latin: book) • liberty • librarian • library • libretto

Lib. (*or* **Lib**) *Politics* Liberal

LIBA Lloyd's Insurance Brokers' Association

lib. cat. library catalogue

Lib Dem Liberal Democrat

LIBID ('lɪbɪd) London Inter-Bank Bid Rate

LIBOR ('liːbɔː) *Finance* London Inter-Bank Offered Rate

Lic. (*or* **Lic**) Licentiate (in degrees, etc.)

LIC *Electronics* linear integrated circuit

LicAc Licentiate of Acupuncture

LICeram Licentiate of the Institute of Ceramics

LicMed Licentiate in Medicine

LICW Licentiate of the Institute of Clerks of Works

lidar ('liːdɑː) light detection and ranging

Lieut Lieutenant

Lieut-Col Lieutenant-Colonel

Lieut-Com Lieutenant-Commander

Lieut-Gen Lieutenant-General

Lieut-Gov Lieutenant-Governor

LIFFE (laɪf) London International Financial Futures and Options Exchange

LIFireE Licentiate of the Institution of Fire Engineers

LIFO ('laɪfəʊ) *Accounting, Computing* last in, first out

LILO last in, last out

lim. limit

LIM linear-induction motor

LIMEAN London Inter-Bank Mean Rate

lin. lineal • linear

linac ('lɪnæk) *Physics* linear accelerator

Lincs Lincolnshire

ling. linguistics

lin-log *Physics, Maths.* linear-logarithmic

Linn. (Carolus) Linnaeus (1707–78, Swedish botanist)

LIOB Licentiate of the Institute of Building

LIP life insurance policy

LIPM Lister Institute of Preventive Medicine

LIPS (*or* **lips**) (lɪps) *Computing* logical inferences per second

liq. liquid • liquor

LISM Licentiate of the Incorporated Society of Musicians

LISP (lɪsp) *Computing* list processing (a programming language)

lit. literal(ly) • literary • literature • litre(s) • little

Lit *symbol for* lira (Italian monetary unit)

LitB Bachelor of Letters *or* Literature (Latin *Litterarum Baccalaureus*)

lit. crit. (lɪt krɪt) *Colloquial* literary criticism

LitD Doctor of Letters *or* Literature (Latin *Litterarum Doctor*)

lith. lithograph(y)

Lith. Lithuania(n)

litho. (*or* **lithog.**) lithograph(ic) • lithography

lithol. lithology

Lit. Hum. Litterae Humaniores (Latin: the humanities; classics course at Oxford University)

LittB Bachelor of Letters *or* Literature (Latin *Litterarum Baccalaureus*)

LittD Doctor of Letters *or* Literature (Latin *Litterarum Doctor*)

LittM Master of Letters *or* Literature (Latin *Litterarum Magister*)

liv. st. livre sterling (French: pound sterling)

LJ Lord Justice

lkge *Commerce* leakage

ll. leaves • leges (Latin: laws) • lines (of written matter)

l.l. loco laudato (Latin: in the place quoted)

LL Late Latin • Law Latin •

(or **£L**, **£Leb.**) *symbol for* Lebanese pound (monetary unit) • *Physics, Maths.* linear-linear • *postcode for* Llandudno • Lord-Lieutenant • Low Latin

LL. lines (of written matter) • Lords

LLA Lady Literate in Arts

LLB (or **LlB**) Bachelor of Laws (Latin *Legum Baccalaureus*)

LLCM Licentiate of London College of Music

LLCO Licentiate of the London College of Osteopathy

LLD (or **LlD**) Doctor of Laws (Latin *Legum Doctor*)

Llds *Insurance* Lloyd's

LLE low-level exposure (to radiation)

LLL Licentiate in Laws

LLM Master of Laws (Latin *Legum Magister*)

LLNW low-level nuclear waste

LLRW low-level radioactive waste

LLW low-level (radioactive) waste

lm *Physics, symbol for* lumen

Lm *symbol for* Maltese lira (monetary unit)

LM Licentiate in Medi-

cine • Licentiate in Midwifery • *Music, Prosody* long metre • Lord Mayor • *Aeronautics* lunar module

LMC Local Medical Committee

LMCC Licentiate of the Medical Council of Canada

LMD *Music, Prosody* long metre double

LME London Metal Exchange

LMed Licentiate in Medicine

LMP *Med.* last menstrual period

LMR *Nuclear engineering* liquid-metal reactor • *Railways* London Midland Region

LMRCP Licentiate in Midwifery of the Royal College of Physicians

LMRSH Licentiate Member of the Royal Society for the Promotion of Health

LMRTPI Legal Member of the Royal Town Planning Institute

LMS Licentiate in Medicine and Surgery • *Education* local management of schools • London Mathematical Society • (or **LMS(R)**) London, Midland and Scottish Railway •

London Missionary Society • *Med.* loss of memory syndrome

LMSSA Licentiate in Medicine and Surgery of the Society of Apothecaries

LMT *Physics* length, mass, time • *Astronomy* local mean time

LMVD (New Zealand) Licensed Motor Vehicle Dealer

LMX London Market Excess of Loss (at Lloyd's)

ln *symbol for* natural logarithm

Ln Lane (in place names)

LN *postcode for* Lincoln

LNat Liberal National

LNER London and North Eastern Railway

LNG liquefied natural gas

LO liaison officer

LOB Location of Offices Bureau

loc. *Grammar* locative

loc. cit. loco citato (*see under* l.c.)

loco. locomotion • locomotive

L of C lines of communication

L of N League of Nations

LOFT (lɒft) low-frequency radio telescope

log (lɒg) logarithm

log. logic(al)

LOI lunar orbit insertion

Lond. London

Londin. Londiniensis (Latin: (Bishop) of London)

long. (*or* **long**) longitude

Lonrho ('lɒnrəʊ) *Finance* London Rhodesian

l.o.p. (*or* **LOP**) *Navigation* line of position

loq. loquitur (Latin: he (*or* she) speaks)

LORCS League of Red Cross and Red Crescent Societies

LOS loss of signal

lot. lotion

Lot (lɒt) Polskie Linie Lotnicze (Polish Air Lines)

LOX (*or* **lox**) (lɒks) liquid oxygen

l.p. long primer (a size of printer's type) • low pressure

Lp Lordship

LP Labour Party • large paper (edition of a book) • life policy • Limited Partnership • long-playing (of a gramophone record) • Lord Provost • low pressure • *Med.* lumbar puncture

L/P letterpress • life policy

LPC Lord President of the Council

LPG liquefied petroleum gas

LPh (*or* **LPH**) Licentiate in Philosophy

LPLC low-pressure liquid chromatography

lpm lines per minute

LPO London Philharmonic Orchestra

L'pool Liverpool

LPS London Philharmonic Society • Lord Privy Seal

LPSO Lloyd's Policy Signing Office

Lpz. Leipzig

LQ *Computing* letter quality (of printed output)

lr lower

Lr *Chem., symbol for* lawrencium

LR Lloyd's Register (of Shipping)

LRAD Licentiate of the Royal Academy of Dancing

LRAM Licentiate of the Royal Academy of Music

LRB London Residuary Body (in local government)

LRC London Rowing Club

LRCM Licentiate of the Royal College of Music

LRCP Licentiate of the Royal College of Physicians

LRCPE (*or* **LRCPEd**) Licentiate of the Royal College of Physicians of Edinburgh

LRCPI Licentiate of the Royal College of Physicians of Ireland

LRCPSGlas Licentiate of the Royal College of Physicians and Surgeons of Glasgow

LRCS Licentiate of the Royal College of Surgeons of England

LRCSE Licentiate of the Royal College of Surgeons of Edinburgh

LRCSI Licentiate of the Royal College of Surgeons in Ireland

LRCVS Licentiate of the Royal College of Veterinary Surgeons

LREC *Med.* Local Research Ethics Committee

LRPS Licentiate of the Royal Photographic Society

LRSC Licentiate of the Royal Society of Chemistry

LRSM Licentiate of the Royal Schools of Music

LRT light rail transit • London Regional Transport

LRTI *Med.* lower respiratory tract infection

LRV lunar roving vehicle

l.s. left side • (or **L.s.**) letter signed • *Law* locus sigilli (Latin: the place of the seal) • lump sum

LS Leading Seaman • *postcode for Leeds* • *international vehicle registration for Lesotho* • Licentiate in Surgery • Linnean Society • locus sigilli (*see under* l.s.) • London Sinfonietta • *Films* long shot • (or **£S, £Syr.**) *symbol for Syrian pound (monetary unit)*

LSA Licence in Agricultural Sciences • Licentiate of the Society of Apothecaries

LS&GCM Long Service and Good Conduct Medal

l.s.c. loco supra citato (Latin: in the place before cited)

LSd (or **£Sd**) *symbol for Sudanese pound (monetary unit)*

LSD *Computing* least significant digit • lysergic acid diethylamide (hallucinogenic drug)

L.S.D. (or **£.s.d., l.s.d.**) librae, solidi, denarii (Latin: pounds, shillings, pence)

LSE London School of Economics and Political Science

L-Sgt Lance-Sergeant

LSHTM London School of Hygiene and Tropical Medicine

LSI Labour and Socialist International • *Electronics* large-scale integration (or integrated)

LSJ London School of Journalism

LSO London Symphony Orchestra

LSS life-support system

LST landing ship (for) tank(s) *or* transport • (or **l.s.t.**) local standard time

LSZ (New Zealand) limited speed zone

lt light

l.t. local time • long ton

Lt Lieutenant • *Military* Light

LT lawn tennis • Licentiate in Teaching • London Transport • *Electrical engineering* low tension • *symbol for Turkish lira (monetary unit)*

LTA Lawn Tennis Association • lighter than air (of an aircraft)

LT & SR London, Tilbury, and Southend Railway

LTB London Tourist Board

Lt-Cdr Lieutenant-Commander

LTCL Licentiate of Trinity College of Music, London

Lt-Col Lieutenant-Colonel

Lt-Com Lieutenant-Commander

Ltd Limited (after the name of a private limited company)

Lt-Gen Lieutenant-General

Lt-Gov Lieutenant-Governor

LTh Licentiate in Theology

LTH *Biochem.* luteotrophic hormone

LTI Licentiate of the Textile Institute

Lt Inf. Light Infantry

LTM Licentiate in Tropical Medicine

LTOM London Traded Options Market

LTP *Science* long-term potentiation

ltr letter • lighter

LTTE (Sri Lanka) Liberation Tigers of Tamil Eelam

l/u *Shipping* laid (or lying) up

Lu *Chem., symbol for* lutetium

LU Liberal Unionist • loudness unit • *postcode for* Luton

LUC London Underwriters Centre

LUG *Computing* local users group

LUNCO Lloyd's Underwriters Non-Marine Claims Office

LUOTC London University Officers' Training Corps

Luth. Lutheran

Lux. Luxembourg

LuxF *symbol for* Luxembourg franc (monetary unit)

lv. leave (of absence, as from military duty) • livre (French: book)

Lv lev (Bulgarian monetary unit)

LV *Med.* left ventricle (*or* ventricular) • licensed victualler • luncheon voucher

LVA Licensed Victuallers' Association

LVLO Local Vehicle Licensing Office

LVO Lieutenant of the Royal Victorian Order

Lw (formerly) *Chem., symbol for* lawrencium (*see under* Lr)

LW *Radio, etc.* long-wave (*or* long waves) • low water

LWL (*or* **lwl**) length (at) waterline (of a ship) • *Shipping* load waterline

LWM (*or* **lwm**) low water mark

LWRA London Waste Regulation Authority

LWT London Weekend Television

lx *Physics*, symbol for lux

LXX *Bible, symbol for* Septuagint (from its 70 translators)

l.y. *Astronomy* light year

Lys (or **lys**) *Biochem.* lysine

M

m (bold ital.) *Physics, symbol for* magnetic moment • (ital.) *Chem., symbol for* mass • *Music* me (in tonic sol-fa) • (ital.) *Chem.* meta (as in **m-dichlorobenzene**) • *symbol for* metre(s) • *symbol for* milli- (prefix indicating 1/1000 (i.e. 10^{-3}), as in **mm**, millimetre) • million

m. *Cricket* maiden (over) • male • mare • *Currency* mark(s) • married • masculine • medicine • meridian • meridies (Latin: noon) • meridional • mile(s) • (USA, Canada) mill(s) (monetary unit) • minim (liquid measure) • minute(s) • *Med.* misce (Latin: mix) • molar (tooth) • month • moon

M *Printing, symbol for* em • *symbol for* loti (monetary unit of Lesotho; pl. maloti) • (ital.; or **M$_v$**) *Physics, symbol for* luminous exitance • *Aeronautics* Mach (followed by a number) • (bold ital.) *Physics, symbol for* magnetization • *international vehicle registration for* Malta • *postcode for* Manchester • (ital.) *symbol for* mass, especially molar mass • *Films* (Australia) mature audience (certification) • medium (size) • *symbol for* mega- (prefix indicating one million, as in **MW**, megawatt; *or* (in computing) 2^{20}, as in **Mbyte**, megabyte) • *Chem., symbol for* metal (in a chemical formula, as in **MOH**) • million • minim (liquid measure) • (bold ital.) *Physics, symbol for* moment of a force • motorway (as in **M1**, **M4**, etc.) • (ital.; *or* **M$_e$**) *Physics, symbol for* radiant exitance • *Roman numeral for* thousand • *Logic, indicating* the middle term of a syllogism

M. (*or* **M**) Magister (Latin: Master) • Majesty • Manitoba • Marquess • Marquis • Master (in titles) • Medieval • Member (in titles) • *Music* metronome • mezzo *or* mezza (Italian: half) • Middle • militia • Monday • Monsieur (French: Mr *or* Sir) • Mountain

m/a *Book-keeping* my account

mA *symbol for* milliampere(s)

Ma (ital.) *Aeronautics, symbol for* Mach number

MA *US postcode for* Massachusetts • Master of Arts • *Psychol.* mental age • Military Academy • military assistant • mobility allowance • *international vehicle registration for* Morocco

MAA Manufacturers'

Agents Association of Great Britain • master-at-arms

MAAF Mediterranean Allied Air Forces

MAAT Member of the Association of Accounting Technicians

Mac. (*or* **Macc.**) Maccabees (books of the Apocrypha)

MAc Master of Accountancy

MAC (mæk) *Television* multiplexed analogue components

MACE Member of the Association of Conference Executives • Member of the Australian College of Education

Maced. Macedonia(n)

mach. machine(ry) • machinist

MACM Member of the Association of Computing Machines

MAD (mæd) magnetic anomaly detection • *Psychiatry* major affective disorder • *Military* mutual assured destruction

Madag. Madagascar

MADO Member of the Association of Dispensing Opticians

MAE Master of Aeronautical Engineering • Master of Art Education • Master of Arts in Education

MA(Ed) Master of Arts in Education

MAEE Marine Aircraft Experimental Establishment

MAFF (mæf) Ministry of Agriculture, Fisheries, and Food

mag. magazine • magnesium • magnet(ic) • magnetism • magneto • magnitude • magnum

Mag. Magyar

MAgEc Master of Agricultural Economics

MAGPI ('mægpaɪ) *Surgery* meatal advancement and glanuloplasty (operation)

MAgr Master of Agriculture

MAI Master of Engineering (Latin *Magister in Arte Ingeniaria*)

MAIB Marine Accident Investigation Branch

maj. major • majority

Maj *Military* Major

Maj-Gen Major-General

Mal. *Bible* Malachi • Malay(an)

MAL *international vehicle registration for* Malaysia

MALD Master of Arts in Law and Diplomacy

MAMEME Member of the Association of Mining Electrical and Mechanical Engineers

man. management • manual(ly)

Man. Manila • Manitoba

Manch. Manchester

mand. *Music* mandolin

M & B May and Baker (pharmaceutical company) • mild and bitter (beer) • Mills and Boon (publisher of romantic fiction)

M & E music and effects

Man. Dir. Managing Director

M&S Marks & Spencer plc

Manit. Manitoba

manuf. (*or* **manufac.**) manufacture(d) • manufacturer • manufacturing

MANWEB ('mænwɛb) Merseyside and North Wales Electricity Board

MAO Master of Obstetric Art • *Biochem., Pharmacol.* monoamine oxidase

MAOI monoamine oxidase inhibitor (antidepressant)

MAOT Member of the Association of Occupational Therapists

MAP Ministry of Aircraft Production

MAPsS Member of the Australian Psychological Society

mar. *Music* marimba • maritime • married

Mar. March

MAR Master of Arts in Religion

MARAC Member of the Australasian Register of Agricultural Consultants

marc. *Music* marcato (Italian: marked; i.e. each note emphasized)

MARC (mɑːk) *Bibliog.* machine-readable cataloguing

March. Marchioness

MArch Master of Architecture

marg. margin(al)

mar. insce. marine insurance

Marq. Marquess • Marquis

MARV (mɑːv) *Military* manoeuvrable re-entry vehicle

mas. (*or* **masc.**) masculine

MASc Master of Applied Science

MASC Member of the

Australian Society of Calligraphers

MASCAM ('mæskæm) *Electronics* masking-pattern adaptive sub-band coding and multiplexing

MASCE Member of the American Society of Civil Engineers

maser ('meɪzə) microwave amplification by stimulated emission of radiation

MASH (mæʃ) (USA) mobile army surgical hospital

Mass. Massachusetts

mat. matinée

MAT *Insurance* marine, aviation, and transport • Master of Arts in Teaching

MATh Master of Arts in Theology

maths. mathematics

MATS *US Air Force* Military Air Transport Service

MATSA Managerial Administrative Technical Staff Association

Matt. *Bible* Matthew

MATV master antenna television

Mau Re (pl. **Mau Rs**) *symbol for* Mauritian rupee (monetary unit)

MAusIMM Member of

the Australasian Institute of Mining and Metallurgy

max. maxim • (or **max**, **MAX**) maximum

mb *Meteorol.*, *symbol for* millibar(s)

m.b. *Med.* misce bene (Latin: mix well)

MB Bachelor of Medicine (Latin *Medicinae Baccalaureus*) • US postcode for Manitoba • mark of the Beast • (Canada) Medal of Bravery • *Computing* megabyte

MBA Master of Business Administration

MBAcA Member of the British Acupuncture Association

mbar *Meteorol.*, *symbol for* millibar(s)

MBASW Member of the British Association of Social Workers

m.b.c. *Med.* maximum breathing capacity

MBC metropolitan borough council • municipal borough council

MBCS Member of the British Computer Society

MBD *Med.* minimal brain dysfunction

MBE Member of the Order of the British Empire

MBG microemulsion-based gel

mbH mit beschränkter Haftung (German: with limited liability)

MBHI Member of the British Horological Institute

MBIFD Member of the British Institute of Funeral Directors

MBKSTS Member of the British Kinematograph, Sound, and Television Society

MBO *Finance* management buyout • management by objectives

MBOU Member of the British Ornithologists' Union

MBP *Med.* mean blood pressure

MBPICS Member of the British Production and Inventory Control Society

MBPsS Member of the British Psychological Society

MBSc Master of Business Science

MBT *Military* main battle tank • (or **m.b.t.**) *Med.* mean body temperature

Mbyte *Computing* megabyte

m/c machine • (*or* **m.c.**) motor cycle

MC Master of Ceremonies • Master of Surgery (Latin *Magister Chirurgiae*) • Member of Council • Military Cross • Missionaries of Charity • *international vehicle registration for* Monaco • Monte Carlo

M/C Manchester

MCA Management Consultants' Association • *Computing, trademark* micro channel architecture • monetary compensatory amount(s)

MCAM Member of the CAM Foundation

MCB Master in Clinical Biochemistry • *Computing* memory control block • miniature circuit breaker • *Military* multiple-cratering bomblets

MCBSI Member of the Chartered Building Societies Institute

MCC Manchester Computer Centre • Marylebone Cricket Club • member of the county council • metropolitan county council

MCCD RCS Member in Clinical Community Dentistry of the Royal College of Surgeons

MCD Master of Civic Design • Movement for Christian Democracy

MCE Master of Civil Engineering

MCFP (Canada) Member of the College of Family Physicians

MCG Melbourne Cricket Ground

MCGA *Computing* multi-colour graphics array

MCh (*or* **MChir**) Master of (*or* in) Surgery (Latin *Magister Chirurgiae*)

MCHC *Med.* mean cell (*or* corpuscular) haemoglobin concentration

MChD Master of Dental Surgery (Latin *Magister Chirurgiae Dentalis*)

MChE Master of Chemical Engineering

MChemA Master in Chemical Analysis

MChOrth Master of Orthopaedic Surgery (Latin *Magister Chirurgiae Orthopaedicae*)

MChS Member of the Society of Chiropodists

mchy machinery

MCIBSE Member of the Chartered Institution of Building Services Engineers

MCIM Member of the Chartered Institute of Marketing

MCIOB Member of the Chartered Institute of Building

MCIS Member of the Institute of Chartered Secretaries and Administrators (formerly Chartered Institute of Secretaries)

MCIT Member of the Chartered Institute of Transport

MCL Master of (*or* in) Civil Law

MCISc Master of Clinical Science

MCMES Member of the Civil and Mechanical Engineers' Society

MCom Master of Commerce

MCommH Master of Community Health

MConsE Member of the Association of Consulting Engineers

MCOphth Member of the College of Ophthalmologists

MCP (*or* m.c.p.) male chauvinist pig • Member of Colonial Parliament • Member of the College of Preceptors

MCPA 2-methyl-4-chlorophenoxyacetic acid (used in herbicides)

MCPB *Chem.* 4-(2-methyl-4-chlorophenoxy)butanoic acid (weedkiller)

MCPP Member of the College of Pharmacy Practice

MCPS Mechanical Copyright Protection Society • Member of the College of Physicians and Surgeons

MCR middle common room (in certain universities)

MCS Madras Civil Service • Malayan Civil Service • Military College of Science

MCSEE Member of the Canadian Society of Electrical Engineers

MCSP Member of the Chartered Society of Physiotherapy

MCST Member of the College of Speech Therapists

MCT mainstream corporation tax • Member of the Association of Corporate Treasurers

MCU *Photog.* medium close-up

Md *Chem., symbol for* mendelevium

Md. Maryland

M/d *Commerce* months after date

MD Doctor of Medicine (Latin *Medicinae Doctor*) • *Music* main droite (French: right hand) • malicious damage • managing director • *Music* mano destra (Italian: right hand) • *US postcode for* Maryland • (*or* **M/D**) *Banking* memorandum of deposit • mentally deficient • Middle Dutch • military district • mini-disc (in sound recording) • musical director

MDA methylenedioxy-amphetamine (hallucinogenic drug; love drug *or* ice) • methylenedioxymeth-amphetamine (hallucinogenic drug; Ecstasy) • *Computing* monochrome display adaptor • Muscular Dystrophy Association

M-day (USA) mobilization day

MDC metropolitan district council • more developed country

MDentSc Master in Dental Science

MDes Master of Design

MDHB Mersey Docks and Harbour Board

mdise merchandise

Mdlle Mademoiselle (French: Miss)

Mdm Madam

MDMA methylenedioxy-methamphetamine (hallucinogenic drug; Ecstasy)

Mdme Madame (French: Mrs)

mdnt midnight

MDP Mongolian Democratic Party

MDR (*or* **m.d.r.**) minimum daily requirement

MDS Master of Dental Surgery

MDSc Master of Dental Science

mdse merchandise

MDT (USA) Mountain Daylight Time

MDu Middle Dutch

Me Maine (USA) • Messerschmitt (German aircraft) • *Chem., symbol for* methyl (used in formulae)

ME *US postcode for* Maine • marine engineer(ing) • Master of Education • Master of Engineering • mechanical engineer(ing) · *postcode for* Medway · Middle East(ern) · Middle English · military engineer · mining engineer(ing) · Most Excellent (in titles) · *Med.* myalgic encephalomyelitis

MEAF Middle East Air Force

meas. measure

MEB Midlands Electricity Board

MEc Master of Economics

MEC Member of the Executive Council · Middle East Command

MECAS Middle East Centre for Arab Studies

mech. mechanical(ly) · mechanics · mechanism

MECI Member of the Institute of Employment Consultants

MECO ('miːkəʊ) *Astronautics* main engine cut off

MEcon Master of Economics

med. medical · medicine · medieval · medium

Med. Mediterranean

MEd Master of Education

MED minimum effective dose

Medit. Mediterranean

med. jur. medical jurisprudence

MedScD Doctor of Medical Science

MEF Middle East Force

meg (mɛg) *Computing* megabyte

MEIC Member of the Engineering Institute of Canada

MELF Middle East Land Forces

mem. member · memento (Latin: remember) · memoir(s) · memorandum · memorial

MENCAP (*or* Mencap) ('mɛnkæp) Royal Society for Mentally Handicapped Children and Adults

MEng Master of Engineering

MEO Marine Engineering Officer

MEP (Sri Lanka) Mahajana Eksath Peramuna (People's United Front) · Master of Engineering Physics · (*or* **m.e.p.**) mean effective pressure · Member of the European Parliament

MEPA Master of Engineering and Public Administration

mer. meridian · meridional

merc. mercantile • mercury

MERLIN ('mɜːlɪn) *Astronomy* Multi-Element Radio-linked Interferometer Network (UK)

Messrs ('mɛsəz) Messieurs (French: gentlemen *or* sirs; used in English as pl. of Mr; *see also under* MM)

met. metallurgical • metallurgist • metallurgy • metaphor • metaphysics • (*or* **met;** mɛt) meteorological (as in **met. office**) • meteorology • metronome • metropolitan

Met (*or* **met**) *Biochem.* methionine • (mɛt) Metropolitan Opera House (New York) • (mɛt) Metropolitan Police

metal. (*or* **metall.**) metallurgical • metallurgy

metaph. metaphor(ical) • metaphysical • metaphysics

MetE Metallurgical Engineer

meteorol. (*or* **meteor.**) meteorological • meteorology

Meth. Methodist

MetR Metropolitan Railway (London)

MeV *symbol for* mega-electronvolt(s)

Mex. Mexican • Mexico

MEX *international vehicle registration for* Mexico

MEXE Military Engineering Experimental Establishment

Mez mezzo-soprano

mf (ital.) *Music* mezzo forte (Italian; moderately loudly)

mF *symbol for* millifarad(s)

MF machine finish(ed) (of paper) • Master of Forestry • *Telecom.* medium frequency • melamine–formaldehyde (as in **MF resin**) • Middle French • *Telecom.* multifrequency

M/F (*or* **m/f**) male or female (in advertisements)

MFA Master of Fine Arts

MFARCS Member of the Faculty of Anaesthetists of the Royal College of Surgeons

MFC Mastership in Food Control

MFCM Member of the Faculty of Community Medicine

mfd manufactured

mfg manufacturing

MFH Master of Foxhounds

MFHom Member of the Faculty of Homeopathy

MFlem Middle Flemish

MFLOPS ('εm,flɒps) *Computing* million floating-point operations per second

MFM *Computing* modified frequency modulation

MFN most favoured nation (in trade agreements)

MFOM Member of the Faculty of Occupational Medicine

MFPA Mouth and Foot Painting Artists

mfr. (*or* **mfre**) manufacture · manufacturer

MFr Middle French

m. ft. *Med.* mistura fiat (Latin: let a mixture be made; in prescriptions)

MFV motor fleet vessel

mg *symbol for* milligram(s)

Mg *Chem., symbol for* magnesium

MG machine glazed (of paper) · machine gun · *Music* main gauche (French: left hand) · Major-General · *Building trades* make good · Morris Garages (sports car; named after its original manufacturer) · *Med.* myasthenia gravis

MGA Major-General in charge of Administration

MGB Ministerstvo Gosudarstvennoi Bezopasnosti (Russian: Ministry of State Security; Soviet secret police, 1946–54) · motor gunboat

MGC Machine Gun Corps

MGDS RCS Member in General Dental Surgery of the Royal College of Surgeons

MGGS Major-General, General Staff

MGI Member of the Institute of Certificated Grocers

MGk Medieval Greek

M. Glam Mid Glamorgan

MGM Metro-Goldwyn-Mayer (film studio)

MGO Master General of the Ordnance · Master of Gynaecology and Obstetrics

Mgr Manager · Monseigneur (French: my lord) · *RC Church* Monsignor

MGr Medieval Greek

Mgrs Managers · *RC Church* Monsignors

mgt management

mH *Physics, symbol for* millihenry(s)

MH Master of Horse · (USA) Medal of Honor

MHA (Australia, Canada) Member of the House of Assembly • Methodist Homes for the Aged

MHCIMA Member of the Hotel Catering and Institutional Management Association

MHD *Physics* magnetohydrodynamics

MHE Master of Home Economics

MHG Middle High German

MHK (Isle of Man) Member of the House of Keys

M.Hon. Most Honourable

MHR (USA, Australia) Member of the House of Representatives

MHRA Modern Humanities Research Association

MHRF Mental Health Research Fund

MHS *Computing* message-handling system

MHW mean high water (of tides)

MHz *symbol for* megahertz

mi. mile • (USA, Canada) mill(s) (monetary unit)

MI *US postcode for* Michigan • Military Intelligence (*see* MI5; MI6) • mounted infantry • *Med.* myocardial infarction

MI5 Military Intelligence, section five (British counter-intelligence agency)

MI6 Military Intelligence, section six (British intelligence and espionage agency)

MIA Master of International Affairs • *Military* missing in action

MIAA&S Member of the Incorporated Association of Architects and Surveyors

MIAeE Member of the Institute of Aeronautical Engineers

MIAgrE Member of the Institution of Agricultural Engineers

MIAM Member of the Institute of Administrative Management

MIBF Member of the Institute of British Foundrymen

MIBiol Member of the Institute of Biology

MIBritE Member of the Institution of British Engineers

MIB(Scot) Member of the Institute of Bankers in Scotland

Mic. *Bible* Micah

MICE Member of the Institution of Civil Engineers

MICEI Member of the Institution of Civil Engineers of Ireland

MICFor Member of the Institute of Chartered Foresters

Mich. Michaelmas · Michigan

MIChemE Member of the Institution of Chemical Engineers

MICorrST Member of the Institution of Corrosion Science and Technology

MICR *Computing* magnetic-ink character recognition

microbiol. microbiology

micros. microscopist · microscopy

MICS Member of the Institute of Chartered Shipbrokers

mid. middle

Mid. Midshipman

MIDAS ('maɪdəs) missile defence alarm system

Middx Middlesex

MIDI (*or* **Midi**) ('mɪdɪ) musical instrument digital interface

Mid. Lat. Middle Latin

MIDPM Member of the Institute of Data Processing Management

MIE(Aust) Member of the Institution of Engineers, Australia

MIED Member of the Institution of Engineering Designers

MIEE Member of the Institution of Electrical Engineers

MIEI Member of the Institution of Engineering Inspection

MIE(Ind) Member of the Institution of Engineers, India

MIES Member of the Institution of Engineers and Shipbuilders, Scotland

MIEx Member of the Institute of Export

MIExpE Member of the Institute of Explosives Engineers

MIF *Immunol.* migration inhibition factor

MIFA Member of the Institute of Field Archaeologists

MIFF Member of the Institute of Freight Forwarders

MIFireE Member of the Institute of Fire Engineers

MiG (mɪg) Mi(koyan and) G(urevich) (Soviet jet

fighter; named after its designers)

MIG (MIG) metal-inert gas (as in **MIG welding**)

MIGasE Member of the Institution of Gas Engineers

MIGeol Member of the Institution of Geologists

MIH Master of Industrial Health • Member of the Institute of Housing

MIHort Member of the Institute of Horticulture

MIHT Member of the Institution of Highways and Transportation

MIIM Member of the Institute of Industrial Managers

MIInfSc Member of the Institute of Information Sciences

mil. military • militia

MIL Member of the Institute of Linguists

MILGA Member of the Institute of Local Government Administrators

milit. military

MILocoE Member of the Institution of Locomotive Engineers

MIM Member of the Institute of Metals

MIMarE Member of the Institute of Marine Engineers

MIMC Member of the Institute of Management Consultants

MIMechE Member of the Institution of Mechanical Engineers

MIMGTechE Member of the Institution of Mechanical and General Technician Engineers

MIMI Member of the Institute of the Motor Industry

MIMinE Member of the Institution of Mining Engineers

MIMM Member of the Institution of Mining and Metallurgy

MIMunE Member of the Institution of Municipal Engineers (now amalgamated with the Institution of Civil Engineers)

min minimum • *symbol for* minute(s)

min. mineralogical • mineralogy • minim (liquid measure) • minimum • mining • minor • minute(s)

Min. Minister • Ministry

MIND *indicating* National Association for Mental Health

mineral. mineralogical • mineralogy

Minn. Minnesota

Min. Plen. Minister Plenipotentiary

MInstAM Member of the Institute of Administrative Management

MInstBE Member of the Institution of British Engineers

MInstD Member of the Institute of Directors

MInstE Member of the Institute of Energy

MInstEnvSci Member of the Institute of Environmental Sciences

MInstMC Member of the Institute of Measurement and Control

MInstME Member of the Institution of Mining Engineers

MInstMM Member of the Institution of Mining and Metallurgy

MInstP Member of the Institute of Physics

MInstPet Member of the Institute of Petroleum

MInstPI Member of the Institute of Patentees and Inventors

MInstPkg Member of the Institute of Packaging

MInstPS Member of the Institute of Purchasing and Supply

MInstR Member of the Institute of Refrigeration

MInstRA Member of the Institute of Registered Architects

MInstT Member of the Institute of Transport

MInstTM Member of the Institute of Travel Managers in Industry and Commerce

MInstWM Member of the Institute of Wastes Management

MINucE Member of the Institution of Nuclear Engineers

MIOSH Member of the Institution of Occupational Safety and Health

m.i.p. mean indicated pressure

MIP marine insurance policy • maximum investment plan • Member of the Institute of Plumbing • monthly investment plan

MIPA Member of the Institute of Practitioners in Advertising

MIPM Member of the Institute of Personnel Management

MIPR Member of the Institute of Public Relations

MIProdE Member of the Institution of Production Engineers

MIPS (*or* **mips**) (mips) *Computing* million instructions per second

MIQ Member of the Institute of Quarrying

MIRAS ('maɪˌræs) mortgage interest relief at source

MIREE(Aust) Member of the Institution of Radio and Electronics Engineers (Australia)

MIRT Member of the Institute of Reprographic Technicians

MIRTE Member of the Institute of Road Transport Engineers

MIRV (mɜːv) *Military* multiple independently targeted re-entry vehicle

MIS management information system • Member of the Institute of Statisticians

misc. miscellaneous • miscellany

MISD *Computing* multiple instruction (stream), single data (stream)

Miss. Mission • Missionary • Mississippi

mist. *Med.* mistura (Latin: mixture)

MIStructE Member of the Institution of Structural Engineers

MITA Member of the Industrial Transport Association

MITD Member of the Institute of Training and Development

MITE Member of the Institution of Electrical and Electronics Technician Engineers

MITI (Japan) Ministry of International Trade and Industry

MITT Member of the Institute of Travel and Tourism

Mitts (mɪts) minutes of telecommunications traffic

MIWEM Member of the Institution of Water and Environmental Management

MJ *symbol for* megajoule(s)

MJI Member of the Institute of Journalists

MJS Member of the Japan Society

MJur Magister Juris (Latin: Master of Law)

mk *Currency* mark

Mk mark (type of car)

MK *symbol for* Malawi kwacha (monetary unit) • *postcode for* Milton Keynes

mks *Currency* marks • (*or* **m.k.s., MKS**) metre kilogram second (as in **mks units**)

mkt market

ml (*or* **mL**) *symbol for* millilitre(s)

ml. mail

ML Licentiate in Medicine (Latin *Medicinae Licentiatus*) • Master of Law(s) • Medieval Latin • *postcode for* Motherwell • motor launch

MLA (*or* **MLArch**) Master of (*or* in) Landscape Architecture • Member of the Legislative Assembly

MLC Meat and Livestock Commission • (India, Australia) Member of the Legislative Council

MLCOM Member of the London College of Osteopathic Medicine

MLD *Pharmacol.* minimal lethal dose

MLF *Military* multilateral (nuclear) force

MLG Middle Low German

MLitt Master of Letters (Latin *Magister Litterarum*)

Mlle Mademoiselle (French: Miss)

MLO military liaison officer

MLR *Banking* minimum lending rate • (ital.) Modern Language Review

MLS Master of Library Science

MLSO Medical Laboratory Scientific Officer

MLW mean low water (of tides)

mm *symbol for* millimetre(s)

m.m. (*or* **M/m**) made merchantable • mutatis mutandis (Latin: with the necessary changes)

MM *Music* Maelzel's metronome (indicating the tempo of a piece) • Majesties • Martyrs • Master Mechanic • Master of Music • mercantile marine • Messieurs (French: gentlemen *or* sirs; used in French as pl. of M (Monsieur); *compare* Messrs) • Military Medal

MMA Metropolitan Museum of Art

MMB Milk Marketing Board

MMC Monopolies and Mergers Commission

MMD (Zambia) Movement for Multiparty Democracy

MMDS *Radio* multipoint microwave distribution system

Mme Madame (French: Mrs)

MME Master of Mechanical Engineering • Master of Mining Engineering • Master of Music Education

MMechE Master of Mechanical Engineering

MMed Master of Medicine

MMedSci Master of Medical Science

MMet Master of Metallurgy

MMetE Master of Metallurgical Engineering

mmf *Physics* magnetomotive force

mmHg millimetre(s) of mercury (unit of pressure)

MMin Master of Ministry

MMM (Canada) Member of the Order of Military Merit

3M Minnesota Mining and Manufacturing Company

MMR measles, mumps, rubella (in **MMR vaccine**)

MMS Marine Meteorological Services • Member of the Institute of Management Services

MMSA Master of Midwifery of the Society of Apothecaries

MMSc Master of Medical Science

MMU *Computing* memory management unit

MMus Master of Music

MMusEd Master of Musical Education

mn. midnight

Mn *Chem.*, symbol for manganese • Modern (of languages)

MN Merchant Navy • *US postcode for* Minnesota

MNA Master of Nursing Administration • Member of the National Assembly (of Quebec)

MNAD Multinational Airmobile Division (of NATO)

MNC multinational company

MnE Modern English

MNE multinational enterprise

MNECInst Member of the North East Coast Institution of Engineers and Shipbuilders

mng managing

mngmt management

mngr manager

MnGr (*or* **MnGk**) Modern Greek

MNI Member of the Nautical Institute

MNR marine nature reserve • Mozambique National Resistance

MNurs Master of Nursing

mo. moment • month

m.o. mail order • modus operandi • money order

m-o months old

Mo *Chem., symbol for* molybdenum

Mo. Missouri • Monday

MO mail order • manually operated • mass observation • Master of Obstetrics • Medical Officer • military operations • *US postcode for* Missouri • modus operandi • money order

MO&G Master of Obstetrics and Gynaecology

MOBS (mobz) multiple-orbit bombardment system (nuclear-weapon system)

MoC mother of the (trade-union) chapel

mod. moderate • *Music* moderato (Italian; at a moderate tempo) • modern • *Maths.* modulus

MoD Ministry of Defence

modem ('məʊdɛm) *Computing* modulator demodulator

mod. praes. *Med.* modo praescripto (Latin: in the manner directed)

Mods Honour Moderations (at Oxford University)

MOEH Medical Officer for Environmental Health

MOH Master of Otter Hounds • Medical Officer of Health

MOI Ministry of Information

mol *Chem., symbol for* mole(s)

mol. molecular • molecule

MOL *Astronautics* manned orbital laboratory

mol. wt. molecular weight

m.o.m. middle of month

MOMI Museum of the Moving Image

mon. monastery • monetary

Mon. Monday

Mont. Montana

mor. *Bookbinding* morocco

Mor. Moroccan • Morocco

MOR middle-of-the-road

MORI (*or* **Mori**) ('mɔːrɪ) Market and Opinion Research Institute (as in **MORI poll**)

morn. morning

morph. (*or* **morphol.**) morphological • morphology

mor. sol. *Med.* more solito (Latin: in the usual manner; in prescriptions)

mos. months

MOT (*or* **MoT**) Ministry of Transport (usually referring to the road-vehicle test, as in **MOT certificate**)

MOVE (muːv) Men Over Violence (association for wife batterers)

movt movement

MOW (New Zealand) Ministry of Works • Movement for the Ordination of Women

MOX mixed oxide (as in **MOX fuel**)

mp melting point • (ital.) *Music* mezzo piano (Italian; moderately softly)

m.p. melting point

MP Member of Parliament • Metropolitan Police • Military Police(man) • Mounted Police(man)

MPA Master of Professional Accounting • Master of Public Administration • Master Printers Association • Member of the Parliamentary Assembly of Northern Ireland

MPBW Ministry of Public Building and Works

MPC maximum permissible concentration

MPD maximum permissible dose

MPE Master of Physical Education • maximum permissible exposure (to radiation)

MPEA Member of the Physical Education Association

mpg miles per gallon

MPG *Education* main professional grade (teacher's basic salary)

mph miles per hour

MPh Master of Philosophy

MPH Master of Public Health

MPhil Master of Philosophy

MPIA Master of Public and International Affairs

MPLA Movimento Popular de Libertação de Angola (Portuguese: Popular Movement for the Liberation of Angola)

MPO management and personnel office • Metropolitan Police Office

MPP Member of the Provincial Parliament (of Ontario)

MPRISA Member of the Public Relations Institute of South Africa

MPRP Mongolian People's Revolutionary Party (communists)

MPS Medical Protection Society • Member of the Philological Society • Member of the Physical Society • *Med.* mucopolysaccharide (as in **MPS disease**)

MPsyMed Master of Psychological Medicine

MQ metol-quinol (photographic developer)

Mr Mister

MR magnetic resonance (as in **MR scanner**) • *Law* Master of the Rolls • (*or* **M/R**) *Commerce* mate's receipt • motivation(al) research • municipal reform

MRA Moral Rearmament

MRAC Member of the Royal Agricultural College

MRACP Member of the Royal Australasian College of Physicians

MRACS Member of the Royal Australasian College of Surgeons

MRAeS Member of the Royal Aeronautical Society

MRAIC Member of the Royal Architectural Institute of Canada

MRAS Member of the Royal Asiatic Society

MRBM *Military* medium-range ballistic missile

MRBS Member of the Royal Botanic Society

MRC Medical Research Council

MRCA multirole combat aircraft

MRCGP Member of the Royal College of General Practitioners

MRC-LMB Medical Research Council Laboratory of Molecular Biology

MRCO Member of the Royal College of Organists

MRCOG Member of the Royal College of Obstetricians and Gynaecologists

MRCP Member of the Royal College of Physicians

MRCPA Member of the Royal College of Pathologists of Australia

MRCPath Member of the Royal College of Pathologists

MRCPE Member of the Royal College of Physicians of Edinburgh

MRCPGlas Member of the Royal College of Physicians and Surgeons of Glasgow

MRCPI Member of the Royal College of Physicians of Ireland

MRCPsych Member of the Royal College of Psychiatrists

MRCS Member of the Royal College of Surgeons

MRCSE Member of the Royal College of Surgeons of Edinburgh

MRCSI Member of the Royal College of Surgeons of Ireland

MRCVS Member of the Royal College of Veterinary Surgeons

MRD machine-readable dictionary

MRe Mauritian rupee (monetary unit)

MRE Master of Religious Education • *Military* meal, ready to eat • Microbiological Research Establishment

MRG Minority Rights Group

MRGS Member of the Royal Geographical Society

MRH Member of the Royal Household

MRHS Member of the Royal Horticultural Society

MRI *Med.* magnetic resonance imaging (*or* image) • Member of the Royal Institution

MRIA Member of the Royal Irish Academy

MRIAI Member of the Royal Institute of the Architects of Ireland

MRIC Member of the Royal Institute of Chemistry (*see* MRSC)

MRIN Member of the Royal Institute of Navigation

MRINA Member of the Royal Institution of Naval Architects

MRIPHH Member of the Royal Institute of Public Health and Hygiene

MRM mechanically recovered meat (in food processing)

MRMetS Member of the Royal Meteorological Society

mRNA *Biochem.* messenger RNA

MRO Member of the Register of Osteopaths

MRP manufacturers' recommended price

MRPharmS Member of the Royal Pharmaceutical Society

Mrs ('mɪsɪz) Mistress (title of a married woman)

MRS *Physics* magnetic resonance spectroscopy

MRSA *Med.* methicillin-resistant *Staphylococcus aureus*

MRSC Member of the Royal Society of Chemistry (formerly MRIC)

MRSH Member of the Royal Society for the Promotion of Health

MRSL Member of the Royal Society of Literature

MRSM Member of the Royal Society of Medicine • Member of the Royal Society of Musicians of Great Britain

MRSPE Member of the Royal Society of Painter-Etchers and Engravers

MRSPP Member of the Royal Society of Portrait Painters

MRST Member of the Royal Society of Teachers

MRTPI Member of the Royal Town Planning Institute

MRUSI Member of the Royal United Service Institution

MRV *Military* multiple re-entry vehicle

MRVA Member of the Rating and Valuation Association

ms manuscript • *symbol for* millisecond(s)

m.s. mail steamer

m/s metre(s) per second • (*or* **M/s**) *Finance* months after sight

m/s² metre(s) per second squared

Ms (mɪz *or* məz) Miss *or* Mrs (unspecified)

MS (*or* **M/S**) mail steamer • *Music* mano sinistra (Italian: left hand) • manuscript • Master of Surgery • *international vehicle registration for* Mauritius • *Photog.* medium shot (*or* mid-shot) • memoriae sacrum (Latin: sacred to the memory of; on gravestones) • *Cartography* milestone • minesweeper • *US postcode for* Mississippi • multiple sclerosis

MSA Master of Science in Agriculture • Member of the Society of Apothecaries • Mineralogical Society of America

MS&R Merchant Shipbuilding and Repairs

MSArch Master of Science in Architecture

MSAutE Member of the Society of Automobile Engineers

MSBA Master of Science in Business Administration

MSBus Master of Science in Business

MSc Master of Science

MSC Manchester Ship Canal • Manpower Services Commission

MScA (*or* **MSc(Ag)**) Master of Science in Agriculture

MSc(Arch) Master of Science in Architecture

MScD Master of Dental Science

MSChE Master of Science in Chemical Engineering

MSCI Index *Finance* Morgan Stanley Capital International World Index

MSD Doctor of Medical Science

MSDent Master of Science in Dentistry

MS-DOS (ˌɛmˌɛsˈdɒs) *Computing, trademark* MicroSoft Disk Operating System

MSE Member of the Society of Engineers

MSEd Master of Science in Education

MSEE Master of Science in Electrical Engineering

MSEM Master of Science in Engineering Mechanics

MSF Manufacturing, Science, and Finance (Union) • Master of Science in Forestry • Médecins sans frontières (French: Doctors Without Frontiers; charitable organization)

MSG monosodium glutamate (food additive)

Msgr Monseigneur (French: my lord) • *RC Church* Monsignor

MSH Master of Staghounds

MSHE (*or* **MSHEc**) Master of Science in Home Economics

MSHyg Master of Science in Hygiene

MSI *Electronics* medium-scale integration

MSIAD Member of the Society of Industrial Artists and Designers

MSIE Master of Science in Industrial Engineering

MSINZ Member of the

Surveyors' Institute of New Zealand

MSJ Master of Science in Journalism

MSL (*or* **msl**) mean sea level

MSM Master of Sacred Music • Meritorious Service Medal

MSME Master of Science in Mechanical Engineering

MSN Master of Science in Nursing

MSO Member of the Society of Osteopaths

MSocSc Master of Social Science(s)

MSPE Master of Science in Physical Education

MSPH Master of Science in Public Health

MSPhar (*or* **MSPharm**) Master of Science in Pharmacy

MSQ managing service quality

MSR Member of the Society of Radiographers • *Military* missile-site radar

MSS (*or* **MS(S), mss**) manuscripts • (*or* **MSSc**) Master of Social Science • Master of Social Service • Member of the Royal Statistical Society

MSTD Member of the Society of Typographic Designers

Mstr Master

MSU *Med.* midstream (specimen of) urine

MSW magnetic surface wave(s) • medical social worker

MSY maximum sustainable yield (of a natural resource)

mt. *Military* megaton

m.t. metric ton(s)

Mt *symbol for* metical (monetary unit of Mozambique) • Mount • Mountain

MT mail transfer • mean time • mechanical transport • *US postcode for* Montana • motor tanker • motor transport

M/T empty (used on gas cylinders) • mail transfer

MTA Music Trades' Association

MTAI Member of the Institute of Travel Agents

MTB motor torpedo boat

MTBE methyl *t*-butyl ether (lead-free antiknock petrol additive)

MTC Mechanized Transport Corps

MTCA Ministry of Transport and Civil Aviation

MTD Midwife Teacher's Diploma

MTech Master of Technology

MTEFL Master in the Teaching of English as a Foreign (*or* Second) Language

mtg meeting • (*or* **mtge**) mortgage

mth month

MTh Master of Theology

mtn motion

MTO made to order

Mt Rev Most Reverend (title of archbishop)

Mts Mountains • Mounts

MTS Master of Theological Studies

MU Musicians' Union

MUF *Telecom.* maximum usable frequency

MUFTI ('mʌftɪ) *Military* minimum use of force tactical intervention

MUGA ('mʌgə) *Med.* multiple-gated arteriography (as in **MUGA scan**)

mun. (*or* **munic.**) municipal(ity)

MUniv Master of the University

mus. museum • music(al)

MusB Bachelor of Music (Latin *Musicae Baccalaureus*)

MusD Doctor of Music (Latin *Musicae Doctor*)

MusM Master of Music (Latin *Musicae Magister*)

mv (ital.) *Music* mezza voce (Italian: half voice; i.e. softly)

m.v. market value • mean variation • motor vessel

mV *symbol for* millivolt(s)

MV *symbol for* megavolt(s) • merchant vessel • (*or* **M/V**) motor vessel • muzzle velocity (of firearms)

MVB Bachelor of Veterinary Medicine

MVD Doctor of Veterinary Medicine • Ministerstvo Vnutrennikh Del (Russian: Ministry of Internal Affairs; Soviet police organization, 1946–60)

MVEE Military Vehicles and Engineering Establishment

MVL motor-vehicle licence

MVO Member of the Royal Victorian Order

MVSc (*or* **MVS**) Master of Veterinary Science

mW *symbol for* milliwatt(s)

MW *international vehicle registration for* Malawi •

Master of Wine • *Radio* medium wave • *symbol for* megawatt(s) • *Chem.* molecular weight • Most Worshipful • Most Worthy

MWeldl Member of the Welding Institute

Mx *Magnetism, symbol for* maxwell • Middlesex

my million years (following a number)

MY motor yacht

myc. (*or* **mycol.**) mycological • mycology

MYOB *Colloquial* mind your own business

MYRA *Finance* multiyear rescheduling agreement

myst. mystery (*or* mysteries)

myth. (*or* **mythol.**) mythological • mythology

N

n (ital.) *Chem., symbol for* amount of substance • *Printing, symbol for* en • (ital.) *Maths, symbol for* indefinite number • *symbol for* nano- (prefix denoting 10^{-9}, as in **nm**, nanometre) • *Physics, symbol for* neutron • (ital.) *Chem.* normal (i.e: unbranched, as in **n-butane**) • *Electronics* n-type (semiconductor)

n. name • natus (Latin: born) • nephew • *Commerce* net • neuter • new • nominative • noon • note • noun • number

N *Printing, symbol for* en • *Chess, symbol for* knight • naira (Nigerian monetary unit) • *Electrical engineering* neutral • *Physics, symbol for* newton(s) • ngultrum (monetary unit of Bhutan; *see also under* Nu) • *Chem., symbol for* nitrogen • north(ern) • *postcode for* north London • *international vehicle registration for* Norway • nuclear (as in **N-**

weapon) • *Physics, symbol for* nucleon • *(ital.) Chem., indicating* substitution on a nitrogen atom (as in **N-phenylhydroxylamine**)

N. (*or* **N**) National(ist) • navigation • Navy • New • Norse • north(ern) • November

n/a not applicable • not available

Na *Chem., symbol for* sodium (Latin *natrium*)

NA *international vehicle registration for* Netherlands Antilles • *Banking* new account • *Med.* Nomina Anatomica (Latin: Anatomical Names; official anatomical terminology) • North America(n)

N/A (*or* **N/a**) *Banking* new account • (*or* **N/A**) *Banking* no account • not available

n.a.a. *Shipping* not always afloat

NAAFI (*or* **Naafi**) ('næfɪ) Navy, Army, and Air Force Institutes

NAAS National Agricultural Advisory Service

NAB National Advisory Body for Public Sector Higher Education • National Assistance Board (former government department) • National Australia Bank

NABC National Association of Boys' Clubs

NABS National Advertising Benevolent Society

NAC National Advisory Council • National Agriculture Centre • National Association for the Childless

NACAB National Association of Citizens Advice Bureaux

NACCB National Accreditation Council for Certification Bodies

NACNE National Advisory Committee on Nutrition Education

NACODS ('neɪkɒdz) National Association of Colliery Overmen, Deputies, and Shotfirers

NACOSS National Approved Council for Security Systems

NACRO (*or* **Nacro**) ('nækrəʊ) National Association for the Care and Resettlement of Offenders

NAD *Biochem.* nicotinamide adenine dinucleotide • *Med.* no abnormality detected

NADEC National Association of Development Education Centres

NADFAS National Association of Decorative and Fine Arts Societies

NADGE NATO Air Defence Ground Environment

NADH *Biochem.*, *indicating* a reduced form of NAD (H is the symbol for hydrogen)

NADP *Biochem.* nicotinamide adenine dinucleotide phosphate

NADW North Atlantic deep water

NAEA National Association of Estate Agents

NAEW NATO Airborne Early Warning

NA f. *symbol for* Netherlands Antillean guilder (monetary unit)

NAFTA ('næftə) New Zealand and Australia Free Trade Agreement

NAGC National Association for Gifted Children

Nah. *Bible* Nahum

Nahal (nə'hɑːl) (Israel) No'ar Halutzi Lohem (Hebrew: Pioneer and Military Youth)

NAHAT National Association of Health Authorities and Trusts

NAHT National Association of Head Teachers

NAI nonaccidental injury

NAIRU ('neɪruː) *Economics* nonaccelerating inflation rate of unemployment

NAITA ('neɪtə) National Association of Independent Travel Agents

NAK (*or* **nak**) (næk) *Telecom.* negative acknowledgment

NALGO ('nælgəu) National and Local Government Officers' Association

N. Am. North America(n)

NAMAS National Measurement and Accreditation Service

NAMCW National Association of Maternal and Child Welfare

NAMH National Association for Mental Health (now called MIND)

NAMMA NATO MRCA Management Agency

NAMS (USA) national air-monitoring sites

NAND (nænd) *Computing, Electronics* not AND (as in **NAND gate, NAND operation**)

N&P National and Provincial (building society)

N and Q notes and queries

NAO National Audit Office

NAPF National Association of Pension Funds

naph. *Chem.* naphtha

NAPO ('næpəʊ) National Association of Probation Officers (trade union)

NAPT National Association for the Prevention of Tuberculosis

NAS naval air station · Noise Abatement Society

NASA (*or* **Nasa**) ('næsə) (USA) National Aeronautics and Space Administration

NASDA ('næsdə) (Japan) National Space Development Agency

NAS/UWT National Association of Schoolmasters/Union of Women Teachers

nat. national(ist) · natural · natus (Latin: born)

N. At. North Atlantic

NATFHE National Association of Teachers in Further and Higher Education

natl national

NATLAS ('nætlæs) National Testing Laboratory Accreditation Scheme

NATO (*or* **Nato**) ('neɪtəʊ) North Atlantic Treaty Organization

NATS (nætz) National Air Traffic Services

nat. sc. (*or* **nat. sci.**) natural science(s)

NATSOPA (næt'səʊpə) National Society of Operative Printers, Graphical and Media Personnel (formerly National Society of Operative Printers and Assistants)

naut. nautical

nav. naval · navigable · navigation · navigator

NAV *Finance* net asset value (of an organization)

Nav.E. Naval Engineer

navig. navigation · navigator

NAVSAT ('næv,sæt) navigational satellite

NAWC National Association of Women's Clubs

NAWO National Alliance of Women's Organizations

NAYC Youth Clubs UK (formerly National Association of Youth Clubs)

NAYT National Association of Youth Theatres

Nazi ('nɑːtsɪ) National-sozialisten (German: National Socialist)

nb (*or* **n.b.**) *Cricket* no ball · nota bene (Latin: note well)

Nb *Chem., symbol for* niobium

NB New Brunswick (Canada) • North Britain (i.e. Scotland) • nota bene (Latin: note well)

NBA Net Book Agreement • North British Academy

NBC National Book Council (*see under* NBL) • (USA) National Broadcasting Company • nuclear, biological, and chemical (of weapons or warfare)

NbE north by east

NBG (*or* **nbg**) *Colloquial* no bloody good

NBI National Benevolent Institution

NBK National Bank of Kuwait

NBL National Book League (formerly Council) • (*or* **nbl**) *Colloquial* not bloody likely

NBPI National Board for Prices and Incomes

NBR *Chem.* nitrilebutadiene rubber

NBRI National Building Research Institute

NBS Newcastle Business School

NBV *Accounting* net book value (of an asset)

NbW north by west

NC National Certificate • *Education* National Curriculum • New Church • *Physics* nickel–cadmium (of electric cells) • no charge • North Carolina (abbrev. *or* postcode) • numerical control *or* numerically controlled (as in **NC machine**)

N/C (*or* **n/c**) new charter • no charge

NCA National Certificate of Agriculture • National Childminding Association • National Cricket Association

NCB National Children's Bureau • National Coal Board (now British Coal Corporation, BCC) • *Insurance* no claim bonus

NCBW nuclear, chemical, and biological warfare

NCC National Computing Centre • National Consumer Council • *Education* National Curriculum Council • Nature Conservancy Council

NCCI National Committee for Commonwealth Immigrants

NCCJ National Conference of Christians and Jews

NCCL National Council for Civil Liberties (now called Liberty)

n.c.d. *Colloquial* no can do

NCDAD National Council for Diplomas in Art and Design

NCDL National Canine Defence League

NCET National Council for Educational Technology

NCI *Finance* New Community Instrument

NCLC National Council of Labour Colleges

NCNC National Convention of Nigeria and the Cameroons • National Convention of Nigerian Citizens (political party)

NCO noncommissioned officer

NCP National Car Parks Ltd • (Australia) National Country Party (now called National Party)

NCPS noncontributory pension scheme

NCR National Cash Register (Company Ltd) • no carbon required (of paper)

NCRL National Chemical Research Laboratory

NCSC (Australia) National Companies and Securities Commission

NCSE National Council for Special Education

NCT National Chamber of Trade • National Childbirth Trust

NCU National Communications Union • National Cyclists' Union

NCV (*or* **n.c.v.**) no commercial value

NCVCCO National Council of Voluntary Child Care Organizations

NCVO National Council for Voluntary Organizations

NCVQ National Council for Vocational Qualifications

NCW National Council of Women (of Great Britain)

n.d. no date (*or* not dated) • *Banking* not drawn

Nd *Chem., symbol for* neodymium

ND Naturopathic Diploma • *Photog.* neutral density • no date • North Dakota (abbrev. *or* postcode)

N-D Notre-Dame (French: Our Lady; in church names, etc.)

NDA National Diploma in Agriculture

N. Dak. North Dakota

NDB *Aeronautics* nondirectional beacon

ndc National Defence College

NDC National Dairy Council

NDCS National Deaf Children's Society

NDD National Diploma in Dairying • National Diploma in Design

NDE near-death experience

NDH National Diploma in Horticulture

NDIC National Defence Industries Council

NDN National District Nurse Certificate

NDP National Democratic Party (of various countries) • *Economics* net domestic product • (Canada) New Democratic Party

NDPS National Data Processing Service

NDSF National Diploma of the Society of Floristry

NDU Nursing Development Unit

n.e. not exceeding

n/e new edition • *Banking* no effects (i.e. no funds)

Ne *Chem., symbol for* neon

NE Naval Engineer • US

postcode for Nebraska • *postcode for* Newcastle • new edition • New England • *Banking* no effects (i.e. no funds) • northeast(ern) • nuclear energy

N/E new edition • *Banking* no effects (i.e. no funds) • *Accounting* not entered

NEAC New English Art Club

NEAF Near East Air Force

NEARELF Near East Land Forces

Neb. (*or* **Nebr.**) Nebraska

NEB National Enterprise Board • New English Bible

NEBSS National Examinations Board for Supervisory Studies

n.e.c. not elsewhere classified

NEC National Executive Committee • National Exhibition Centre (Birmingham) • (Japan) Nippon Electric Company

NECCTA National Educational Closed Circuit Television Association

NECInst North East Coast Institution of Engineers and Shipbuilders

NEDC National Economic Development Council (*or*

Neddy) • North East Development Council

NEDO National Economic Development Office

NEEB North Eastern Electricity Board

neg. negative(ly) • negligence

NEG negative (in transformational grammar)

Neh. *Bible* Nehemiah

NEH National Endowment for the Humanities

NEL National Engineering Laboratory

nem. con. (*or* **dis.**) nemine contradicente (*or* dissentiente) (Latin: no-one opposing; unanimously)

N. Eng. northern England

n.e.p. new edition pending

Nep. Neptune (planet)

NEQ *Electronics* nonequivalence (as in **NEQ gate**)

NERC Natural Environment Research Council

n.e.s. not elsewhere specified

Neth. Netherlands

n. et m. *Med.* nocte et mane (Latin: night and morning; in prescriptions)

neurol. neurological • neurology

Nev. Nevada

Newf. Newfoundland

New M New Mexico

New Test. New Testament

n.f. noun feminine

NF National Front • Newfoundland • (*or* **N/F**) *Banking* no funds • Norman French (language)

NFBTE National Federation of Building Trades Employers

NFC National Freight Consortium

NFCO National Federation of Community Organization

Nfd Newfoundland

NFD Newfoundland • no fixed date

NFDM nonfat dry milk

NFER National Foundation for Educational Research

NFFO nonfossil-fuel obligation (for electricity companies)

NFFPT National Federation of Fruit and Potato Trades

NFHA National Federation of Housing Associations

NFL (USA, Canada) National Football League

Nfld Newfoundland

NFMS National Federation of Music Societies

NFS National Fire Service • *Computing* network file service (*or* system) • not for sale

NFSE National Federation of Self-Employed (and Small Businesses)

NFT National Film Theatre

NFU National Farmers' Union

NFWI National Federation of Women's Institutes

NG New Guinea • nitroglycerine • (*or* **n.g.**) no good • *postcode for* Nottingham

NGA National Graphical Association (*see* GPMU)

NGC *Astronomy* New General Catalogue (prefixed to a number to designate a Catalogue object)

NGk New Greek

NGNP nominal gross national product

NGO (India) nongazetted officer • nongovernmental organization

NGS nuclear generating station

NGTE National Gas Turbine Establishment

NGU *Med.* nongonococcal urethritis

NGV natural-gas vehicle

NH New Hampshire (abbrev. *or* postcode) • northern hemisphere

NHBC National House-Building Council

NHBRC National House-Builders' Registration Certificate

N.Heb. (*or* **NHeb**) New Hebrew • New Hebrides

NHG New High German

NHI National Health Insurance

NHK Nippon Hōsō Kyōkai (Japan Broadcasting Corporation)

NHR National Housewives Register

NHS National Health Service

NHTPC National Housing and Town Planning Council

Ni *Chem., symbol for* nickel

NI National Insurance • Native Infantry • Northern Ireland • North Island (New Zealand)

NIAB National Institute of Agricultural Botany

NIACRO Northern Ireland Association for the

Care and Resettlement of Offenders

NIAE National Institute of Agricultural Engineering

NIAID National Institute of Allergy and Infectious Diseases

Nibmar (*or* **NIBMAR**) ('nɪb,mɑː) no independence before majority African rule

NIBSC National Institute for Biological Standards Control

NIC National Incomes Commission • (*or* **nic**) National Insurance contribution • newly industrialized country • *international vehicle registration for* Nicaragua

NiCad (*or* **NiCd, Ni/Cd**) nickel–cadmium (battery)

NICAM ('naɪkæm) *Electronics* near-instantaneous companded audio multiplex (for digital coding of audio signals)

NICEC National Institute for Careers Education and Counselling

NICG Nationalized Industries Chairmen's Group

NICRA Northern Ireland Civil Rights Association

NICS Northern Ireland Civil Service

NICU *Med.* neonatal intensive care unit

NID National Institute for the Deaf • (India) National Institute of Design • Naval Intelligence Division • Northern Ireland District

NIDD non-insulin-dependent diabetes

NIES Northern Ireland Electricity Service

NIESR National Institute of Economic and Social Research

NIF *Finance* note issuance facility

NIHCA Northern Ireland Hotels and Caterers Association

NIHE (Ireland) National Institute for Higher Education

NII Nuclear Installations Inspectorate

Nikkei Nihou Keizi Shimbun (share index on Tokyo Stock Exchange)

NILP Northern Ireland Labour Party

nimby ('nɪmbɪ) *Colloquial* not in my back yard (indicating liberals, reformers, etc., in principle but not in practice)

NIMH National Institute of Medical Herbalists

NIMR National Institute for Medical Research

NINO ('ni:nəʊ) no inspector, no operator (system)

Nip. Nippon(ese)

N. Ir. Northern Ireland

NIR Nauchno-Issledovatel'skaya Rabota (Russian colour-television system) • nonionizing radiation

NIRC National Industrial Relations Court

N. Ire. Northern Ireland

NIREX ('naɪrɛks) Nuclear Industry Radioactive Waste Executive

NIS *symbol for* new Israeli shekel (monetary unit)

NISTRO Northern Ireland Science and Technology Regional Organization

NISW National Institute for Social Work

NIT negative income tax

NJ New Jersey (abbrev. or postcode)

NK *Immunol.* natural killer (as in **NK cell**) • not known

NKC *Immunol.* natural killer cell

NKGB Narodny Komissariat Gosudarstvennoi Bezopasnosti (Russian: People's Commissariat of State Security; Soviet agency, 1943–46)

NKr *symbol for* Norwegian krone (monetary unit)

NKVD Narodny Komissariat Vnutrennikh Del (Russian: People's Commissariat of Internal Affairs; Soviet agency, 1934–46)

NKz *symbol for* new kwanza (Angolan monetary unit)

n.l. (*or* **nl**) *Printing* new line • non licet (Latin: it is not permitted) • non liquet (Latin: it is not clear)

NL National Liberal • *international vehicle registration for* Netherlands • New Latin • (Australia) no liability (after the name of a public limited company; equivalent to plc) • (*or* **N.Lat.**) north latitude

NLC National Liberal Club

NLCS North London Collegiate School

NLD (Burma) National League for Democracy

NLF National Liberal Federation • National Liberation Front • National Loans Fund

NLLST National Lending Library for Science and Technology

NLP *Computing* natural language processing • *Computing* neurolinguistic programming

NLQ *Computing* near letter quality

NLS National Library of Scotland

n.l.t. not later than • not less than

NLW National Library of Wales

NLYL National League of Young Liberals

nm *symbol for* nanometre(s)

n.m. nautical mile(s) • non-metallic • noun masculine

N/m no mark(s) (on a bill of lading)

NM New Mexico (abbrev. or postcode) • nuclear medicine

N. Mex. New Mexico

n mile nautical mile

NMP *Economics* net material product

n.m.t. not more than

NMU National Maritime Union

NMW national minimum wage (as in **NMW policy**)

NN *postcode for* Northampton

NNE north-northeast

NNEB National Nursery Examination Board

NNHT Nuffield Nursing Homes Trust

NNI noise and number index (to evaluate aircraft noise)

NNMA Nigerian National Merit Award

NNOM Nigerian National Order of Merit

NNP *Economics* net national product

NNR National Nature Reserve

NNT nuclear nonproliferation treaty

NNW north-northwest

no. north(ern) • number (from Italian *numero*)

n.o. *Cricket* not out

No *Chem., symbol for* nobelium

No. north(ern) • number (from Italian *numero*)

NO naval officer

n.o.c. not otherwise classified

NOC National Olympic Committee • not otherwise classified

NOCD *Colloquial* not our class, dear

noct. *Med.* nocte (Latin: at night)

NODA National Operatic and Dramatic Association

NODC non-OPEC developing country

n.o.i.b.n. not otherwise indexed by name

n.o.k. next of kin

nol. pros. *Law* nolle prosequi (Latin: do not prosecute; procedure for ending criminal proceedings)

nom. nominal · nominative

noncom. noncommissioned

Noncon. Nonconformist

non obst. non obstante (Latin: notwithstanding)

non pros. *Law* non prosequitur (Latin: he does not prosecute; former judgment in favour of defendant)

non seq. non sequitur (Latin: (a statement that) does not follow logically)

n.o.p. not otherwise provided (for)

NOP National Opinion Poll · not our publication

Nor. Norman · (*or* **nor.**) north · Norway · Norwegian

NOR (nɔː) *Computing, Electronics* not OR (as in **NOR gate, NOR operation**)

NORAD ('nɔːræd) North

American Air Defense Command

Norf. Norfolk

norm. normal

Norm. Norman

Northants Northamptonshire

Northd (*or* **Northumb.**) Northumberland

Norvic. Norvicensis (Latin: (Bishop) of Norwich)

Norw. Norway · Norwegian

NORWEB ('nɔːwɛb) North Western Electricity Board

n.o.s. not otherwise specified

Nos. (*or* **nos.**) numbers (from Italian *numeros*)

NOT (nɒt) *Computing, Electronics* not (from its sense in logic, as in **NOT gate, NOT operation**)

NOTAR (*or* **Notar**) ('nəʊtɑː) no-tail rotor (of an aircraft)

NOTB National Ophthalmic Treatment Board

Nottm Nottingham

Notts Nottinghamshire

nov. novel(ist) · novice

Nov. (*or* **Nov**) November

NOX (nɒks) nitrogen oxide(s)

np *Printing* new paragraph • new pence

n.p. *Law* net personalty • (*or* **n/p**) net proceeds • *Printing* new paragraph • nisi prius (Latin: unless previously) • nonparticipating • *Bibliog.* no place of publication given • no printer • no publisher • normal pitch • not paginated

Np *Telecom.*, symbol for neper • *Chem.*, symbol for neptunium

NP national park • National Power plc • neuropsychiatric • neuropsychiatry • *postcode for* Newport • Notary Public • noun phrase

NPA National Park Authority • Newspaper Publishers' Association

NPC no-player character (in the game Dungeons and Dragons)

NPD Nationaldemokratische Partei Deutschlands (German: National Democratic Party; neo-Nazis) • *Marketing* new product development • *Astronomy* north polar distance

n.p.f. not provided for

NPF (Syria) National Progressive Front

NPFA National Playing Fields Association

NPG National Portrait Gallery

NPK nitrogen, phosphorus, and potassium (in fertilizers; from the chemical symbols of these elements)

n.p.n.a. *Commerce* no protest for nonacceptance

n.p. or d. no place or date

n.p.p. no passed proof

NPP nuclear power plant

NPS nuclear power source • nuclear power station

NPT non-proliferation treaty

NPU *Med.* not passed urine

NPV *Finance* net present value • no par value (of shares)

NPW nuclear-powered warship

NQOC *Colloquial* not quite our class

nr near

NR natural rubber • *postcode for* Norwich

NRA National Recreation Area • National Rifle Association • National Rivers Authority • nuclear-reaction analysis

NRC National Research Council

NRCC National Research Council of Canada

NRD National Register of Designers (*or* Registered Designer)

NRDC National Research Development Corporation

NRDS *Med.* neonatal respiratory distress syndrome

NREM *Physiol.* non-rapid eye movement (as in **NREM sleep**)

NRM (Uganda) National Resistance Movement

NRMA (Australia) National Roads and Motorists Association

NROTC Naval Reserve Officer Training Corps

NRP nuclear reprocessing plant

NRPB National Radiological Protection Board

NRR Northern Rhodesia Regiment

NRs *symbol for* Nepalese rupee (monetary unit)

NRT (*or* **n.r.t.**) net registered tonnage

NRV *Finance* net realizable value

ns *symbol for* nanosecond(s) • (Graduate of the Royal) Naval Staff (College, Greenwich)

n.s. near side • not specified • *Banking* not sufficient (funds)

n/s nonsmoker • *Banking* not sufficient (funds)

NS National Service • National Society • new series • Newspaper Society • New Style (method of reckoning dates) • (*or* **N/S**) nonsmoker • not significant • Nova Scotia • nuclear ship

NSA National Skating Association

NSAID *Med.* nonsteroidal anti-inflammatory drug

NSB National Savings Bank

NSC National Safety Council • National Sporting Club

NSCR National Society for Cancer Relief

NSF (*or* **N/S/F, n.s.f.**) *Banking* not sufficient funds • Nuclear Structure Facility (Daresbury, Cheshire)

NSG *Education* nonstatutory guidelines (concerning the National Curriculum)

NSHEB North of Scotland Hydroelectric Board

NSL National Sporting League

NSM new smoking material • nonstipendiary minister

NSPCC National Society for the Prevention of Cruelty to Children

n.s.p.f. not specially provided for

NSRA National Smallbore Rifle Association

NSU *Med.* nonspecific urethritis

NSW New South Wales

n.t. net terms • net tonnage

NT (Ireland) National Teacher • National Theatre • National Trust • New Testament • Northern Territory (Australia) • *Bridge* notrump(s) • Nurse Teacher

NTA net tangible assets

NTB *Economics* nontariff barrier

NTD *Colloquial* not top drawer

NTDA National Trade Development Association

NTG North Thames Gas

Nth North

NTI noise transmission impairment

NTP *Physics* normal temperature and pressure

NTS National Trust for Scotland • not to scale

NTVLRO National Television Licence Records Office

nt. wt. (*or* nt wt) net weight

n.u. name unknown

Nu *symbol for* ngultrum (monetary unit of Bhutan)

NU natural uranium • number unobtainable

NUAAW National Union of Agricultural and Allied Workers

NUCPS National Union of Civil and Public Servants

NUCUA National Union of Conservative and Unionists Associations

NUFLAT National Union of Footwear, Leather, and Allied Trades (now amalgamated with the NUHKW to form the National Union of Knitwear, Footwear, and Apparel Trades)

NUHKW National Union of Hosiery and Knitwear Workers (*see* NUFLAT)

NUI National University of Ireland

NUIW National Union of Insurance Workers

NUJ National Union of Journalists

NUJMB Northern Universities Joint Matriculation Board

num. number • numeral(s)

Num. *Bible* Numbers

NUM National Union of Mineworkers

NUMAST ('njuːmæst) National Union of Marine, Aviation, and Shipping Transport Officers

numis. (*or* **numism.**) numismatic(s)

NUPE ('njuːpɪ) National Union of Public Employees

NUR National Union of Railwaymen (*see* RMT)

NUS National Union of Seamen (*see* RMT) • National Union of Students

NUT National Union of Teachers

NUTG National Union of Townswomen's Guilds

NUTGW (*or* **NUT&GW**) National Union of Tailors and Garment Workers (now amalgamated with the GMB)

NUTN National Union of Trained Nurses

NUU New University of Ulster

NV (Netherlands) Naamloze Vennootschap (after the name of a company; equivalent to plc) • *US postcode for* Nevada • New Version • nonvintage (of wine, etc.) • (*or* **n.v.**) *Finance* nonvoting (shares)

N/V nonvintage (of wine etc.) • *Banking* no value

NVG *Military* night-vision goggles

NVI nonvalue indicator (type of postage stamp)

NVM Nativity of the Virgin Mary

NVQ National Vocational Qualification

NW net worth • northwest(ern) • *postcode for* northwest London

NWFP North-West Frontier Province (Pakistan)

NWP North-Western Province (India)

n. wt. net weight

NWT Northwest Territories (Canada)

NY New York (abbrev. *or* state postcode)

NYC New York City

NYD *Med.* not yet diagnosed

NYMT National Youth Music Theatre

NYO National Youth Orchestra

NYOS National Youth Orchestra of Scotland

NYP not yet published

NYT National Youth Theatre

NZ New Zealand (abbrev. *or* IVR)

NZBC New Zealand Broadcasting Corporation

N. Zeal. New Zealand

NZEFIP New Zealand Expeditionary Force in the Pacific (in World War II)

NZEI New Zealand Educational Institute

NZIA New Zealand Institute of Architects

NZLR New Zealand Law Reports

NZMA New Zealand Medical Association

NZPA New Zealand Press Association

NZRFU New Zealand Rugby Football Union

NZRN New Zealand Registered Nurse.

O

o (ital.) *Chem.* ortho (as in **o-cresol**)

o. *Printing* octavo • old • only • order

O *Slang* opium • *Chem., symbol for* oxygen • *Pharmacol.* pint (Latin *octarius*) • *Med.,* indicating a blood group (see also under ABO) • *Logic, indicating* a particular negative categorial proposition

O. (*or* **O**) Ocean • *Printing* octavo • October • *Med.* oculus (Latin: eye) • Oddfellows • Office • Ohio • old • order (of knighthood, etc.) • Orient • Osten (German: east) • ouest (French: west)

o/a on account (of) • on or about

OA objective analysis • (*or* **o.a.**) office automation • Officier d'Académie (French: Officer of the Academy; award for services in education) • *Banking* old account • operational analysis • osteoarthritis • (*or* **o.a.**) overall

OAA Outdoor Advertising Association of Great Britain

o.a.d. overall depth

o.a.h. overall height

OAM Medal of the Order of Australia

O & C Oxford and Cambridge (Schools Examination Board)

O & M organization and method(s)

O & O Oriental and Occidental Steamship Company

OAO one and only • Orbiting Astronomical Observatory

OAP old age pension(er)

OAPEC (əʊˈeɪpɛk) Organization of Arab Petroleum-Exporting Countries

OAR *RC Church* (of the) Order of Augustinian Recollects

OAS on active service • Organization of American States

OASIS (əʊˈeɪsɪs) optimal aircraft sequencing using intelligent systems

OAU Organization of African Unity

ob. obiit (Latin: he *or* she died) • obiter (Latin: incidentally) • oboe • observation • obstetric(s)

o.b. ordinary building (grade; of timber)

o/b on or before (preceding a date)

Ob. *Bible* Obadiah

OB off Broadway • old bonded (whisky) • old boy • Order of Barbados • order of battle • ordinary business (in life-assurance policies) • outside broadcast

OBA optical bleaching agent (in detergents)

Obad. *Bible* Obadiah

obb. (*or* **obbl.**) *Music* obbligato (Italian: obligatory)

obdt obedient

OBE Officer of the Order of the British Empire • out-of-the-body experience

ob-gyn (*or* **ob-gyne**) obstetrics–gynaecology

OBI Order of British India

obit. obituary

obj. *Grammar* object(ive) • (*or* **objn**) objection

obl. oblique • oblong

OBM *Surveying* Ordnance benchmark

Obogs ('əʊbɒgz) *Military* on-board oxygen-generating system

ob. ph. *Surveying* oblique photograph(y)

obs. obscure • observation • observatory • observe(d) • obsolete

obsc. obscure

obscd obscured

obstet. obstetric(s) • obstetrician

obstn obstruction

OBU One Big Union

o.c. *Architect.* on centre • (*or* **oc**) only child • *Shipping* open charter • opere citato (*see* op. cit.)

o/c officer commanding • overcharge

Oc. Ocean

OC Officer Commanding • *Electrical engineering* operating characteristic • operations centre • oral contraceptive • (Officer of the)

Order of Canada • *Philately* original cover • overseas country

OCA Old Comrades Association

O.Carm. (of the) Order of Carmelites

O.Cart. (of the) Order of Carthusians

Oc.B/L *Shipping* ocean bill of lading

occ. (*or* **occn**) occasion • (*or* **occas.**) occasional(ly) • occident(al) • occupation • occurrence

OCD *Med.* obsessive compulsive disorder • Ordo (*or* Ordinis) Carmelitarum Discalceatorum (Latin: (of the) Order of Discalced Carmelites; Discalced Carmelite Fathers)

oceanog. oceanography

OCF Officiating Chaplain to the Forces

OCR *Computing* optical character recognition (*or* reader) • Ordo (*or* Ordinis) Cisterciensium Reformatorum (Latin: (of the) Order of Reformed Cistercians; Trappists)

OCS (USA) Officer Candidate School

OCSO (of the) Order of

Cistercians of the Strict Observance (Trappists)

oct. *Music* octave · *Printing* octavo

Oct (*or* **Oct.**) October

OCTU ('ɒktuː) Officer Cadet Training Unit

OCU Operational Conversion Unit

o.d. *Med.* oculus dexter (Latin: right eye) · *Military* olive drab · outer (*or* outside) diameter

OD *Med.* oculus dexter (Latin: right eye) · officer of the day · Old Dutch (language) · *Military* olive drab · ordinary seaman · Ordnance datum (standard sea level of the Ordnance Survey) · ordnance department · organization development · outer (*or* outside) diameter · (*or* **o/d**) overdose

O/D (*or* **O/d, o/d**) on deck · *Banking* on demand · *Banking* overdraft (*or* overdrawn)

ODA *Med.* Operating Department Assistant · Overseas Development Administration (formerly Ministry of Overseas Development, ODM)

ODan Old Danish

ODAS Ocean Data Station

ODC (of the) Order of Discalced Carmelites

ODESSA (əʊˈdɛsə) Organisation der SS-Angehörigen (German: Organization of SS members)

ODI Overseas Development Institute

ODM Ministry of Overseas Development (*see under* ODA)

ODV *Colloquial* eau de vie (French: cognac)

o.e. omissions excepted

Oe *Physics, symbol for* oersted

OE Old English (language)

OEA Overseas Education Association

OECD Organization for Economic Cooperation and Development

OED (ital.) Oxford English Dictionary

OEEC Organization for European Economic Cooperation (superseded by OECD)

OEM *Computing* original equipment manufacturer

OES Order of the Eastern Star

OF Oddfellows · oil-filled · oil-fired · *Printing* old-face (type) · Old French (language) • Order of the Founder (of the Salvation Army) • oxidizing flame

OFA *Med.* oncofetal antigen

O factor *Psychol.* oscillation factor

off. offer(ed) • office • (*or* **offr**) officer • (*or* **offcl**) official • officinal

OFFER (*or* **Offer**) ('ɒfə) Office of Electricity Regulation

OFGAS (*or* **Ofgas**) ('ɒf,gæs) Office of Gas Supply

OFM (of the) Order of Friars Minor (Franciscans)

OFMCap. (of the) Order of Friars Minor Capuchin (Franciscan order)

OFMConv. (of the) Order of Friars Minor Conventual (Franciscan order)

OFr Old French

OFR Order of the Federal Republic of Nigeria

OFris Old Frisian

OFS Orange Free State

OFT Office of Fair Trading

OFTEL (*or* **Oftel**) ('ɒf,tɛl) Office of Telecommunications

OFWAT (*or* **Ofwat**) ('ɒf,wɒt) Office of Water Services

o.g. *Philately* original gum • *Sport* own goal

OG Officer of the Guard • *Architect.* ogee • *Philately* original gum

OGael Old Gaelic

OGL *Commerce* open general licence

OGM ordinary general meeting

Ogpu (*or* **OGPU**) ('ɒgpuː) Obyedinyonnoye Gosudarstvennoye Politicheskoye Upravleniye (Russian: United State Political Administration; Soviet state security system, 1923–34)

OGS Oratory of the Good Shepherd

OH *US postcode for* Ohio

OHC (*or* **o.h.c.**) overhead cam (*or* camshaft)

OHG Old High German

OHMS On Her (*or* His) Majesty's Service

OHN occupational health nurse

OHNC occupational health nursing certificate

OHP overhead projector

OHS occupational health service • *Metallurgy* open-hearth steel

OHV (*or* **o.h.v.**) overhead valve

OIC (*or* **O i/c**) officer in charge

OIr Old Irish

OIt Old Italian

OJ Order of Jamaica

OJT on-the-job training

OK all correct (from *orl korrect*, phonetic spelling) • *US postcode for* Oklahoma

OKH Oberkommando der Heeres (German Army High Command, World War II)

Okla. Oklahoma

ol. *Med.* oil (Latin *oleum*)

Ol. Olympiad

OL (*or* **o.l.**) *Med.* oculus laevus (Latin: left eye) • *postcode for* Oldham • Old Latin • *Computing* on-line • operating licence • (Officer of the) Order of Leopold

Old Test. Old Testament

OLE *Computing* object linking and embedding

O level *Education* Ordinary level (replaced by GCSE)

OLG Old Low German

o.m. old measurement

OM old man • optical microscopy • Order of Merit • organic matter

OMC operation and maintenance costs

OMCS Office of the Minister for the Civil Service

OMI Oblate(s) of Mary Immaculate

OMM (Canada) Officer of the Order of Military Merit

omn. hor. *Med.* omni hora (Latin: every hour)

OMO one-man operator *or* operation (of buses)

o.n. *Med.* omni nocte (Latin: every night)

ON octane number • Old Norse • Ontario • (Jamaica) Order of the Nation

ONC Ordinary National Certificate • Orthopaedic Nursing Certificate

OND Ophthalmic Nursing Diploma • Ordinary National Diploma

ONF Old Norman (*or* Northern) French

ONG organisation non-gouvernementale (French: nongovernmental organization)

o.n.o. or near(est) offer

Ont. Ontario

ONZ Order of New Zealand

o/o (*or* **o.o.**) on order

O/o offers over

OO *Colloquial* once-over

(i.e. a preliminary inspection)

OOD *Computing* object-oriented design • officer of the day • officer of the deck

OOL *Computing* object-oriented language

OON Officer of the Order of the Niger

OOP *Computing* object-oriented programming

OOT out of town

OOW officer of the watch

op. opera (Latin: works) • operation • operator • opposite • optical • opus (Latin: a work; *see also* Op.)

o.p. *Theatre* opposite prompt side (i.e. actor's right) • out of print • overproof (of alcohol)

Op. *Music* Opus (preceding a number; indicating a piece by a particular composer)

OP *Military* observation post • old prices • *Insurance* open policy • *Theatre* opposite prompt side (i.e. actor's right) • Ordo (*or* Ordinis) Praedictatorum (Latin: (of the) Order of Preachers; Dominicans) • osmotic pressure • *Colloquial* other people's • other people's; *see also under* OPM; OP's) • out of

print • outpatient • overproof (of alcohol)

op-amp *Electronics* operational amplifier

op art optical art

OPAS Occupational Pensions Advisory Service

OPB Occupational Pensions Board

OPC (*or* opc) ordinary Portland cement

op. cit. opere citato (Latin: in the work cited; used in textual annotations)

OPCON ('ɒp,kɒn) operational control

OPCS Office of Population Censuses and Surveys

OPEC ('əʊ,pεk) Organization of Petroleum-Exporting Countries

OPers Old Persian

OPEX ('əʊ,pεks) operational, executive, and administrative personnel (in the UN)

ophthal. (*or* oph.) ophthalmic • (*or* **ophthalmol.**) ophthalmologist • (*or* **ophthalmol.**) ophthalmology

OPM *Colloquial* (USA) other people's money • output per man

o.p.n. ora pro nobis (Latin: pray for us)

OPO one-person operator *or* operation (of buses)

opp. (*or* **Opp.**) opuses (*or* opera; *see also under* Op.) • opposed • opposite • opposition

OPP oriented polypropene (in **OPP film**, used for packaging)

OPQ occupational personality questionnaire

OPr (*or* **OProv**) Old Provençal

OPruss Old Prussian

ops. operations

OP's *Colloquial* other people's (as in **OP's cigarettes**)

opt. *Grammar* optative • optical • optician • optics • optimal • optimum • optional

OQ Officer of the National Order of Quebec

or. orange • orient(al)

o.r. *Insurance* owner's risk

OR official receiver • operational (*or* operations) requirement • operational (*or* operations) research • *Electronics* or (from its sense in logic, as in **OR gate**, **OR operation**) • *US postcode for* Oregon • *Military* other ranks • *Insurance* owner's risk

Oracle ('ɒrək°l) optional reception of announcements by coded line electronics (teletext service of Independent Television)

o.r.b. *Insurance* owner's risk of breakage

orch. orchestra(l) • (*or* **orchd**) orchestrated by

ord. ordain(ed) • order • ordinal • ordinance • ordinary • ordnance

o.r.d. *Insurance* owner's risk of damage

ordn. ordnance

Ore. (*or* **Oreg.**) Oregon

org. organic • organization • organized

orig. origin • original(ly) • originate(d)

ORL *Med.* otorhinolaryngology (ear, nose, and throat specialty; ENT)

ornithol. (*or* **ornith.**) ornithological • ornithology

OROM *Computing* optical read-only memory

ors. others

ORS Operational Research Society

ORSL Order of the Republic of Sierra Leone

Orth. Orthodox (religion)

o.s. *Med.* oculus sinister (Latin: left eye) • old se-

ries • (*or* **os**) only son • outside (measurement)

o/s (*or* **O/s**) out of stock •
outsize (of clothing) • (*or*
O/s) *Banking* outstanding

Os *Chem., symbol for* os-
mium

OS *Med.* oculus sinister
(Latin: left eye) • Old
Saxon (language) • Old
School • Old Style (method
of reckoning dates) • *Computing* operating system (*see
also* OS/2) • Ordinary Seaman • Ordnance Survey •
out of stock • outsize (of
clothing)

OS/2 *Computing* Operating System/2 (produced by
IBM and Microsoft)

OSA (of the) Order of St
Augustine (Augustinians)

OSB (of the) Order of St
Benedict (Benedictines)

osc *Military* (graduate of)
overseas staff college

OSC (of the) Order of St
Clare (Poor Clares)

OSCAR ('ɒskə) Orbital
Satellites Carrying Amateur
Radio • Organization for
Sickle Cell Anaemia Re-
search

OSD (of the) Order of St
Dominic (Dominicans)

OSE operational support
equipment

OSF *Computing* Open Software Foundation • (of the)
Order of St Francis (Franciscans)

OSFC (of the) Order of St
Francis, Capuchin

O/Sig Ordinary Signalman

OSI (*or* **OSlav**) Old Slavonic

OSM (of the) Order of the
Servants of Mary (Servites)

OSNC Orient Steam Navigation Company

OSO orbiting solar observatory

o.s.p. obiit sine prole
(Latin: died without issue)

OSp Old Spanish

O.SS.S Ordo (*or* Ordinis)
Sanctissimi Salvatoris
(Latin: (of the) Order of the
Most Holy Saviour; Bridget-
tines)

O.SS.T Ordo (*or* Ordinis)
Sanctissimae Trinitatis
Redemptionis Captivorum
(Latin: (of the) Order of the
Most Holy Trinity for the
Redemption of Captives;
Trinitarians)

OST (USA) Office of Science and Technology

osteo. osteopath(ic)

OStJ Officer of the Order of St John of Jerusalem

OSU (of the) Order of St Ursula (Ursulines)

OSUK Ophthalmological Society of the United Kingdom

OT occupational therapy (*or* therapist) • Old Testament • *Med.* operating theatre • (Australia) Overland Telegraph (from Adelaide to Darwin) • overtime

OTB (USA) off-track betting

OTC Officers' Training Corps • one-stop-inclusive tour charter • Organization for Trade Cooperation • over the counter (as in **OTC market** (in securities), **OTC medicines**) • oxytetracycline (an antibiotic)

OTE on-target earnings (for a salesman)

OTEC ('əʊtɛk) ocean thermal-energy conversion

OTeut Old Teutonic

OTH *Telecom.* over the horizon (as in **OTH radar**)

OTS *Advertising* opportunities to see

ott. *Music* ottava (Italian: octave)

OTT *Colloquial* over the top (i.e. excessive)

OTU operational training unit

OTurk Old Turkish

OU Open University • Oxford University

OUDS ('əʊ'juː 'diː 'ɛs *or* aʊdz) Oxford University Dramatic Society

OUP (Northern Ireland) Official Unionist Party • Oxford University Press

OURT Order of the United Republic of Tanzania

ov. overture

o.v.c. other valuable consideration (in contract law)

o.v.n.o. or very near offer

Ovra Opera di vigilanza e di repressione dell'antifascismo (Italian secret police of the Fascist regime)

O/W oil in water (emulsion)

OX *postcode for* Oxford

Oxbridge ('ɒks,brɪdʒ) Oxford and Cambridge (Universities; regarded collectively)

OXFAM (*or* **Oxfam**) ('ɒksfæm) Oxford Committee for Famine Relief

Oxon Oxfordshire (Latin *Oxonia*) • Oxoniensis (Latin: of Oxford)

oz (*or* **oz.**) ounce(s) (Italian *onza*)

oz T troy ounce.

•••••••••••••••••••••••••••••••••••••••

P

p (bold ital.) *Physics, symbol for electric dipole moment* • (ital.) *Physics, symbol for* momentum (bold ital. in vector equations) • (ital.) *Chem.* para (as in **p-cresol**) • *symbol for* penny (*or* pence) • (ital.) *Music* piano (Italian; softly, quietly) • *symbol for* pico- (prefix indicating 10^{-9} as in **ps**, picosecond) • (ital.) *Physics, symbol for* pressure • *Physics, symbol for* proton • *Electronics* p-type (semiconductor)

p. page • part • participle • partim (Latin: in part) • pass(ed) • *Nautical* passing showers • past • per (Latin: by, for) • *Grammar* person • pint • pipe • pius (Latin: holy) • population • post (Latin: after) • primus (Latin: first) • pro (Latin:

for, in favour of) • *Knitting* purl

P *medieval Roman numeral for* four hundred • (ital.) *Physics, symbol for* parity • *symbol for* parking (on road signs) • *Chess, symbol for* pawn • *symbol for* peta- (prefix indicating 10^{-15} as in **PJ**, petajoule) • pharmacy (on medicines obtained without a prescription from a pharmacy) • *Biochem., symbol for* phosphate • *Chem., symbol for* phosphorus • *Physics, symbol for* poise • *Computing* polynomial (referring to a class of formal languages recognizable in polynomial time) • *international vehicle registration for* Portugal • Post Office (on maps) • (ital.) *Physics, symbol for* power •

(ital.) *Physics*, symbol for pressure • proprietary (product) • *symbol for* pula (monetary unit of Botswana)

P. (or **P**) *RC Church* Papa (Latin: Pope) • Pastor • pater (Latin: father) • *Music* pedal • *Ecclesiast.* Père (French: Father) • *Horticulture* perennial • populus (Latin: people) • post • President • Priest • Prince • Progressive (party, movement, etc.) • *Theatre* prompt side (i.e. the actor's left)

P45 *indicating* a form relating to unemployment benefit issued by the DSS

pa. past

p.a. participial adjective • per annum • press agent

p/a *Book-keeping* personal account

Pa *Physics*, symbol for pascal • *Chem.*, symbol for protactinium

Pa. Pennsylvania

PA *postcode for* Paisley • Pakistan Army • *international vehicle registration for* Panama • (or **P/A**) *Insurance* particular average • *US postcode for* Pennsylvania • *Med.* pernicious anaemia • *Insurance* personal accident • *Accounting* personal account • *Taxation* personal allowance • personal appearance • personal assistant • Pierre Allain (climbing boot; named after its inventor) • Piper Aircraft (as in **PA-28**) • political agent • *Military* Post Adjutant • power amplifier • (or **P/A**) power of attorney • press agent • Press Association • (or **P/A**) *Banking, Bookkeeping* private account • programme assistant • public address (system) • publicity agent • Publishers Association • purchasing agent

PABA ('pɑːbə) *Biochem., Pharmacol.* p-aminobenzoic acid

PABX *Telephony* private automatic branch exchange

pac passed (final examination of the) advanced class (of the Military College of Science)

Pac. Pacific

PAC Pan-African(ist) Congress • Public Accounts Committee • *Stock exchange* put-and-call (option)

P-A-C *Psychol.* parent, adult, child (in transactional analysis)

PACE (peɪs) Police and Criminal Evidence Act

(1984) • Protestant and Catholic Encounter

PACT (*or* **Pact**) (pækt) Producers' Alliance for Cinema and Television

PaD Pennsylvania Dutch

PAD (pæd) passive air defence

p. ae. *Pharmacol.* partes aequales (Latin: equal parts)

PaG Pennsylvania German

PAg Professional Agronomist

PAGB Proprietary Association of Great Britain

PAICV (Cape Verde) Partido Africano da Independencia de Cabo Verde (Portuguese: African Party for the Independence of Cape Verde)

Pak. Pakistan(i)

Pak Re Pakistan rupee (monetary unit)

pal. palaeography • palaeontology

Pal. Palace • Palestine

PAL (pæl) *Television* phase alternation line

palaeontol. palaeontology

pam. (*or* **pamph.**) pamphlet

Pan. Panama

PAN peroxyacetyl nitrate

(atmospheric pollutant) • polyacrylonitrile (polymer)

P&E plant and equipment

P & F chart point-and-figure chart

P & L profit and loss

P & O Peninsular and Oriental (Steamship Company)

P&OSNCo Peninsular and Oriental Steam Navigation Company

p & p postage and packing

PAO Prince Albert's Own (regiment) • public affairs officer

par. paragraph • parallel • parenthesis • parish

Par. Paraguay

PAR (pɑː) *Military* perimeter acquisition radar • phased-array radar • *Aeronautics* precision approach radar • programme analysis review

para. paragraph

par. aff. *Pharmacol.* pars affecta (Latin: (to the) part affected)

paren. parenthesis

parens. parentheses

Parl. Parliament • (*or* **parl.**) parliamentary

parl. proc. parliamentary procedure

Parly Sec. Parliamentary Secretary

part. participle • particular • partner(ship)

PAS public-address system

PASCAL (*or* **Pascal**) ('pæs,kæl) *Computing*, indicating a programming language (named after Blaise Pascal (1623–62), French philosopher, mathematician, and physicist)

pass. passage • passenger • passim (Latin: here and there throughout) • *Grammar* passive

pat. patent(ed)

PAT *Banking* pre-authorized automatic transfer • Professional Association of Teachers

patd patented

path. (*or* **pathol.**) pathological • pathology

Pat. Off. Patent Office

pat. pend. patent pending

PAU Pan American Union

PAX *Telephony* private automatic exchange

PAYE pay as you earn (income tax) • pay as you enter

payt payment

PAYV pay as you view

Pb *Chem., symbol for* lead (Latin *plumbum*)

PB pass book • *Athletics* personal best • Pharmacopoeia Britannica (Latin: British Pharmacopoeia) • *Pharmacol.* phenobarbitone • plastic-bonded • Plymouth Brethren • power brakes • Prayer Book • *Knitting* purl into back of stitch

PBA *Colloquial* poor bloody assistant

PBAB please bring a bottle

PBB *Chem.* polybrominated biphenyl (toxic constituent of plastics, etc.)

PBI *Colloquial* poor bloody infantry(man)

pbk paperback (book)

PBM *Surveying* permanent benchmark • play by mail (of games)

PBR payment by results

PBS Public Broadcasting Service

PBX *Telephony* private branch exchange

pc *Astronomy, symbol for* parsec

pc. piece • price

p.c. per cent • postcard • *Med.* post cibum (Latin: after meals; in prescriptions)

PC Panama Canal • Parish

Council(lor) • Parliamentary Commissioner (ombudsman) • Past Commander • (Ireland) Peace Commissioner • perpetual curate • personal computer • *Politics* Plaid Cymru • Police Constable • (USA) politically correct (*or* political correctness) • *Chem.* polycarbonate • *Chem.* polypropylene (*or* polypropene) carbonate (plastic) • Post Commander • potentially correct • Prince Consort • *Electronics* printed circuit • Privy Council(lor) • process control • (Canada) Progressive Conservative • propositional calculus • *Chem.* propylene (*or* propene) carbonate

P/C (*or* **p/c**) petty cash • price(s) current

PCB petty cash book • *Chem.* polychlorinated biphenyl (toxic constituent of plastics, etc.) • (*or* **pcb**) *Electronics* printed-circuit board • *Insurance* private car benefits

PCC parochial church council • Press Complaints Commission

PCE Postgraduate Certificate of Education

P-Celtic *Linguistics, indicating* one of two main groups of languages that developed from Common Celtic. *See also* Q-Celtic

pcf pounds per cubic foot

PCFC Polytechnics and Colleges Funding Council

pci pounds per cubic inch

PCL *Computing* printer control language

pcm per calendar month

PCM phase-contrast microscope • photochemical machinery • protein-calorie malnutrition • *Telecom.* pulse-code modulation

PCMO Principal Colonial Medical Officer

PCN *Computing* personal communications network

PCOD polycystic ovary disease

p-code *Computing, indicating* an intermediate language designed as the target language for UCSD Pascal

PCP *Chem.* pentachlorophenol (wood preservative) • phencyclohexylpiperidine (the drug phencylidine; angel dust) • *Med. Pneumocystis carinii* pneumonia (complication of Aids) • prime commercial paper

pcs. pieces • prices

PCS (Scotland) Principal Clerk of Session

pct per cent

PCTE *Computing* portable common tool environment

p.c.u. passenger car unit

pd paid • passed

p.d. per diem (Latin: daily) • (*or* **p/d**) post-dated • *Physics* potential difference

Pd *Chem., symbol for* palladium

PD per diem (Latin: daily) • Pharmacopoeia Dublinensis (Latin: Dublin Pharmacopoeia) • (USA) Police Department • port dues • postal district • preventive detention (*or* detainee) • probability of detection • (Ireland) Progressive Democrat(s) • progressive disease • *Insurance* property damage • *Computing* public domain (software)

P/D price–dividend (in **P/D ratio**)

PDA *Computing* personal digital assistant

PDGF *Med., Biochem.* platelet-derived growth factor

pdl *Physics, symbol for* poundal

PDL *Computing* page description language • poverty datum line

PDM physical distribution management

PDN public data network

PDPA People's Democratic Party of Afghanistan

pdq (*or* **PDQ**) *Colloquial* pretty damn quick

PDR People's Democratic Republic • price–dividend ratio

PDRA postdoctoral research assistant

P/D ratio price–dividend ratio

PDS Parkinson's Disease Society

PDSA People's Dispensary for Sick Animals

PDT Pacific Daylight Time • personal development technology

PDTC Professional Dancer's Training Course Diploma

p.e. *Law* personal estate • printer's error

PE *Insurance* personal effects • *international vehicle registration for* Peru • *postcode for* Peterborough • Pharmacopoeia Edinburgensis (Latin: Edinburgh

Pharmacopoeia • *Computing* phase-encoded (of tape format) • physical education • plastic explosive • polyeth(yl)ene • Port Elizabeth (South Africa) • *Physics* potential energy • Presiding Elder • printer's error • *Statistics* probable error • procurement executive • Protestant Episcopal

P/E (*or* p/e) price–earnings (in **P/E ratio**)

PEA Physical Education Association of Great Britain and Northern Ireland

PEC (*or* **p.e.c.**) photoelectric cell

ped. pedal • pedestal • pedestrian

PEDir Director of Physical Education

PEI (Canada) Prince Edward Island

pen. peninsula(r)

Pen. Peninsula

PEN (pɛn) International Association of Poets, Playwrights, Editors, Essayists, and Novelists

PEng Member of the Society of Professional Engineers

Penn. Pennsylvania

Pent. Pentecost

PEP *Radio* peak envelope power • (*or* **Pep**; pɛp) personal equity plan • political and economic planning

per. percentile • period • person

Per. Persia(n)

PER price–earnings ratio • Professional and Executive Recruitment

PERA Production Engineering Research Association of Great Britain

per an. (*or* **per ann.**) per annum (Latin: yearly)

P/E ratio price–earnings ratio

perc. *Music* percussion

per con *Book-keeping* per contra (Latin: on the other side)

perf. perfect • perforated • perforation • performed (by)

perp. perpendicular

per pro. per procurationem (*see under* pp)

pers. person • personal(ly) • (*or* **persp.**) perspective

Pers. Persia(n)

pert. pertaining

PERT (pɜːt) *Computing, Management* project (*or* programme, performance) evaluation and review technique

Peruv. Peruvian

PEST (pest) Political, Environmental, Social, and Technological (framework for analysing these aspects of a business environment) • Pressure for Economic and Social Toryism (left-wing Conservative group)

pet. petroleum

Pet. *Bible* Peter

PET *Chem.* polyeth(yl)ene terephthalate (plastic used in food packaging) • (pet) *Med.* positron-emission tomography (as in **PET scan**) • *Taxation* potentially exempt transfer

PETN pentaerythritol tetranitrate (explosive)

PETRAS ('petrəs) Polytechnic Educational Technology Resources Advisory Service

Petriburg. Petriburgensis (Latin: (Bishop) of Peterborough)

petrog. petrography

petrol. petrology

PEX *indicating* a discounted airline fare (probably a back formation from APEX, advance-purchase excursion)

pf pfennig (German currency) • *Music* piano (instrument; from *pianoforte*)

pf. perfect • *Finance* preferred (stock) • proof

p.f. (ital.) *Music* piano e forte (Italian; soft and then loud) • (ital.) *Music* più forte (Italian; louder) • pro forma (invoice)

pF *Physics, symbol for* picofarad(s)

PF Patriotic Front • Procurator-Fiscal

PFA Professional Footballers' Association • pulverized fuel ash

pfc passed flying college (in the RAF)

PFC polychlorinated fluorocarbon (synthetic resin)

pfd *Finance* preferred

pfg pfennig (German currency)

PFLO Popular Front for the Liberation of Oman

PFLP Popular Front for the Liberation of Palestine

PFP personal financial planning

pg. page

p.g. paying guest • proof gallon (of alcohol)

Pg. Portugal • Portuguese

PG *Films* parental guidance

(certification) • paying guest • postgraduate • *Pharmacol.* prostaglandin (as in **PGE₁**, etc.)

PGA Professional Golfers' Association

PGCE Postgraduate Certificate of Education

PG Cert Postgraduate Certificate

PG Dip Postgraduate Diploma

PgDn page down (on a keyboard)

PGDRS psychogeriatric dependency rating scale

PGF *Med.* polypeptide growth factor

PGL *Med.* persistent generalized lymphadenopathy (a stage of Aids)

PGM precision-guided munition

PGR *Films* (Australia) parental guidance recommended (certification) • *Psychol.* psychogalvanic response

PgUp page up (on a keyboard)

ph *Optics, symbol for* phot(s)

ph. phase

pH *Chem.* potential of hydrogen ions (measure of acidity or alkalinity)

Ph *Chem., symbol for* phenyl group (in formulae) • (*or* **Ph.**) Philosophy (in degrees)

PH *postcode for* Perth • public health

PHAB (fæb) Physically Handicapped and Able-Bodied

phar. pharmaceutical • pharmacist • (*or* **Phar.**) pharmacopoeia • pharmacy

PharB (*or* **PharmB**) Bachelor of Pharmacy (Latin *Pharmaciae Baccalaureus*)

PharD (*or* **PharmD**) Doctor of Pharmacy (Latin *Pharmaciae Doctor*)

PharM (*or* **PharmM**) Master of Pharmacy (Latin *Pharmaciae Magister*)

pharmacol. pharmacology

PhB Bachelor of Philosophy (Latin *Philosophiae Baccalaureus*)

PHC Pharmaceutical Chemist • primary health care

PhD Doctor of Philosophy (Latin *Philosophiae Doctor*)

Phe (*or* **phe**) *Biochem.* phenylalanine

PHE Public Health Engineer

PHI permanent health insurance

phil. philological • philology • philosopher • philosophical • philosophy

Phil. (*or* **Phila.**) Philadelphia • Philharmonic • *Bible* Philippians • Philippines

Philem. *Bible* Philemon

Phil. I. (*or* **Phil. Is.**) Philippine Islands

philol. philological • philology

philos. philosopher • philosophical • philosophy

Phil. Trans. (ital.) Philosophical Transactions of the Royal Society of London

PhL Licentiate in (*or* of) Philosophy

PHLS Public Health Laboratory Service

PhM Master of Philosophy (Latin *Philosophiae Magister*)

PhmB Bachelor of Pharmacy

phon. (*or* **phonet.**) phonetics • (*or* **phonol.**) phonology

phot. (*or* **photog.**) photograph(ic) • photographer • photography

photom. photometry

phr. phrase

phren. (*or* **phrenol.**) phrenological • phrenology

phys. physical(ly) • physician • physicist • physics • physiological • physiology

phys. ed. physical education

physiol. physiological • physiologist • physiology

p.i. *Insurance* professional indemnity (policy)

PI *Med.* parainfluenza virus • Philippine Islands • private investigator

PIA Pakistan International Airlines Corporation • Personal Investment Authority

PIARC Permanent International Association of Road Congresses

PIB Prices and Incomes Board (superseded by NBPI)

PIBOR ('piːbɔː) *Finance* Paris Interbank Offered Rate

pic. *Music* piccolo • (*or* **pict.**) pictorial

PIC *Computing* programmable interrupt controller

PID pelvic inflammatory disease • *Computing* personal identification device • prolapsed intervertebral disc (slipped disc)

PIDS (pɪdz) *Med.* primary immune deficiency syndrome

PIE Proto-Indo-European (language)

PIH pregnancy-induced hypertension

PIK payment in kind

pil. pilula (Latin: pill; in prescriptions)

PILL (pɪl) *Computing* programmed instruction language learning

PILOT ('paɪlɒt) *Computing* programmed inquiry, learning, or teaching

PIM *Computing* personal information manager

PIMS profit impact of market strategy

p-i-n *Electronics* p-type, intrinsic, n-type (semiconductor)

PIN (pɪn) personal identification number (used, with cash or credit card, to access computer-based bank accounts, etc.)

pinx. pinxit (Latin: he *or* she painted it)

PIPPY (*or* **Pippy**) ('pɪpiː) *Colloquial* person inheriting parent's property

PIRA Paper Industries Research Association

PITCOM ('pɪtkɒm) Parliamentary Information Technology Committee

pixel ('pɪksəl) *Computing* picture element

pizz. *Music* pizzicato (Italian: pinched *or* plucked)

p.j. (*or* **p-j**) *Colloquial* pyjama

PJ Presiding Judge • Probate Judge • *Colloquial* pyjama

pk pack • package • park • peak • peck (unit)

pK *Chem.* potential of *K* (symbol for the dissociation constant; a measure of the strength of acids)

PK *international vehicle registration for* Pakistan • personal knowledge • *Immunol.* Prausnitz-Küstner (as in **PK test**) • psychokinesis

pkg. (*or* **pkge**) package

PKI Partai Komunis Indonésia (Indonesian Communist Party)

pkt packet • pocket

pkwy (USA) parkway

pl. place • plate • platoon • plural • pole (measure)

Pl. Place (in street names)

PL Paymaster Lieutenant • Pharmacopoeia Londiniensis (Latin: Pharmacopoeia of London) • Plimsoll line (on a ship) • *postcode for* Plymouth • Poet Laureate • *international vehicle registration for* Poland • Primrose League • (*or* **P/L**) *Law* product liability • product licence (on labels of medicinal products) • *Computing* programming language (as in **PL/I**, **PL/M**, etc.) • public law • public library

PL/I (*or* **PL/1**) *Computing* Programming Language I

p.l.a. passengers' luggage in advance

PLA (China) People's Liberation Army • Port of London Authority

plat. plateau • platoon

PLATO (*or* **Plato**) ('pleɪtəʊ) *Computing* programmed logic for automatic teaching operation

plc public limited company (following the name of a company)

PLC *Marketing* product life cycle • public limited company (following the name of a company)

Plen. Plenipotentiary

plf (*or* **plff**) plaintiff

PLG private/light goods (vehicle)

PLI President of the Landscape Institute

PLM Paris–Lyons–Mediterranean (Railway)

PL/M *Computing* Programming Language for Microcomputers

PLO Palestine Liberation Organization

PLP Parliamentary Labour Party

PLR public lending right

PLSS (plɪs) *Astronautics* personal (*or* portable) life-support system

pltf plaintiff

PLU *Colloquial* people like us

Pluna (*or* **PLUNA**) ('pluːnə) Primeras Líneas Uruguayas de Navegación Aérea (Uruguayan airline)

plup. (*or* **plupf.**) pluperfect

plur. plural • plurality

PL/Z *Computing* Programming Language Zilog

pm. premium

p.m. post meridiem (Latin: after noon) • postmortem (examination)

Pm *Chem.*, symbol for promethium

PM *Music* particular (*or* peculiar, proper) metre • Past Master (of a fraternity) • Paymaster • Police Magistrate • Postmaster • post

meridiem (*see under* p.m.) •
postmortem (examination) • Prime Minister • *Military* Provost Marshal

PMA *Dentistry* papillary, marginal, attached (gingivitis; in **PMA index**) • paramethoxyamphetamine (hallucinogenic drug) • personal military assistant • *Chem.* polymethyl acrylate (synthetic polymer)

PMBX *Telephony* private manual branch exchange

PMC Personnel Management Centre

PMG Paymaster General • Postmaster General • *Military* Provost Marshal General

p.m.h. per man-hour

PMH previous medical history

pmk postmark

PML *Insurance* probable maximum loss

PMO Principal Medical Officer

PMRAFNS Princess Mary's Royal Air Force Nursing Service

PMS *Med.* premenstrual syndrome • President of the Miniature Society

pmt payment

PMT *Photog.* photomechanical transfer • *Med.* premenstrual tension

PMX *Telephony* private manual exchange

pn (*or* **p-n**) *Electronics* p-type n-type semiconductor (as in **pn junction**)

p.n. please note • *Commerce* promissory note • *Physics* proton number

PN *Med.* postnatal • (*or* **P/N**) *Commerce* promissory note • *Computing* pseudonoise (as in **PN sequence**) • psychoneurotic

PNA Psychiatric Nurses Association

PNB Philippine National Bank

PNdB *symbol for* perceived noise decibel(s)

PNEU Parents' National Educational Union

PNG Papua New Guinea (abbrev. *or* IVR)

PNI *Med.* psychoneuroimmunology

pnp (*or* **p-n-p**) *Electronics* p-type n-type p-type semiconductor (as in **pnp transistor**)

PNS *Med.* parasympathetic nervous system

PNV (Spain) Partido

Nacional Vasco (Basque Nationalist Party)

pnxt pinxit (Latin: (he *or* she) painted it)

p.o. *Med.* per os (Latin: by mouth; in prescriptions)

Po *Chem., symbol for* polonium

PO parole officer • personnel officer • petty officer • Philharmonic Orchestra • pilot officer • *postcode for* Portsmouth • postal order • Post Office

POA primary optical area (in graphic design) • Prison Officers' Association (trade union)

POB Post Office Box

POC (*or* **p.o.c.**) port of call

POD pay(ment) on delivery • (ital.) Pocket Oxford Dictionary • port of debarkation

POE port of embarkation • port of entry

poet. poetic(al) • poetry

POETS day ('pəʊɪtz) *Colloquial, indicating* Friday (piss off early tomorrow's Saturday)

POEU Post Office Engineers Union

P. of W. Prince of Wales

POGO ('pəʊgəʊ) Polar Orbiting Geophysical Observatory

pol. political • politics

Pol. Poland • Polish

POL petroleum, oil, and lubricants

pol. econ. political economy

polit. political • politics

POM prescription-only medicine (*or* medication)

POMEF Political Office Middle East Force

Ponsi ('pɒnsɪ) *Military slang* person of no strategical importance

Ponti ('pɒntɪ) *Military slang* person of no tactical importance

POO Post Office order

pop. popular(ly) • population

POP plaster of Paris • (*or* **p.o.p.**) point of purchase • Post Office preferred (size of envelopes, etc.) • *Photog.* printing-out paper • proof of purchase

p.o.r. pay(able) on receipt • pay on return • port of refuge

Port. Portugal • Portuguese

pos. position • positive

POS point of sale

poss. possession • *Grammar* possessive • possible • possibly

POSSLQ ('pɒsəl,kju:) *Colloquial* (USA) person of the opposite sex sharing living quarters

Possum ('pɒsəm) patient-operated selector mechanism (phonetic spelling of POSM)

POST (pəʊst) Parliamentary Office of Science and Technology • point-of-sales terminal (in supermarkets, etc.)

posth. (*or* **posthum.**) posthumous(ly)

pot. potassium • potential • potentiometer

POUNC Post Office Users' National Council

POV *Films* point of view

POW Prince of Wales • prisoner of war

pp past participle • per curationem (Latin: by authority of; in correspondence, used by signatory on behalf of someone else) • (ital.) *Music* pianissimo (Italian; very quietly)

pp. pages

p.p. parcel post • per person • per procurationem (*see under* pp) • post-paid •

Med. post prandium (Latin: after a meal; in prescriptions) • prepaid • privately printed

PP parcel post • parish priest • Past President • Patres (Latin: Fathers) • *Med.* pellagra-preventive (in **PP factor**, former name for the vitamin nicotinic acid) • *Chem.* polyprop(yl)ene • prepositional phrase

PPA Periodical Publishers' Association • Pre-School Playgroups Association

ppb parts per billion

PPB paper, printing, and binding • party political broadcast • planning-programming-budgeting (system)

PPBS planning-programming-budgeting system

PPC Patres Conscripti (Latin: Conscript Fathers, members of the Roman Senate) • (*or* **p.p.c.**) pour prendre congé (French: to take leave) • *Med.* progressive patient care

PPCLI Princess Patricia's Canadian Light Infantry

ppd post-paid • prepaid

PPD *Med.* purified protein derivative (of tuberculin)

PPE personal protective equipment • philosophy, politics, and economics (course at Oxford University)

pph. pamphlet

PPH *Med.* post-partum haemorrhage

PPI *Radar* plan-position indicator • *Insurance* policy proof of interest

PPInstHE Past President of the Institute of Highway Engineers

PPIStructE Past President of the Institution of Structural Engineers

PPITB Printing and Publishing Industry Training Board

PPL Phonographic Performance Limited

ppm pages per minute • parts per million • pulse per minute

PPM *Electronics* peak programme meter

PPMA Produce Packaging and Marketing Association

PPN *Computing* public packet network

ppp (ital.) *Music* pianissimo (Italian; as quietly as possible)

PPP Pakistan's People's Party • personal pension plan • private patients plan • *Economics* purchasing power parity

PPPS (*or* **ppps**) post post postscriptum (Latin: third postscript)

ppr (*or* **p.pr.**) present participle

PPR printed paper rate (of postage)

PPRA Past President of the Royal Academy

PPRBA Past President of the Royal Society of British Artists

PPRBS Past President of the Royal Society of British Sculptors

PPRE Past President of the Royal Society of Painter-Etchers and Engravers

p.pro. per procurationem (*see under* pp)

PPROI Past President of the Royal Institute of Oil Painters

PPRTPI Past President of the Royal Town Planning Institute

PPS Parliamentary Private Secretary • *Med.* pelvic pain syndrome • (*or* **pps**) post postscriptum (Latin: further postscript) • (Australia) prescribed payments system • Principal Private Secretary

PPSIAD Past President of the Society of Industrial Artists and Designers

ppt. *Chem.* precipitate

PPTA (New Zealand) Post-primary Teachers Association

PPU Peace Pledge Union

pq previous (*or* preceding) question

PQ parliamentary question • Province of Quebec

pr pair • paper • power

pr. present • price • print(ed) • printer • printing • pronoun

p.r. *Med.* per rectum (Latin: by the rectum)

Pr *Chem., symbol for* praseodymium • *Chem., symbol for* propyl group (in formulae)

Pr. Priest • Prince • Provençal

PR parliamentary report • (*or* **P/R**) payroll • percentile rank • *Law* personal representative • photographic reconnaissance • Populus Romanus (Latin: the Roman people) • Pre-Raphaelite • press release • *postcode for* Preston • *Boxing*

prize ring • profit rate • proportional representation • public relations • Puerto Rican • Puerto Rico

PRA President of the Royal Academy • (USA) Public Roads Administration

PRB Pre-Raphaelite Brotherhood

PRBS President of the Royal Society of British Sculptors

PRC People's Republic of China

PRCS President of the Royal College of Surgeons

PRE President of the Royal Society of Painter-Etchers and Engravers

Preb. Prebend(ary)

prec. preceding

pred. predicate

pref. preface • prefatory • preferably • preference • preferred • prefix

prelim. preliminary

prem. premium

prep. preparation • preparatory • preposition

PREPP *Med.* Post-Registration Education and Practice Project (for establishing standards of nursing practice)

pres. present (time) • presidency • presidential • presumed

Pres. (or **Presb.**) Presbyter(ian) • President

pret. *Grammar* preterite

prev. previous(ly)

PRF *Electronics* pulse repetition (or recurrence) frequency

PRHA President of the Royal Hibernian Academy

PRI Plastics and Rubber Institute • President of the Royal Institute of Painters in Water Colours

PRIA President of the Royal Irish Academy

PRIAS President of the Royal Incorporation of Architects in Scotland

PRIBA President of the Royal Institute of British Architects

prim. primary • primitive

prin. principal • principle

Prin. Principal

print. printing

PRISA Public Relations Institute of South Africa

priv. private • privative

p.r.n. *Med.* pro re nata (Latin: as the situation demands; in prescriptions)

pro. profession(al)

Pro (or **pro**) *Biochem.* proline

Pr.O Press Officer

PRO Public Record Office • public relations officer

prob. probable • probably • problem

proc. procedure • proceedings • process

Proc. Proceedings • Proctor

prod. produce(d) • producer • product • production

prof. profession(al)

Prof. Professor

prog. prognosis • *Computing* program • programme • progress • progressive

Prog. Progressive (party, movement, etc.)

PROI President of the Royal Institute of Oil Painters

PROLOG (or **Prolog**) ('prəʊlɒg) *Computing* programming in logic (a programming language)

prom. promontory

PROM (prɒm) *Computing* programmable read-only memory

pron. pronominal • pro-

noun • pronounce(d) • pronunciation

PRONED ('prəʊˌnɛd)
Promotion of Non-Execu-
tive Directors

prop. proper(ly) • property • proposition • proprietary • proprietor

PROP Preservation of the
Rights of Prisoners

propr proprietor

PRORM Pay and Records
Office, Royal Marines

pros. prosody

Pros. Atty Prosecuting
Attorney

Prot. Protectorate • Protestant

pro tem. pro tempore
(Latin: for the time being)

prov. proverb • (or
provb.) proverbial(ly) •
province • provincial • provi-
sional

Prov. Provençal • Prov-
ence • *Bible* Proverbs • Province • Provost

prox. proximo (Latin: in
(*or* of) the next (month))

prox. acc. proxime
accessit (Latin: (he *or* she)
came nearest; next in order
of merit to the winner)

PRP profit- (*or* performance-)related pay

prs pairs

PRs *symbol for* Pakistan
rupee (monetary unit)

PRS Performing Right Society Ltd • President of the
Royal Society

PRSA President of the
Royal Scottish Academy •
Public Relations Society of
America

PRSE President of the
Royal Society of Edinburgh

PRSH President of the
Royal Society for the Promotion of Health

PRSW President of the
Royal Scottish Water Col-
our Society

PRT petroleum revenue tax

PRUAA President of the
Royal Ulster Academy of
Arts

Prus. Prussia(n)

PRWA President of the
Royal West of England
Academy

PRWS President of the
Royal Society of Painters in
Water Colours

ps *Military* passed school
of instruction (of officers) •
Physics, symbol for pico-
second(s) • postscript

ps. pieces • pseudonym

Ps *Physics, symbol for* positronium

Ps. *Bible* (Book of) Psalms • Psalm

PS paddle steamer • Parliamentary Secretary • passenger steamer • Pastel Society • Permanent Secretary • *Linguistics* phrase structure • Police Sergeant • *Chem.* polystyrene • postscript • power steering • private secretary • Privy Seal • *Theatre* prompt side (i.e. the actor's left) • (Australia) public service (equivalent to the civil service)

psa *indicating* Graduate of RAF Staff College

Psa. *Bible* (Book of) Psalms • Psalm

PSA Petty Sessions Area • pleasant Sunday afternoon • President of the Society of Antiquaries • (Australia) Prices Surveillance Authority • Property Services Agency • *Med.* prostatic specific antigen • (New Zealand) Public Service Association

p's and q's *Colloquial, indicating* manners (phonetic spelling of p(lea)se and (than)k you's)

PSB (Japan) Postal Savings Bureau

PSBR public sector borrowing requirement

psc *Military* passed staff college

PSD *Law* Petty Sessional Divison

PSDR public sector debt requirement

PSE Pacific Stock Exchange • pale soft exudate (in meat processing) • Pidgin Sign English • psychological stress evaluator (lie detector)

pseud. pseudonym

psf (*or* **p.s.f.**) pounds per square foot

PSG *Linguistics* phrase-structure grammar

PSHFA Public Servants Housing Finance Association

psi (*or* **p.s.i.**) pounds (*or* pound-force) per square inch

PSI Policy Studies Institute

psia pounds per square inch, absolute

PSIAD President of the Society of Industrial Artists and Designers

psid pounds per square inch, differential

psig pounds per square inch, gauge

PSIS Permanent Secretaries Committee on the Intelligence Services

PSK *Telecom.* phase shift keying

PSL *Economics* private-sector liquidity • public-sector loan(s)

psm passed school of music (Certificate of the Royal Military School of Music)

PSMA President of the Society of Marine Artists

PSNC Pacific Steam Navigation Company

PSO personal staff officer • Principal Scientific Officer

PSP *Med.* phenolsulphonphthalein (in **PSP test** for kidney function)

Pss Psalms

PSS *Computing* Packet Switch Stream (PPN of British Telecom) • (*or* **pss.**) postscripts

PSSC Personal Social Services Council

psso *Knitting* pass slipped stitch over

PST (USA, Canada) Pacific Standard Time

PSTN public switched telephone network

PSV public service vehicle

PSW psychiatric social worker

psych. psychological • psychology

psychoanal. psycho-analysis

psychol. psychological • psychologist • psychology

pt part • patient • payment • pint (abbrev. *or* symbol) • point (abbrev. *or* (in printing) symbol) • port

pt. *Grammar* preterite

p.t. part time • past tense • pro tempore (Latin: for the time being)

Pt *Chem., symbol for* platinum • Point (in place names) • Port (in place names)

PT (USA) Pacific Time • (USA) patrol torpedo (in **PT boat**) • physical therapy • physical training • physiotherapist • postal telegraph • post town • pupil teacher • purchase tax

Pta *symbol for* peseta (Spanish monetary unit)

PTA Parent–Teacher Association • Passenger Transport Authority

PT boat (USA) patrol torpedo boat

PTC *Med.* percutaneous transhepatic cholangiography • *Genetics* phenylthiocarbamide (referring to the inherited ability to taste it) • *Med.* plasma thromboplastin component

PTCA *Med.* percutaneous transluminal coronary angioplasty

Pte *Military* Private • (India, etc.) private limited company (after company name; equivalent to Ltd)

PTE Passenger Transport Executive

PTFE polytetrafluoroeth(yl)ene

ptg printing

PTI physical training instructor • Press Trust of India • *Computing* public tool interface

PTM *Telecom.* pulse-time modulation

PTN *Colloquial* pay through the nose • public telephone network (of British Telecom) • public transportation network

PTO (*or* **pto**) please turn over • *Astronautics* power takeoff • public telecommu-

nications operator • Public Trustee Office

ptp past participle

pts parts • payments • pints • points • ports

Pts. Portsmouth

PTS Philatelic Traders' Society

ptsc *Military* passed technical staff college

PTSD *Med.* post-traumatic stress disorder

PTT Postal, Telegraph, and Telephone Administration

Pty (Australia, South Africa, etc.) Proprietary (after a company name; equivalent to Ltd)

p.u. paid up

Pu *Chem., symbol for* plutonium

PU *Med.* passed urine • pick-up • *Chem.* polyurethane

pub. public • publican • publication • publish(ed) • publisher • publishing

pubd published

pub. doc. public document

publ. public • publication • publicity • published • publisher

pubn publication

pubr publisher

pulv. *Pharmacol.* pulvis (Latin: powder)

PUO *Med.* pyrexia (fever) of unknown origin

pur. (*or* **purch.**) purchase(r)

PUS Permanent Undersecretary

PUVA ('puːvə) *Med.* psoralen ultraviolet A (treatment for psoriasis)

p.v. *Med.* per vaginam (Latin: by the vagina)

PV petite vitesse (French: goods *or* slow train)

PVA polyvinyl acetate (synthetic resin) • *Chem.* polyvinyl alcohol

PVC polyvinyl chloride (synthetic resin)

PVD *Med.* peripheral vascular disease

PVF polyvinyl fluoride (synthetic resin)

PVP polyvinyl pyrrolidone (synthetic resin)

PVS *Med.* persistent vegetative state • *Med.* postviral syndrome (myalgic encephalomyelitis)

PVSM (India) Param Vishishc Seva Medal

Pvt. *Military* Private

p.w. per week

PW policewoman • prisoner of war • public works

PWA *Med.* person with Aids

PWD Public Works Department

PWE Political Welfare Executive

PWLB Public Works Loan Board

pwt pennyweight

px Pedro Ximénez (grape; referring to sweet wines and sherries)

PX please exchange • (USA) Post Exchange (army or navy retail store) • *Telephony* private exchange

pxt pinxit (Latin: (he *or* she) painted it)

py *Chem.* pyridine (used in formulae)

PY *international vehicle registration for* Paraguay

pyo (*or* **PYO**) pick your own (fruit, etc.)

PZI *Med.* protamine zinc insulin (diabetes treatment)

PZS President of the Zoological Society

Q

q *Physics, symbol for* quark • (ital.) *symbol for* quintal (100 kg)

q. quaere (Latin: inquire) • quaque (Latin: every) • quart • quarter • quarterly • query • question • quire

Q *Electronics* quality (in **Q factor**) • (ital.) *Physics, symbol for* quantity of heat • *Chess, symbol for* queen • *symbol for* quetzal (Guatemalan monetary unit) • *indicating* the highest level of security according to the Nuclear Regulatory Commission (as in **Q clearance**)

Q. (*or* **Q**) quarterly • Quartermaster • quarter-page (in advertisement placing) • Quarto (Shakespeare manuscript) • Quebec • Queen (*or* Queen's) • question • *pseudonym of* (Sir Arthur Thomas) Quiller-Couch (1863–1944, British writer)

QA quality assurance

QAB *Church of England* Queen Anne's Bounty

QAIMNS Queen Alexandra's Imperial Military Nursing Service

QAM *Telecom.* quadrature amplitude modulation

Q & A question and answer

Qantas ('kwɒntəs) Queensland and Northern Territory Aerial Service (Australian national airline)

QARANC Queen Alexandra's Royal Army Nursing Corps

QARNNS Queen Alexandra's Royal Naval Nursing Service

QB *Law* Queen's Bench • *Chess* queen's bishop

QBD Queen's Bench Division

QBI *Slang* quite bloody impossible

QBP *Chess* queen's bishop's pawn

QC quality control • Quartermaster Corps • Queen's Counsel

Q-Celtic *Linguistics, indicating* one of two main

groups of languages developed from Common Celtic. *See also* P-Celtic

QCVSA Queen's Commendation for Valuable Service in the Air

q.d. *Med.* quaque die (Latin: every day)

q.d.s. *Med.* quater in die sumendus (Latin: to be taken four times a day)

q.e. quod est (Latin: which is)

QE2 (ital.) Queen Elizabeth II (passenger liner)

QED *Physics* quantum electrodynamics • quod erat demonstrandum (Latin: which was to be proved)

QEF quod erat faciendum (Latin: which was to be done)

QEH Queen Elizabeth Hall (London)

QEI quod erat inveniendum (Latin: which was to be discovered *or* found out)

QEO Queen Elizabeth's Own

QF quick-firing

QFD *Physics* quantum flavourdynamics

QFSM Queen's Fire Service Medal for Distinguished Service

QGM Queen's Gallantry Medal

q.h. *Med.* quaque hora (Latin: every hour)

QHC Queen's Honorary Chaplain

QHDS Queen's Honorary Dental Surgeon

QHNS Queen's Honorary Nursing Sister

QHP Queen's Honorary Physician

QHS Queen's Honorary Surgeon

QI quartz–iodine (in **QI lamp**)

q.i.d. *Med.* quater in die (Latin: four times a day)

QISAM *Computing* queued indexed sequential access method

QKt *Chess* queen's knight

QKtP *Chess* queen's knight's pawn

ql quintal (100 kg)

q.l. *Med.* quantum libet (Latin: as much as you please; in prescriptions)

QL *Computing* query language

Qld (*or* **QLD**) Queensland

qlty quality

qly quarterly

qm. quomodo (Latin: by what means)

q.m. *Med.* quaque mane (Latin: every morning; in prescriptions)

QM *Physics* quantum mechanics • Quartermaster • Queen's Messenger

QMAAC Queen Mary's Army Auxiliary Corps

QMC Quartermaster Corps

Q. Mess. Queen's Messenger

QMG Quartermaster-General

Qmr Quartermaster

QMS Quartermaster Sergeant

q.n. quaque nocte (Latin: every night; in prescriptions)

QN *Chess* queen's knight

QNI Queen's Nursing Institute

QNP *Chess* queen's knight's pawn

qnt. quintet

QO qualified officer

QOOH Queen's Own Oxfordshire Hussars

Q(ops) Quartering (operations)

q.p. *Med.* quantum placet (*see* q.pl.)

QP *Chess* queen's pawn

q.pl. *Med.* quantum placet (Latin: as much as seems good; in prescriptions)

QPM Queen's Police Medal

QPR Queen's Park Rangers (football club)

qq. questions

Qq. Quartos (Shakespeare manuscripts)

qq. hor. *Med.* quaque hora (Latin: every hour; in prescriptions)

qq.v. quae vide (Latin: which (words, items, etc.) see; textual cross reference)

qr. quarter • quarterly • quire

QR *Chess* queen's rook • *Marketing* quick response • *symbol for* riyal (monetary unit of Qatar)

QRIH Queen's Royal Irish Hussars

QRP *Chess* queen's rook's pawn

qrs quarters

QRV Qualified Valuer, Real Estate Institute of New South Wales

q.s. *Med.* quantum sufficit (Latin: as much as will suffice; in prescriptions) • quarter section (of land)

QS quadraphonic-stereophonic (of audio equipment) • quantity sur-

veyor • quarter sessions •
Queen's Scholar

QSM (New Zealand)
Queen's Service Medal

QSO *Astronomy* quasistellar object (i.e. a quasar) •
(New Zealand) Queen's
Service Order

QSS *Astronomy* quasistellar source

QSTOL ('kjuː,stɒl) *Aeronautics* quiet short takeoff
and landing

qt *symbol for* quart

qt. quantity • quartet

q.t. (*or* **QT**) *Colloquial* quiet
(as in **on the q.t.**)

qtly quarterly

qto quarto

QTOL ('kjuː,tɒl) *Aeronautics* quiet takeoff and landing

qtr quarter

qty quantity

qu. quart • quarter • quarterly • queen • query • question

quad. quadrant • quadraphonic • quadrilateral • (*or*
quadr., quadrupl.) quadruplicate

qualn qualification

quango ('kwæŋgəʊ) quasi-autonomous nongovernmental (*or* national government) organization

quar. (*or* **quart.**) quarter • quarterly

quasar ('kweɪzɑː) *Astronomy* quasistellar object

quat. *Med.* four (Latin *quattuor*; in prescriptions)

Que. Quebec

ques. question

quint. quintuplicate

quor. quorum

quot. quotation

quotid. *Med.* quotidie
(Latin: daily)

q.v. *Med.* quantum vis
(Latin: as much as you
wish) • quod vide (Latin:
which (word, item, etc.)
see; textual cross reference)

QWERTY ('kwɜːtɪ) *indicating* a standard keyboard
in English-speaking countries (from the first six of
the upper row of keys on a
typewriter)

QWL quality of work(ing)
life

qy query

R

r (ital.) *Electricity, symbol for* internal resistance • (ital.) *symbol for* radius • (bold ital.) *Maths., symbol for* radius vector • *Music* ray (in tonic solfa)

r. radius • railway • rain • range • rare • *Commerce* received • recipe • *Printing* recto • replacing • residence • resides • right • rises • river • road • rod (unit of length) • rouble • *Cards* rubber • ruled • *Cricket, Baseball, etc.* run(s) • rupee

R *Medieval Roman numeral for* eighty • (ital.) *Chem., symbol for* molar gas constant • *Chem., symbol for a* radical (in formulae, as in **ROH**) • *symbol for* radius • *symbol for* rand (South African monetary unit) • *Maths., symbol for* ratio • *Physics, symbol for* Réaumur (temperature scale) • *Electrical engineering, symbol for* resistance • *Films (Australia, USA)* restricted (certifi-cation) • reverse (on selector mechanism of vehicle with automatic transmission) • *Physics, symbol for* roentgen • *Chess, symbol for* rook • *Microbiol.* rough (in **R-form** of a bacterial colony)

R. (*or* **R**) rabbi • *Politics* Radical • radius • railway • rector • Regiment • Regina (Latin: Queen) • registered • Regius • regular (clothing size) • Republican • reserve • response (in Christian liturgy) • Respublica (Latin: Republic) • Rex (Latin: King) • right *or* (in the theatre) stage right • River • road • rouble • Royal • Rue (French: street)

3 (*or* **three**) **Rs** reading, (w)riting, and (a)rithmetic

Ra *Chem., symbol for* radium

RA *international vehicle registration for* Argentina • Rear-Admiral • Royal Academy (*or* Academician) • Royal Artillery

R/A *Finance* refer to acceptor (on a bill of exchange)

RAA Regional Arts Association • Royal Academy of Arts

RAAF Royal Australian Air Force • Royal Auxiliary Air Force

RAAMC Royal Australian Army Medical Corps

Rabb. Rabbinic(al)

RABDF Royal Association of British Dairy Farmers

RABI Royal Agricultural Benevolent Institution

RAC Royal Agricultural College • Royal Armoured Corps • Royal Automobile Club

RACE (reɪs) Research and Development in Advanced Communication Technologies for Europe

RACGP Royal Australian College of General Practitioners

RAChD Royal Army Chaplains' Department

RACI Royal Australian Chemical Institute

RACO Royal Australian College of Ophthalmologists

RACOG Royal Australian College of Obstetricians and Gynaecologists

RACP Royal Australasian College of Physicians

RACS Royal Arsenal Co-operative Society • Royal Australasian College of Surgeons

rad *Maths., symbol for* radian

rad. radiator • radical • radius • *Maths., Anatomy* radix

Rad. *Politics* Radical

RAD Royal Academy of Dancing

RADA ('rɑːdə) Royal Academy of Dramatic Art

radar ('reɪdɑː) radio detection and ranging

RADAR Royal Association for Disability and Rehabilitation

RADC Royal Army Dental Corps

RADIUS ('reɪdɪəs) Religious Drama Society of Great Britain

RAdm (*or* **RADM**) Rear-Admiral

RAE Royal Aerospace (formerly Aircraft) Establishment • Royal Australian Engineers

RAEC Royal Army Educational Corps

RAeroC Royal Aero Club of the United Kingdom

RAeS Royal Aeronautical Society

RAF Royal Air Force

RAFA Royal Air Forces Association

RAFBF Royal Air Force Benevolent Fund

RAFG Royal Air Force Germany

RAFRO Royal Air Force Reserve of Officers

RAFVR Royal Air Force Volunteer Reserve

RAHS Royal Australian Historical Society

RAI Radiotelevisione Italiana (Italian broadcasting corporation; originally Radio Audizioni Italiane) • Royal Anthropological Institute

RAIA Royal Australian Institute of Architects

RAIC Reception of Adults into the (Catholic) Church • Royal Architectural Institute of Canada

rall. *Music* rallentando (Italian: becoming slow)

r.a.m. relative atomic mass

RAM (ræm) *Computing* random-access memory • (Member of the) Royal Academy of Music

RAMC Royal Army Medical Corps

RAN Royal Australian Navy

R & A Royal and Ancient (Golf Club, St Andrews)

R & B (*or* **r & b**) rhythm and blues

r. & c.c. riot and civil commotion

R & D research and development

R & I Regina et Imperatrix (Latin: Queen and Empress) • Rex et Imperator (Latin: King and Emperor)

R & M reliability and marketing

R & R (*or* **R and R**) *Med.* rescue and resuscitation • rest and recreation • rock and roll

R&VA Rating and Valuation Association

RANR Royal Australian Naval Reserve

RANVR Royal Australian Naval Volunteer Reserve

RAOB Royal Antediluvian Order of Buffaloes

RAOC Royal Army Ordnance Corps

RAP Regimental Aid Post

RAPC Royal Army Pay Corps

RAPID ('ræpɪd) Register for the Ascertainment and Prevention of Inherited Diseases

RAR Royal Australian Regiment

RARDE Royal Armament Research and Development Establishment

RARO Regular Army Reserve of Officers

RAS Royal Agricultural Society • Royal Asiatic Society • Royal Astronomical Society

RASC Royal Army Service Corps (now called Royal Corps of Transport, RCT)

RASE Royal Agricultural Society of England

RATO ('reɪtəʊ) rocket-assisted takeoff

RAuxAF Royal Auxiliary Air Force

RAVC Royal Army Veterinary Corps

RAX *Telephony* rural automatic exchange

Rb *Chem., symbol for* rubidium

RB reconnaissance bomber (aircraft; as in **RB-57**) • *international vehicle registration for* Republic of Botswana • Rifle Brigade • Royal Ballet

RBA (Member of the) Royal Society of British Artists

RBC *Med.* red blood cell •

Med. red blood (cell) count • Royal British Colonial Society of Artists

RBE relative biological effectiveness (of radiation)

RBK&C Royal Borough of Kensington and Chelsea

rbl. rouble

RBNA Royal British Nurses' Association

RBS Royal Society of British Sculptors

RBSA (Member of the) Royal Birmingham Society of Artists

RBT random breath testing

RBY Royal Bucks Yeomanry

RC *Med.* red (blood) cell • Red Cross • reinforced concrete • Reserve Corps • *Photog.* resin-coated (as in **RC paper**) • *Electronics* resistor-capacitor (*or* resistance-capacitance) • Roman Catholic • *international vehicle registration for* Taiwan (Republic of China)

RCA *international vehicle registration for* Central African Republic • Radio Corporation of America • (Member of the) Royal Cambrian Academy • (Member of the) Royal Ca-

nadian Academy of Arts •
Royal College of Art

RCAC Royal Canadian
Armoured Corps

RCAF Royal Canadian Air
Force

RCamA (Member of the)
Royal Cambrian Academy

RCAMC Royal Canadian
Army Medical Corps

RCB *Theatre* right centre
back (of stage)

RCB(CG) *international vehicle registration for* Republic
of the Congo

RCC (*or* **RCCh**) Roman
Catholic Church

rcd received

RCD Regional Cooperation for Development (association of Asian countries) •
Electronics residual current
device

RCDS Royal College of
Defence Studies

RCGP Royal College of
General Practitioners

RCH *international vehicle
registration for* Republic of
Chile

RCHA Royal Canadian
Horse Artillery

RCHM Royal Commission on Historical Monuments

RCM radar (*or* radio) countermeasures • regimental
court martial • Royal College of Midwives • (Member of the) Royal College of
Music

RCMP Royal Canadian
Mounted Police (formerly
Royal Northwest Mounted
Police, RNWMP)

RCN Royal Canadian
Navy • (*or* **Rcn**) Royal College of Nursing

RCNC Royal Corps of
Naval Constructors

RCNR Royal Canadian
Naval Reserve

RCNT Registered Clinical
Nurse Teacher

RCNVR Royal Canadian
Naval Volunteer Reserve

RCO Royal College of Organists

RCOG Royal College of
Obstetricians and Gynaecologists

RCP Royal College of Physicians

RCPath Royal College of
Pathologists

RCPE (*or* **RCPEd**) Royal
College of Physicians, Edinburgh

RCPI Royal College of
Physicians of Ireland

RCPSG Royal College of Physicians and Surgeons of Glasgow

RCPsych Royal College of Psychiatrists

rcpt receipt

RCR Royal College of Radiologists

RCS Royal College of Science • Royal College of Surgeons of England • Royal Commonwealth Society • Royal Corps of Signals

RCSB Royal Commonwealth Society for the Blind

RCSE (or **RCSEd**) Royal College of Surgeons of Edinburgh

RCSI Royal College of Surgeons in Ireland

rct receipt • recruit

RCT remote control transmitter (for TV operation, etc.) • Royal Corps of Transport

rcvr receiver

RCVS Royal College of Veterinary Surgeons

rd rendered • road • round • *Physics, symbol for* rutherford

r.d. *Physics* relative density

Rd Road

RD récemment dégorgé (French: recently disgorged;

referring to wines having a longer ageing period on their first cork) • (or **R/D**) refer to drawer (on a cheque) • Royal Dragoons • Royal Naval and Royal Marine Forces Reserve Decoration • Rural Dean • (New Zealand) Rural Delivery

RDA Rassemblement Démocratique Africain (French: African Democratic Rally; political party) • recommended dietary (or daily) allowance (of nutrients) • Royal Defence Academy

RD&D research, development, and demonstration

RD&E research, development, and engineering

RDAT (or **R-DAT**) rotary-head digital audio tape

RDB *Military* Research and Development Board

RDBMS *Computing* relational database management system

RDC Royal Defence Corps • Rural District Council

RDF radio direction finder (or finding) • *Military* (USA) Rapid Deployment Force • Royal Dublin Fusiliers

RDI Royal Designer for Industry (of the Royal Society of Arts)

RDS radio data system (for automatic tuning of receivers) • *Med.* respiratory distress syndrome • Royal Drawing Society • Royal Dublin Society

RDT&E research, development, testing, and engineering

RDV (or **rdv**) rendezvous

RDX Research Department Explosive (cyclonite)

Re (ital.) *Physics, symbol for* Reynolds number • *Chem., symbol for* rhenium • *symbol for* rupee (Indian monetary unit; *see also* Rs)

RE Reformed Episcopal • religious education • Right Excellent • Royal Engineers • Royal Exchange • Royal Society of Painter-Etchers and Engravers

REACH (riːtʃ) Retired Executives' Action Clearing House

react (rɪˈækt) research education and aid for children with potentially terminal illness

Rear-Adm. Rear-Admiral

rec. receipt • recipe • record(ed) • recorder • recording • recreation

REC (rɛk) regional electricity company

recd received

recit. *Music* recitative

recon. (or **recond.**) recondition

REconS Royal Economic Society

recpt receipt

recryst. *Chem.* recrystallized

rec. sec. recording secretary

rect. receipt • rectangle • rectangular

Rect. Rector(y)

red. *Finance* redeemable • reduce(d) • reduction

redox (ˈrɛdɒks) *Chem.* reduction–oxidation

Red R Register of Engineers for Disaster Relief

redupl. reduplicate • reduplication

ref. refer(red) • referee • reference • reform(ed) • refrigerated ship

Ref. Ch. Reformed Church

refl. reflect(ion) • reflective • reflexive

Ref. Pres. Reformed Presbyterian

refrig. refrigeration • refrigerator

Ref. Sp. Reformed Spelling

reg. regiment • region • register(ed) • registrar • registration • registry • regular(ly) • regulation • regulator

Reg. Regent • Regina (Latin: Queen)

regd registered

Reg-Gen. Registrar-General

Reg. Prof. Regius Professor

regr. registrar

Regt Regent • Regiment

rel. relating • relation • relative(ly) • release(d) • *Bibliog.* relié (French: bound) • religion • religious • reliquiae (Latin: relics)

rel. pron. relative pronoun

rem (rɛm) roentgen equivalent man (former unit of radioactivity)

rem. remark(s)

REM (rɛm *or* 'ɑː 'iː 'ɛm) *Physiol.* rapid eye movement (as in **REM sleep**)

REME ('riːmiː) Royal Electrical and Mechanical Engineers

remitt. remittance

REN *Telecom.* ringer equivalence number

REngDes Registered Engineering Designer

rep. repair • repeat • *Med.* repetatur (Latin: let it be repeated; in prescriptions) • report(ed) • reporter • representative • reprint

Rep. (USA) Representative • Republic • (USA) Republican

REPC Regional Economic Planning Council

repr. represented • representing • reprint(ed)

repro. reproduction

rept receipt • report

Repub. Republic • (USA) Republican

req. request • require(d) • requisition

RERO Royal Engineers Reserve of Officers

res. research(er) • reserve(d) • residence • resident • reside(s) • resigned • resolution

RES Royal Entomological Society of London

resp. respective(ly) • respondent

ret. retain • retire(d) • return(ed)

retd retained • retired • returned

R. et I. Regina et Imperatrix (Latin: Queen and Empress) • Rex et Imperator (Latin: King and Emperor)

rev. revenue • reverse(d) • review(ed) • revise(d) • revision • revolution • revolving

Rev. *Bible* Revelation • (*or* **Rev**) Reverend • Review

rev. a/c revenue account(s)

Revd Reverend

Rev. Stat. Revised Statutes

Rev. Ver. Revised Version (of the Bible)

rf. *Music* rinforzando (Italian: reinforcing)

r.f. radio frequency

Rf *symbol for* rufiyaa (monetary unit of Maldives) • *Chem., symbol for* rutherfordium

RF radio frequency • reconnaissance fighter (aircraft; as in **RF-4E**) • research foundation • *symbol for* Rwanda franc (monetary unit)

RFA Royal Field Artillery • Royal Fleet Auxiliary

RFC Royal Flying Corps • Rugby Football Club

RFH Royal Festival Hall (London)

RFI radio-frequency interference

RFN Registered Fever Nurse

RFQ *Commerce* request for quotation

RFS Registry of Friendly Societies • Royal Forestry Society

RFU Rugby Football Union

RG *postcode for* Reading

RGA Royal Garrison Artillery

RGB *Electrical engineering, Image technol.* red green blue (as in **RGB signals**)

RGG Royal Grenadier Guards

RGI Royal Glasgow Institute of the Fine Arts

RGJ Royal Green Jackets

RGN Registered General Nurse (formerly SRN)

RGNP *Economics* real gross national product

RGO Royal Greenwich Observatory (now in Cambridge)

RGS Royal Geographical Society

RGSA Royal Geographical Society of Australasia

Rgt Regiment

r.h. right hand(ed)

Rh *Med.* rhesus (factor) (as in **Rh positive**) • *Chem., symbol for* rhodium

RH *postcode for* Redhill • *international vehicle registration for* Republic of Haiti • right hand(ed) • Royal Highness

RHA Regional Health Authority • Road Haulage Association • Royal Hibernian Academy • Royal Horse Artillery

RHAS Royal Highland and Agricultural Society of Scotland

RHB Regional Hospital Board

r.h.d. right-hand drive (of a motor vehicle)

rheo. rheostat

rhet. rhetoric(al)

RHF Royal Highland Fusiliers

RHG Royal Horse Guards

RHHI Royal Hospital and Home for Incurables (Putney)

RHistS Royal Historical Society

RHM Ranks Hovis McDougall

RHR Royal Highland Regiment (Black Watch)

RHS Royal Highland Show • Royal Historical Society • Royal Horticultural Society • Royal Humane Society

RHV Registered Health Visitor

RI Railway Inspectorate • Regina et Imperatrix (Latin: Queen and Empress) • (*or* **R/I**) reinsurance • religious instruction • *international vehicle registration for* Republic of Indonesia • Rex et Imperator (Latin: King and Emperor) • Rhode Island (abbrev. *or* postcode) • Rotary International • Royal Institution

RIA Royal Irish Academy

RIAA Recording Industry Association of America

RIAF Royal Indian Air Force

RIAI Royal Institute of the Architects of Ireland

RIAM Royal Irish Academy of Music

RIAS Royal Incorporation of Architects in Scotland

RIASC Royal Indian Army Service Corps

RIB rigid-hull inflatable boat

RIBA Member of the Royal Institute of British Architects • (or **Riba**) Royal Institute of British Architects

RIBI Rotary International in Great Britain and Ireland

RIC Royal Institute of Chemistry (now called Royal Society of Chemistry, RSC) • Royal Irish Constabulary

RICA Research Institute for Consumer Affairs

RICE (rais) rest, ice, compression, elevation (for treating sports injuries)

RICS Royal Institution of Chartered Surveyors

RIE *Commerce* recognized investment exchange • Royal Indian Engineering (College)

RIF *Military* reduction in force • Royal Inniskilling Fusiliers

RIFF resource interchange file format

RIIA Royal Institute of International Affairs

RIM *international vehicle registration for* Islamic Republic of Mauritania • Royal Indian Marines

RIN Royal Indian Navy

RINA Royal Institution of Naval Architects

RINVR Royal Indian Naval Volunteer Reserve

RIOP Royal Institute of Oil Painters

RIP *Computing* raster input processor • requiescat (or requiescant) in pace (Latin: may (he, she, or they) rest in peace)

RIPA Royal Institute of Public Administration

RIPH&H (or **RIPHH**) Royal Institute of Public Health and Hygiene

RIrF Royal Irish Fusiliers

rit. *Music* ritardando (Italian: holding back) • *Music* ritenuto (Italian: held back)

riv. (or **Riv.**) river

RJ *Military* road junction

RK *Med.* radical keratotomy (used in treatment of shortsightedness) • religious knowledge

RKO (USA) Radio-Keith-Orpheum (film studio, now broadcasting company)

RL *international vehicle registration for* Republic of Lebanon • Rugby League

RLO returned letter office

(formerly dead letter office, DLO)

RLPO Royal Liverpool Philharmonic Orchestra

RLPS Royal Liverpool Philharmonic Society

Rls *symbol for* rial (monetary unit of Iran)

RLS Robert Louis Stevenson (1850–94, Scottish writer)

RLSS Royal Life Saving Society

rly (*or* **Rly**) railway

rm ream • room

RM *international vehicle registration for* Madagascar • Registered Midwife • *symbol for* Reichsmark (former German currency) • Resident Magistrate • *postcode for* Romford • Royal Mail • Royal Marines

RMA Royal Marine Artillery • Royal Military Academy (Sandhurst; formerly Woolwich) • Royal Musical Association

RMB (*or* **Rmb**) (China) renminbi (Chinese: people's money (the currency used by the indigenous population); *compare* FEC, Foreign Exchange Certificate)

RMCM (Member of the) Royal Manchester College of Music

RMCS Royal Military College of Science

RMedSoc Royal Medical Society, Edinburgh

RMetS Royal Meteorological Society

RMFVR Royal Marine Forces Volunteer Reserves

RMI Resource Management Initiative (for the NHS)

RMIT Royal Melbourne Institute of Technology

RMLI Royal Marine Light Infantry

r.m.m. *Chem.* relative molecular mass

RMM *international vehicle registration for* Republic of Mali

RMN Registered Mental Nurse

RMO resident medical officer

RMP Royal Military Police

RMPA Royal Medico-Psychological Association

rms *Maths.* root mean square

RMS *Maths.* root mean square • Royal Mail Service • Royal Mail Ship (*or* Steamer) • Royal Microscopical Society • Royal Society of Miniature Painters

RMSM Royal Military School of Music

RMT National Union of Rail, Maritime, and Transport Workers (formed by amalgamation of the NUR with the NUS)

Rn *Chem., symbol for* radon

RN (USA) Registered Nurse • *international vehicle registration for* Republic of Niger • Royal Navy (*or* Naval)

RNA *Biochem.* ribonucleic acid • Royal Naval Association

RNAS Royal Naval Air Service • Royal Naval Air Station

RNase (*or* **RNAase**) *Biochem.* ribonuclease

RNAY Royal Naval Aircraft Yard

R 'n' B rhythm and blues

RNBT Royal Naval Benevolent Trust

RNC Royal Naval College

RNCM (Member of the) Royal Northern College of Music

rnd round

RND Royal Naval Division

RNEC Royal Naval Engineering College

RNIB Royal National Institute for the Blind

RNID Royal National Institute for the Deaf

RNLI Royal National Lifeboat Institution

RNLO Royal Naval Liaison Officer

RNMDSF Royal National Mission to Deep Sea Fishermen

RNMH Registered Nurse for the Mentally Handicapped

RNPFN Royal National Pension Fund for Nurses

R 'n' R rock and roll

RNR Royal Naval Reserve

RNS Royal Numismatic Society

RNSA Royal Naval Sailing Association

RNSC Royal Naval Staff College

RNT Registered Nurse Tutor • Royal National Theatre

RNTNEH Royal National Throat, Nose, and Ear Hospital

RNVR Royal Naval Volunteer Reserve

RNVSR Royal Naval Volunteer Supplementary Reserve

RNXS Royal Naval Auxiliary Service

RNZAC Royal New Zealand Armoured Corps

RNZAF Royal New Zealand Air Force

RNZIR Royal New Zealand Infantry Regiment

RNZN Royal New Zealand Navy

RNZNVR Royal New Zealand Naval Volunteer Reserve

ro. (*or* **r°**) *Printing* recto • roan

r.o. *Cricket* run out

RO Radio Orchestra • receiving office(r) • receiving order • record(s) office • regimental order • relieving officer • returning officer • *symbol for* rial Omani (monetary unit of Oman) • *international vehicle registration for* Romania

ROA (*or* **RoA**) *Education* record of achievement • *Finance* return on assets

ROC Royal Observer Corps

ROCE *Finance* return on capital employed

ROE *Finance* return on

equity • Royal Observatory, Edinburgh

ROF Royal Ordnance Factory

R of O Reserve of Officers

ROG (*or* **r.o.g.**) receipt of goods

ROI *Finance* return on investment • (Member of the) Royal Institute of Oil Painters

ROK *international vehicle registration for* Republic of Korea

rom. roman (type)

Rom. Roman • Romance *or* Romanic (languages) • Romania(n) • *Bible* Romans

ROM (rɒm) *Computing* read-only memory

Rom. Cath. Roman Catholic

RONA *Finance* return on net assets

ROP *Advertising* run of paper (as in **ROP printing**)

RORC Royal Ocean Racing Club

ro-ro (*or* **RORO**) (ˈrəʊrəʊ) roll-on/roll-off (ferry)

ROSE *Computing* Research Open Systems in Europe

ROSLA ('rɒzlə) raising of school-leaving age

RoSPA (*or* **Rospa**) ('rɒspə) Royal Society for the Prevention of Accidents

rot (rɒt) *Maths.*, *symbol for* curl (of a function)

rot. rotating · rotation

ROU *international vehicle registration for* Republic of Uruguay

Rp *symbol for* rupiah (Indonesian monetary unit)

RP (*or* **rp**) Received Pronunciation · recommended price · Reformed Presbyterian · Regimental Police(man) · Regius Professor · reply paid · (*or* **R/P**) reprint(ing) · República Portuguesa (Republic of Portugal) · *international vehicle registration for* Republic of the Philippines · *Insurance* return (of) premium · Révérend Père (French: Reverend Father) · (Member of the) Royal Society of Portrait Painters

RPB *Finance* recognized professional body

RPC Royal Pioneer Corps

RPE Reformed Protestant Episcopal

RPG *Computing* report program generator · *Military*

rocket-propelled grenade · role-playing game

RPI retail price index

rpm revolutions per minute

RPM reliability performance measure · resale price maintenance

RPMS Royal Postgraduate Medical School

RPN *Computing*, *Maths.* reverse Polish notation

RPO Royal Philharmonic Orchestra

RPR (France) Rassemblement pour la République (French: Rally for the Republic; Gaullists)

rps revolutions per second

RPS Royal Philharmonic Society · Royal Photographic Society

RPSGB Royal Pharmaceutical Society of Great Britain

rpt repeat · report

RPV *Military* remotely piloted vehicle

RQ (*or* **r.q.**) regraded (*or* remoulded) quality (of tyres) · (*or* **R/Q**) *Commerce* request for quotation · *Med.* respiratory quotient

RQMS regimental quartermaster sergeant

RR Right Reverend • (*or* R-R) Rolls-Royce

RRC (Lady of the) Royal Red Cross

RRF Royal Regiment of Fusiliers

rRNA *Biochem.* ribosomal RNA

RRP recommended retail price

RR. PP. Révérends Pères (French: Reverend Fathers)

3 (*or* **three**) **Rs** reading, (w)riting, and (a)rithmetic

RRS Royal Research Ship

r.s. right side

Rs *symbol for* rupees (*see also under* Re)

RS Received Standard (English) • Reformed Spelling • *Med.* respiratory system • *Law* Revised Statutes • *Military* Royal Scots • Royal Society

RSA Republic of South Africa • *Computing* Rivest, Shamir, and Adelman (denoting a method of encryption, as in **RSA cipher**, **RSA system**) • Royal Scottish Academy (*or* Academician) • Royal Society for the Encouragement of Arts, Manufactures, and Commerce • Royal Society of Arts

RSAA Royal Society for Asian Affairs

RSAD Royal Surgical Aid Society

RSAF Royal Small Arms Factory

RSAI Royal Society of Antiquaries of Ireland

RSAMD Royal Scottish Academy of Music and Drama

RSAS Royal Surgical Aid Society

RSC Royal Shakespeare Company • Royal Society of Canada • Royal Society of Chemistry • Rules of the Supreme Court

RSCDS Royal Scottish Country Dance Society

RSCJ Religiosae Sacratissimi Cordis Jesu (Latin: Nuns of the Most Sacred Heart of Jesus; Sacred Heart Society)

RSCM Royal School of Church Music

RSCN Registered Sick Children's Nurse (formerly SRCN)

RSD Royal Society of Dublin

RSE Received Standard English • Royal Society of Edinburgh

RSF Royal Scots Fusiliers

RSFSR (formerly) Russian Soviet Federative Socialist Republic

RSG rate-support grant • regional seat of government (in civil defence)

RSGB Radio Society of Great Britain (amateur radio operators)

RSGS Royal Scottish Geographical Society

RSH Royal Society for the Promotion of Health

RSHA Reichssicherheitshauptamt (Reich Security Central Office; in Nazi Germany)

RSI *Med.* repetitive strain (*or* stress) injury

R. Signals Royal Corps of Signals

RSJ *Building trades* rolled-steel joist

RSL (Australia) Returned Services League • Royal Society of Literature

RSLA raising of school-leaving age

RSM regimental sergeant major • *international vehicle registration for* Republic of San Marino • Royal School of Mines • Royal Society of Medicine • Royal Society of Musicians of Great Britain

RSMA Royal Society of Marine Artists

RSME Royal School of Military Engineering

RSNC Royal Society for Nature Conservation

RSNZ Royal Society of New Zealand

RSO Radio Symphony Orchestra • railway sorting office • resident surgical officer • Royal Scottish Orchestra • rural suboffice

RSocMed Royal Society of Medicine

RSPB Royal Society for the Protection of Birds

RSPCA Royal Society for the Prevention of Cruelty to Animals

RSPP Royal Society of Portrait Painters

RSRE Royal Signals and Radar Establishment (formerly Royal Radar Establishment, RRE)

RSS Fellow of the Royal Society (Latin *Regiae Societatis Socius*) • Royal Statistical Society

RSSA Royal Scottish Society of Arts

RSSPCC Royal Scottish Society for the Prevention of Cruelty to Children

RSTM&H Royal Society of Tropical Medicine and Hygiene

RSUA Royal Society of Ulster Architects

RSV Revised Standard Version (of the Bible)

RSVP répondez s'il vous plaît (French: please reply)

RSW (Member of the) Royal Scottish Society of Painters in Water Colours

rt right

RT (or **R/T**) radio telegraph (or telegraphy) • radio telephone (or telephony) • received text

RTBA rate to be agreed

RTC (India) Road Transport Corporation • Round Table Conference

rte route

RTE Radio Telefis Éireann (Gaelic: Irish Radio and Television) • *Computing* real-time execution

Rt Hon. Right Honourable

RTITB Road Transport Industry Training Board

RTL *Computing* real-time language • *Electronics* resistor-transistor logic

rtn return

rtng returning

RTO railway transport officer

RTOL ('ɑː,tɒl) *Aeronautics* reduced takeoff and landing

RTPI Royal Town Planning Institute

RTR Royal Tank Regiment

Rt Rev. Right Reverend

RTS Religious Tract Society • Royal Television Society • Royal Toxophilite Society

RTT (or **RTTY**) radioteletype

RTU *Military* returned to unit

RTYC Royal Thames Yacht Club

RTZ Rio Tinto Zinc Corporation Limited

Ru *Chem., symbol for* ruthenium

RU *international vehicle registration for* Republic of Burundi • *Med., Pharmacol.* Roussel-Uclaf (French pharmaceutical company; in **RU-486**, abortion pill) • Rugby Union

RUA Royal Ulster Academy of Painting, Sculpture, and Architecture

RUBISCO (ruːˈbɪskəʊ) *Botany* RuBP carboxylase

RUC Royal Ulster Constabulary

RUF *Banking* revolving underwriting facility

RUG *Computing* restricted users group

RUI Royal University of Ireland

RUKBA (*or* **Rukba**) Royal United Kingdom Beneficent Association

rumpie ('rʌmpɪ) *Colloquial* rural upwardly mobile professional

RUR Royal Ulster Regiment

RURAL ('rʊərəl) Society for the Responsible Use of Resources in Agriculture and on the Land

Rus. Russia(n)

RUSI Royal United Services Institute for Defence Studies (formerly Royal United Service Institution)

Russ. Russia(n)

r.v. *Statistics* random variable • rendezvous

RV rateable value • rendezvous • Revised Version (of the Bible)

RVC Royal Veterinary College

RVCI Royal Veterinary College of Ireland

RVSVP répondez vite, s'il vous plaît (French: please reply quickly)

RW (*or* **R/W**) right of way • Right Worshipful • Right Worthy

RWA (Member of the) Royal West of England Academy • *international vehicle registration for* Rwanda

RWAFF Royal West African Frontier Force

r.w.d. rear-wheel drive

RWF Royal Welch Fusiliers

RwFr Rwanda franc

RWS (Member of the) Royal Society of Painters in Water Colours

rwy (*or* **Rwy**) railway

ry (*or* **Ry**) railway

RYA Royal Yachting Association

RYS Royal Yacht Squadron

RZSScot (*or* **RZSS**) Royal Zoological Society of Scotland

S

s *symbol for* second(s) • (ital.) *Chem.* secondary (isomer; as in **s-butyl alcohol**) • *Music* soh (in tonic sol-fa) • *Chem.* solid (as in **NaCl(s)**) • *Physics* strange (a quark flavour)

s. school • section • see • semi- • series • sets • shilling • sign(ed) • sine (Latin: without) • *Grammar* singular • sinister (Latin: left) • sire • small • snow • society • solidus (Latin: shilling) • solo • son • *Music* soprano (instrument) • spherical • steamer • sets • stratus (cloud) • *Grammar* substantive • succeeded • sun(ny)

s/ sur (French: on; in place names)

S (ital.) *Physics, symbol for* entropy • *symbol for* Schilling (Austrian monetary unit) • *Medieval Roman numeral for* seven (*or* seventy) • *postcode for* Sheffield • *Electrical engineering, symbol for* siemens • *Med.* signā (*see*

under Sig.) • *Geology* Silurian • slow (on a clock or watch regulator) • small (size) • south(ern) • sucre (Ecuadorian monetary unit) • *Chem., symbol for* sulphur • *international vehicle registration for* Sweden

S. (*or* **S**) Sabbath • *Heraldry* sable • *Anatomy* sacral (of vertebrae) • Saint • satisfactory • Saturday • Saxon • School • Sea • (ital.) *Music* segno (Italian: sign) • Senate • sentence • September • sepultus (Latin: buried) • series • ship • signature • Signor (Italian: Mr) • Socialist • Society • Socius (Latin: Fellow; in titles) • *Music* soprano (voice) • south(ern) • *Cards* spades • sun • Sunday

sa. *Heraldry* sable

s.a. *Med.* secundum artem (Latin: by skill) • *Horticulture* semiannual • sex appeal • sine anno (Latin: without date; undated) • subject to approval

Sa *Chem., symbol for* samarium

SA Salvation Army • seaman apprentice • *Horticulture* semiannual • sex appeal • Society of Antiquaries • Society of Arts • Society of Authors • Soil Association • South Africa(n) • South America(n) • South Australia(n) • Sturmabteilung (German: storm troopers; Nazi terrorist militia) • *postcode for* Swansea

S/A subject to acceptance

SAA small arms ammunition • South African Airways • *Computing* systems application architecture

SAAB (*or* **Saab**) (saːb) Svensk Aeroplan Aktiebolag (Swedish aircraft and car company)

SAAF South African Air Force

SAAFA Special Arab Assistance Fund for Africa

Sab. Sabbath

SAB Society of American Bacteriologists

SABC South African Broadcasting Corporation

Sabena (*or* **SABENA**) (sə'biːnə) Société anonyme belge d'exploitation de la navigation aérienne (Belgian World Airlines)

sac *Military, indicating* qualified at a small-arms technical long course

SAC Senior Aircraftman • (USA) Strategic Air Command

SACEUR (*or* **Saceur**) ('sæk,juə) Supreme Allied Commander Europe

SACLANT ('sæk,lænt) Supreme Allied Commander Atlantic

SACSEA ('sæk,siː) Supreme Allied Command, SE Asia

SACW Senior Aircraftwoman

SAD *Psychiatry* seasonal affective disorder

SAE (*or* **s.a.e.**) self-addressed envelope • stamped addressed envelope

SAEF Stock Exchange Automatic Execution Facility

S. Afr. South Africa(n)

S.Afr.D. South African Dutch

SAGB Spiritualist Association of Great Britain

SAGE (seɪdʒ) *Military* (USA, Canada) semiautomatic ground environment

SAH Supreme Allied Head-quarters

SAIDS (seɪdz) simian ac-quired immune deficiency syndrome

SAL South Arabian League

SALR South African Law Reports

SALT (sɔːlt) Strategic Arms Limitation Talks (*or* Treaty)

salv. salvage

Salv. Salvador

Sam. Samaritan · *Bible* Samuel

S. Am. South America(n)

SAM (sæm) surface-to-air missile

Samar. Samaritan

SAMC South African Medical Corps

S. Amer. South Ameri-ca(n)

san. sanitary

SAN *Chem.* styrene–acrylo-nitrile (polymer)

sand. sandwich

S&F *Insurance* stock and fixtures

S&H (*or* **S and H**) ship-ping and handling (charges)

S & M sadism and maso-chism · *Insurance* stock and machinery

s & s *Colloquial* sex and shopping (type of popular fiction)

SANDS (*or* **Sands**) (sændz) Stillbirth and Neo-natal Death Society

s. & s.c. sized and super-calendered (of paper)

S & T Salmon & Trout As-sociation

Sane (seɪn) Schizophrenia – A National Emergency

sanit. sanitary · sanitation

SANROC ('sæn,rɒk) South African Non-Racial Olympics Committee

Sans. (*or* **Sansk.**) San-skrit

sapfu ('sæpfuː) *Slang* sur-passing all previous foul-ups (*or* fuck-ups)

s.a.p.l. *Shipping* sailed as per list (i.e. Lloyd's List)

Sar. Sardinia(n)

SAR search and rescue · Sons of the American Revo-lution

SARAH ('sɛərə) search and rescue homing (radar system) · surgery assistant robot acting on the head (in brain surgery)

Sarl. (*or* **Sàrl.**) (France, Belgium, Luxembourg, Switzerland) société à

responsabilité limitée (private limited company; Ltd)

SARSAT ('saːsæt) search and rescue satellite-aided tracking

Sarum. Sarumensis (Latin: (Bishop) of Salisbury)

SAS Fellow of the Society of Antiquaries (Latin *Societatis Antiquariorum Socius*) • Scandinavian Airline System • *Military* Special Air Service

SASC Small Arms School Corps

Sask. Saskatchewan

SASO Senior Air Staff Officer

sat. saturate(d)

Sat. Saturday • *Astronomy* Saturn

SAT Senior Member of the Association of Accounting Technicians • South Australian Time • (sæt) *Education* standard assessment task

SATB *Music* soprano, alto, tenor, bass

SATRO Science and Technology Regional Organization

SATS South African Transport Services

S. Aus. (*or* **S. Austral.**) South Australia(n)

s.a.v. stock at valuation

SAVAK (*or* **Savak**) ('sævæk *or* 'saːvæk) (Iran) Sāzmān-i-Attalāt Va Amnīyat-i-Keshvar (National Security and Intelligence Organization, 1957–79)

sax. saxophone

Sax. Saxon • Saxony

SAYE save as you earn (savings scheme)

sb *Grammar* substantive

s.b. single-breasted • small bore (rifle)

Sb *Chem., symbol for* antimony (Latin *stibium*)

SB Sam Browne (military officer's belt and strap) • *Commerce* short bill (of exchange) • simultaneous broadcast(ing) • Special Branch (of police) • *Med.* stillborn • stretcher bearer

SBA sick-bay (*or* -berth) attendant • *Aeronautics* standard beam approach

SBAA Sovereign Base Areas Administration

SBAC Society of British Aerospace Companies (formerly Aircraft Constructors

SBC single-board computer

SbE south by east

SBM single buoy mooring

SBN Standard Book Number (replaced by ISBN)

SBP *Med.* systolic blood pressure

SBR styrene–butadiene rubber

SBS *Med.* sick-building syndrome • *Military* Special Boat Service

SBStJ Serving Brother of the Order of St John of Jerusalem

SBU strategic business unit

SbW south by west

sc *Printing* small capitals • *Military* (student at the) staff college

sc. scale • scene • science • scientific • scilicet (namely *or* that is; from Latin *scire licet*) • screw • scruple (unit of weight) • sculpsit (Latin: (he *or* she) carved (*or* engraved) this)

s.c. salvage charges • *Printing* small capitals • supercalendered (of paper)

s/c self-contained

Sc *Chem.*, symbol for scandium

Sc. Scotch • Scots • Scottish

SC *Law* same case • (Australia, New Zealand) School Certificate • Security Council (of the UN) • self-contained • Senatus Consultum (Latin: decree of the Senate) • Senior Counsel • *Law* Sessions Cases • Signal Corps • social club • South Carolina (abbrev. *or* postcode) • Special Constable (*or* Constabulary) • staff college • Staff Corps • (Canada) Star of Courage • supercalendered (paper) • Supreme Court

SCA sickle-cell anaemia

Scand. (*or* **Scan.**) Scandinavia(n)

SCAO Senior Civil Affairs Officer

SCAP (skæp) Supreme Command (*or* Commander) Allied Powers

SCAPA Society for Checking the Abuses of Public Advertising

s. caps *Printing* small capitals

ScB Bachelor of Science (Latin *Scientiae Baccalaureus*)

SCB Solicitors Complaints Bureau

ScBC Bachelor of Science in Chemistry

ScBE Bachelor of Science in Engineering

SCBU *Med.* special-care baby unit

s.c.c. *Printing* single column centimetre

SCC Sea Cadet Corps

SCCL Scottish Council for Civil Liberties

ScD Doctor of Science (Latin *Scientiae Doctor*)

SCDA Scottish Community Drama Association

SCDC Schools Curriculum Development Committee

ScDHyg Doctor of Science in Hygiene

ScDMed Doctor of Science in Medicine

SCE Scottish Certificate of Education

SCF Save the Children Fund • Senior Chaplain to the Forces

scfh standard cubic feet per hour

scfm standard cubic feet per minute

SCG Sydney Cricket Ground

SCGB Ski Club of Great Britain

sch. scholar • school • schooner

Sch. Schilling (Austrian monetary unit) • School

sched. schedule

scherz. *Music* scherzando (Italian: playful, humorous)

SchMusB Bachelor of School Music

schol. scholar • scholarship

sci. science • scientific

SCID (*or* **skid**) (skɪd) *Med.* severe combined immunodeficiency disease

sci. fa. scire facias (Latin: that you cause to know)

sci-fi ('saɪ'faɪ) *Colloquial* science fiction

scil. scilicet (*see under* sc.)

SCIT Special Commissioners of Income Tax

SCL Student in (*or* of) Civil Law

ScM Master of Science (Latin *Scientiae Magister*)

SCM State Certified Midwife (replaced by RM, Registered Midwife) • Student Christian Movement

ScMHyg Master of Science in Hygiene

SCOBEC ('skəʊbek) Scottish Business Education Council

SCONUL Standing Con

ference of National and University Libraries

Scot. Scotch (whisky) · Scotland · Scottish

ScotBIC ('skɒt,bɪk) Scottish Business in the Community

SCOTEC ('skəʊtɛk) Scottish Technical Education Council

SCOTVEC ('skɒt,vɛk) Scottish Vocational Education Council

SCOUT (skaʊt) *Commerce* Shared Currency Option Under Tender

SCP single-cell protein (in food technology)

SCPS Society of Civil and Public Servants

scr. *Finance* scrip · scruple (unit of weight)

SCR senior common room (in a university) · *Electronics* silicon-controlled rectifier

Script. Scriptural · Scripture(s)

SCSI ('skuːzɪ) small computer systems interface

SCUA Suez Canal Users' Association

scuba ('skjuːbə) self-contained underwater breathing apparatus

sculp. (*or* **sculps.,**

sculpt.) sculpsit (*see under* sc.) · sculptor (*or* sculptress) · sculptural · sculpture

SCWS Scottish Co-operative Wholesale Society

sd sailed · sewed (of books) · signed · sound

s.d. safe deposit · semi-detached · *Philosophy* sense datum · *Commerce* short delivery · sine die (Latin: without a day (being fixed)) · *Statistics* standard deviation

SD Doctor of Science (Latin *Scientiae Doctor*) · salutem dicit (Latin: (he *or* she) sends greeting) · sea-damaged · semi-detached · *Med.* senile dementia · Senior Deacon · sequence date · *Commerce* short delivery · Sicherheitsdienst (German: Security Service; in Nazi Germany) · *Finance* sight draft · South Dakota (abbrev. *or* postcode) · special delivery · staff duties · *Statistics* standard deviation · structural description (in transformational grammar) · *international vehicle registration for* Swaziland

S/D *Finance* sight draft

SDA Scottish Development Agency · Scottish Diploma in Agriculture · Seventh Day Adventists • Social Democratic Alliance

S. Dak. South Dakota

SDAT *Med.* senile dementia of the Alzheimer type

S-DAT stationary digital audio tape

SDC Society of Dyers and Colourists

SDD Scottish Development Department • *Telephony* subscriber direct dialling

SDF Social Democratic Federation

SDI Strategic Defense Initiative (US Star Wars programme)

SDIO (USA) Strategic Defense Initiative Office

SDLP (Northern Ireland) Social Democratic and Labour Party

SDO subdivisional officer

SDP Social Democratic Party • *Insurance* social, domestic, and pleasure

SDR *Finance* special drawing right(s)

SDS sodium dodecyl sulphate (detergent) • (Germany) Sozialistischer Deutscher Studentenbund (Federation of Socialist Stu-

dents) • (USA) Students for a Democratic Society

SDT Society of Dairy Technology

s.e. *Statistics* standard error

Se *Chem., symbol for* selenium

SE Society of Engineers • southeast(ern) • *postcode for* southeast London • Standard English • Stirling engine • (*or* **S/E**) stock exchange

SEAC ('siːæk) School Examination and Assessment Council • South-East Asia Command • Standard Eastern Automatic Computer

SEALF South-East Asia Land Forces

SEAQ ('siːæk) Stock Exchange Automated Quotations

SEATO ('siːtəu) South-east Asia Treaty Organization (1954–77)

sec (sɛk) *Maths.* secant

sec. second (of time or an angle) • secondary • (*or* **Sec.**) secretary • section • sector • secundum (Latin: according to)

SECAM ('siː,kæm) séquentiel couleur à mémoire (colour-television broadcasting system developed in France)

SECC Scottish Exhibition and Conference Centre

Sec. Gen. (*or* **Sec-Gen**) Secretary General

sec. leg. secundum legem (Latin: according to law)

sec. reg. secundum regulam (Latin: according to rule)

sect. section

secy (*or* **Secy**) secretary

sed. sedative • sediment

SED Scottish Education Department • shipper's export declaration

sedt sediment

SEEB (*or* **Seeboard**) Southeastern Electricity Board

seg. segment

SEG socioeconomic grade

seismol. seismological • seismology

sel. select(ed) • selection

sem. semester • semicolon

Sem. Seminary • Semitic

s.e.(m.) (*or* **SE(M)**) *Statistics* standard error (of the mean)

SEM scanning electron microscope (*or* microscopy)

semp. *Music* sempre (Italian: always)

Sen. Senate • Senator • Senior

SEN special educational needs • (formerly) State Enrolled Nurse (*see* EN(G))

Senr Senior

SEO Society of Education Officers

sep. sepal • separable • separate(d) • separation

Sep. (*or* **Sep**) September • Septuagint

SEPM Society of Economic Palaeontologists and Mineralogists

sepn separation

SEPON ('siːpɒn) Stock Exchange Pool Nominees Ltd

Sept. (*or* **Sept**) September • Septuagint

seq. sequel • sequence • sequens (Latin: the following (one)) • sequente (Latin: and in what follows) • sequitur (Latin: it follows)

seq. luce *Med.* sequenti luce (Latin: the following day; in prescriptions)

seqq. sequentia (Latin: the following (ones)) • sequentibus (Latin: in the following places)

ser. serial • series • sermon • service

Ser (*or* **ser**) *Biochem.* serine

SERA Socialist Environment and Resources Association

Serb. Serbia(n)

SERC (s3ːk) Science and Engineering Research Council (formerly SRC)

Serg. (*or* **Sergt**) Sergeant

Serj. (*or* **Serjt**) Serjeant

SERPS (*or* **Serps**) (s3ːps) State Earnings-Related Pension Scheme

SERT Society of Electronic and Radio Technicians

serv. servant • service

SES Singapore Stock Exchange

SESDAQ ('sɛsdæk) Stock Exchange of Singapore Dealing and Automated Quotation System

SESI Stock Exchange of Singapore Index

SESO Senior Equipment Staff Officer

sess. session

SET ('ɛs 'iː 'tiː *or* sɛt) selective employment tax (1966–73)

SETI ('sɛtɪ) *Astronomy*

search for extraterrestrial intelligence

sett. settembre (Italian: September)

sev. (*or* **sevl**) several

sf (*or* **sf.**) *Music* sforzando (Italian; strongly accented)

s.f. (*or* **s-f**) science fiction • *Finance* sinking fund • sub finem (Latin: towards the end)

Sf *symbol for* Suriname guilder (monetary unit)

SF *international vehicle registration for* Finland • San Francisco • science fiction • *Telecom.* signal frequency • *Finance* sinking fund • Sinn Fein

SFA Scottish Football Association • *Colloquial* sweet Fanny Adams (i.e. nothing)

SFC specific fuel consumption (of jet engines)

SFInstE Senior Fellow, Institute of Energy

sfm surface feet per minute

SFO Serious Fraud Office • Superannuation Funds Office

sfp *Music* sforzato-piano (Italian; strong accent, followed immediately by soft)

SFr Swiss franc

SFT supercritical fluid technology

SFTCD Senior Fellow, Trinity College Dublin

SFU suitable for upgrade (on airline tickets)

sfz (or **sfz.**) *Music* sforzando (*see under* sf)

sg. *Grammar* singular

s.g. specific gravity

SG Secretary General • ship and goods • singular (in transformational grammar) • Society of Genealogists • Solicitor General • *postcode for* Stevenage • Surgeon General

SGA (Member of the) Society of Graphic Art

SGBI Schoolmistresses' and Governesses' Benevolent Institution

sgd signed

SGF Scottish Grocers' Federation

SGHWR steam-generating heavy-water reactor

S. Glam South Glamorgan

SGML *Computing* standard generalized markup language

SGP *international vehicle registration for* Singapore

Sgt Sergeant

SGT Society of Glass Technology

Sgt Maj. Sergeant Major

sh. *Stock exchange* share • sheep • *Bookbinding* sheet • shilling

s.h. second-hand

SHA Secondary Heads Association • *Astronomy, Navigation* sidereal hour angle • Special Health Authority

SHAEF (ʃeɪf) Supreme Headquarters Allied Expeditionary Forces

Shak. (or **Shaks.**) William Shakespeare (1564–1616, English dramatist and poet)

SH&MA Scottish Horse and Motormen's Association

SHAPE (ʃeɪp) Supreme Headquarters Allied Powers Europe (of NATO)

S/HE *Shipping* Sundays and holidays excepted

SHEX *Shipping* Sundays and holidays excepted

Sh.F. shareholders' funds

SHF *Radio, etc.* superhigh frequency

SHHD Scottish Home and Health Department

SHM *Physics* simple harmonic motion

SHO Senior House Officer

shoran ('ʃɔːræn) short-range navigation

shp shaft horsepower (of an engine)

SHP *Horticulture* single-flowered hardy perennial (*or* hybrid perpetual) (rose)

shpg shipping

shpt shipment

shr. share(s)

sht *Bookbinding* sheet

SHT single-flowered hybrid tea (rose)

shtg. shortage

s.h.v. sub hac voce (*or* hoc verbo) (Latin: under this word)

s.i. sum insured

Si *Chem.*, *symbol for* silicon

SI Sandwich Islands (former name for Hawaii) • Shetland Isles • South Island (New Zealand) • (Order of the) Star of India • Staten Island (New York) • *Chem.* styrene-isoprene (polymer) • Système International (d'Unités; French: International System of Units; in **SI unit(s)**)

SIA Society of Investment Analysts • Spinal Injuries Association

SIAD Society of Industrial Artists and Designers (now called Chartered Society of Designers, CSD)

Sib. Siberia(n)

SIB Securities and Investments Board • *Med.* self-injurious behaviour • Shipbuilding Industry Board

SIBOR ('siːbɔː) *Finance* Singapore Inter-Bank Offered Rate

sic. *Pharmacol.* siccus (Latin: dry)

Sic. Sicilian • Sicily

SIC Standard Industrial Classification

SID (*or* **s.i.d.**) *Radio* sudden ionospheric disturbance

SIDS (sɪdz) *Med.* sudden infant death syndrome (cot death)

SIESO Society of Industrial and Emergency Service Officers

sig. signal • signature • signetur (Latin: let it be written *or* labelled)

Sig. *Med.* signā (Latin: write; in prescriptions, preceding instructions to be written on the label for the patient's use) • Signor (Italian: Mr) • Signore (Italian: Sir)

SIG special-interest group

sig. fig. *Maths.* significant figures

SIGINT (*or* **Sigint**) ('sɪgɪnt) signals intelligence (gathering network)

sig. n. pro. *Med.* signa nomine proprio (Latin: label with the proper name)

sim. similar(ly) • simile

SIM Société internationale de musicologie (French: International Musicological Society)

SIMA Scientific Instrument Manufacturers' Association of Great Britain • *Psychiatry* system for identifying motivated abilities

SIMC Société internationale pour la musique contemporaine (French: International Society for Contemporary Music)

SIMCA (*or* **Simca**) ('sɪmkə) Société industrielle de mécanique et carrosserie automobiles (French car manufacturers)

SIME Security Intelligence Middle East

SIMG International Society of General Medicine (Latin *Societas Internationalis Medicinae Generalis*)

SIMM *Computing, Electron-* ics single in-line memory module

sin (saɪn) *Maths.* sine

SinDrs Doctor of Chinese

sing. *Grammar* singular

sinh (saɪn) *Maths.* hyperbolic sine

SINS (sɪnz) ship's inertial navigation system

SIO *Computing* serial input/output

SIPO *Computing* serial in, parallel out

SIPRI Stockholm International Peace Research Institute

SIS Secret Intelligence Service (MI6)

sit. sitting room • situation

SITA Société internationale de télécommunications aéronautiques (French: International Society of Aeronautical Telecommunications)

SITC Standard International Trade Classification

SITPRO ('sɪtprəʊ) Simpler Trade Procedures Board (formerly Simplification of International Trade Procedures)

sit. vac. (pl. **sits vac.**) situation vacant

SIW self-inflicted wound

SJ Society of Jesus • supersonic jet

SJA St John Ambulance (Brigade *or* Association)

SJAA St John Ambulance Association

SJAB St John Ambulance Brigade

SJC (USA) Supreme Judicial Court

SJD Doctor of Juristic (*or* Juridical) Science (Latin *Scientiae Juridicae Doctor*)

sk sack

SK Saskatchewan • *postcode for* Stockport

skid (skɪd) *Med. see* SCID

s.k.p.o. *Knitting* slip one, knit one, pass slipped stitch over

SKr *symbol for* Swedish krona (monetary unit)

Skt (*or* **Skr.**) Sanskrit

s.l. *Insurance* salvage loss • *Bibliog.* sine loco (Latin: without place (of publication))

SL Serjeant-at-Law • *postcode for* Slough • Solicitor-at-Law • source language • south latitude

SLA Symbionese Liberation Army

SLAC Stanford Linear Accelerator Center

SLADE (sleɪd) Society of Lithographic Artists, Designers, Engravers, and Process Workers

SLAET Society of Licensed Aircraft Engineers and Technologists

SLAM (*or* **Slam**) (slæm) standoff land-attack missile

s.l.a.n. sine loco, anno, vel nomine (Latin: without place, year, name (of printer))

SLAR (*or* **Slar**) (slɑː) *Military* side-looking airborne radar

SLAS Society for Latin American Studies

S. Lat. south latitude

Slav. Slavonian • Slavonic (*or* Slavic)

SLBM submarine-launched ballistic missile

SLC Stanford Linear Collider (at SLAC)

SLCM sea- (*or* ship-, submarine-)launched cruise missile

sld sailed • sealed • sold

SLD self-locking device • Social and Liberal Democrats

s.l. et a. sine loco et anno (Latin: without place and year (of publication))

S level *Education* Special (formerly Scholarship) level

SLF Scottish Landowners' Federation

SLIM South London Industrial Mission

Slipar ('slaɪpɑː) *Military* short light pulse alerting receiver (in an aircraft)

SLORC (Burma) State Law and Order Restoration Council

s.l.p. sine legitime prole (Latin: without lawful issue)

SLP Scottish Labour Party

SLR satellite laser ranging • self-loading rifle • single-lens reflex (camera)

SL Rs *symbol for* Sri Lanka rupee (monetary unit)

Slud (slʌd) *Military slang* salivate, lachrymate, urinate, defecate (effects of chemical weapons)

sly southerly

sm. small

s-m (*or* **s/m**) sadomasochism (*or* sadomasochist)

Sm *Chem.*, *symbol for* samarium

SM Master of Science (Latin *Scientiae Magister*) • (*or* **S-M**) sadomasochism (*or* sadomasochist) • sales

manager • sanctae memoriae (Latin: of holy memory) • Sergeant Major • *Music* short metre • silver medal(list) • Society of Miniaturists • Staff Major • stage manager • (officer qualified for) Submarine Duties • *postcode for* Sutton (Surrey)

SMATV satellite (formerly small) master antenna television

SMB Bachelor of Sacred Music

SMBG *Med.* self-monitoring of blood glucose (for diabetics)

SMC Scottish Mountaineering Club

sm. caps. *Printing* small capitals

SMD Doctor of Sacred Music • *Med.* senile macular degeneration • *Music* short metre double

SME Sancta Mater Ecclesia (Latin: Holy Mother Church) • *international vehicle registration for* Suriname

SMERSH (*or* **Smersh**) Smert Shpionam (Russian: death to spies; section of KGB)

SMHO (Malta) Sovereign Military Hospitaller Order

Smith. Inst. Smithsonian Institution (Washington, DC)

SMLE short magazine Lee-Enfield (rifle)

SMM Master of Sacred Music • Sancta Mater Maria (Latin: Holy Mother Mary)

SMMT Society of Motor Manufacturers and Traders Ltd

SMO Senior Medical Officer • Sovereign Military Order

SMON (smɒn) *Med.* subacute myelo-opticoneuropathy

s.m.p. sine mascula prole (Latin: without male issue)

SMP statutory maternity pay

SMR standard Malaysian rubber • *Med.* standard metabolic rate

SMRTB Ship and Marine Requirements Technology Board

s.n. secundum naturam (Latin: according to nature, naturally) • sine nomine (Latin: without name) • sub nomine (Latin: under a specified name)

Sn *Chem.* symbol for tin (Latin *stannum*)

SN *international vehicle registration for* Senegal • *postcode for* Swindon

S/N *Electronics* signal-to-noise (in **S/N ratio**) • *Engineering* stress-number (in **S/N curve**)

SNA *Computing* systems network architecture

snafu (snæˈfuː) *Slang* situation normal, all fouled (*or* fucked) up

SNAP (snæp) systems for nuclear auxiliary power

SNB *Stock exchange* sellers no buyers

SNCB Société nationale des chemins de fer belges (Belgian National Railways)

SNCC (snɪk) (USA) Student Nonviolent (later National) Coordinating Committee

SNCF (France) Société nationale des chemins de fer français (state railway authority or system)

SND Sisters of Notre Dame

SNG substitute (*or* synthetic) natural gas

SNH Scottish National Heritage

SNIF *Finance* short-term note issuance facility

SNIG sustainable non-inflationary growth

SNO (formerly) Scottish National Orchestra (renamed Royal Scottish Orchestra, RSO) • Senior Naval Officer

SNOBOL ('snəʊ,bɒl) *Computing, indicating* a programming language designed for text manipulation

SNP Scottish National Party

Snr Senior

SNR *Electronics* signal-to-noise ratio • Society for Nautical Research • *Astronomy* supernova remnant

s 'n' s *Colloquial* sex and shopping (type of popular fiction)

SNTS Society for New Testament Studies

SNU (snjuː) *Astronomy* solar neutrino unit

so. south(ern)

s.o. seller's option • shipping order • substance of (specifying weight of paper)

So. south(ern)

SO Scientific Officer • Signal Officer • *postcode for* Southampton • special order • Staff Officer • standing order • Stationery Office • suboffice • Symphony Orchestra

S/O shipowner

SOA state of the art

SOAP (səʊp) *Med.* subjective, objective, analysis, plan (method of compiling patients' records)

SOB *Colloquial* silly old bastard (*or* blighter) • (*or* **s.o.b.**) *Colloquial* son of a bitch

soc. socialist • society • sociology

Soc. Socialist • Society

SocCE(France) Société des ingénieurs civils de France (Society of Civil Engineers of France)

sociol. sociological • sociologist • sociology

SOCO scene-of-crime officer (in the police)

SOCS Society of County Secretaries

socy (*or* **Socy**) society

SODAC Society of Dyers and Colourists

SODEPAX ('səʊdɪ,pæks) Committee on Society, Development, and Peace

SOE Special Operations

Executive (in World War II) • state-owned enterprise

SOED (ital.) Shorter Oxford English Dictionary

SOF Films sound on a film

SOFFEX ('sɒfɛks) Swiss Options and Financial Futures Exchange

S of F Ltd Society of Floristry Limited

S. of S. Secretary of State • Bible Song of Songs

S. of Sol. Bible Song of Solomon

SOGAT ('səʊgæt) Society of Graphical and Allied Trades (see GPMU)

sol. solicitor • soluble • solution

s.o.l. Insurance shipowner's liability

Sol. Solicitor • Bible Song of Solomon

SOLACE (or **Solace**) ('sɒlɪs) Society of Local Authority Chief Executives

Sol. Gen. Solicitor General

soln solution

solr (or **Solr**) solicitor

Som. Somerset

SOM Society of Occupational Medicine

Som.Sh. Somali shilling (monetary unit)

sonar ('səʊnɑː) sound navigation and ranging

sop. soprano

SOP standard operating procedure • Computing sum of products (in **SOP expression**)

SoR (or **SOR**) sale or return

s.o.s. Med. si opus sit (Latin: if necessary; in prescriptions)

SOS save our souls (also, the clearest letters to transmit and receive in Morse code) • (or **SoS**) Secretary of State

SOSc Society of Ordained Scientists

SoSh symbol for Somali shilling (monetary unit)

sost. Music sostenuto (Italian: sustained)

SOTS Society for Old Testament Study

Sou. (or **sou.**) south(ern)

sov. sovereign

SOV Linguistics subject-object-verb (in **SOV language**)

sowc senior officers' war course

Soweto (sə'wɛtəʊ) Southwestern Townships (South Africa)

sp. special • *Biology* species • specific • specimen • spelling • spirit

s.p. self-propelled • sine prole (Latin: without issue) • starting price

Sp. Spain • Spaniard • Spanish

SP *postcode for* Salisbury • Self-Propelled (Antitank Regiment) • shore patrol • starting price (odds in a race) • submarine patrol • *Finance* supra protest

SpA (Italy) società per azioni (public limited company; plc)

SPAB Society for the Protection of Ancient Buildings

Sp. Am. Spanish American

Span. Spaniard • Spanish

Sp. Ar. Spanish Arabic

SPARC (spɑːk) *Computing* scalable processor architecture

SPC *Telecom.* stored-program control (as in **SPC exchange**)

SPCK Society for Promoting Christian Knowledge

SPD Salisbury Plain District • Sozialdemokratische Partei Deutschlands (Social Democratic Party of Germany)

SPDA single-premium deferred annuity

SPE Society for Pure English

spec. special(ly) • specific(ally) • specification

specif. specifically • specification

SPECT *Med.* single photon emission computed tomography

SPF sun protection factor (of sunscreening preparations)

SPG Society for the Propagation of the Gospel (*see* USPG) • Special Patrol Group

SPGB Socialist Party of Great Britain

sp. gr. specific gravity

sp. ht specific heat

spirit. *Music* spiritoso (Italian: in a spirited manner)

s.p.l. sine prole legitima (Latin: without legitimate issue)

SPLA Sudan People's Liberation Army

s.p.m. sine prole mascula (Latin: without male issue)

SPMO Senior Principal Medical Officer

SPNM Society for the Promotion of New Music

SPOD Sexual Problems of the Disabled (department of the Royal Association for Disability and Rehabilitation)

sport. sporting

spp. *Biology* species (plural)

SPQR Senatus Populusque Romanus (Latin: the Senate and People of Rome) • small profits and quick returns

spr. spring

Spr *Military* Sapper

SPR Society for Psychical Research

SPRC Society for the Prevention and Relief of Cancer

SPREd Society of Picture Researchers and Editors

SPRL Society for the Promotion of Religion and Learning

s.p.s. sine prole supersite (Latin: without surviving issue)

SPS syndiotactic polystyrene (a plastic)

SPSO Senior Principal Scientific Officer

spt seaport

SPTL Society of Public Teachers of Law

SPUC (*or* **Spuc**) (spʌk) Society for the Protection of the Unborn Child

SPURV (spɜːv) self-propelled underwater research vehicle

sq *Military* staff qualified

sq. sequence • sequens (*see under* seq.) • squadron • square

Sq. Squadron • Square (in place names)

SQ sick quarters • stereophonic-quadraphonic (of audio equipment)

SQA *Computing* software quality assurance

sq cm square centimetre(s)

sqd squad

sqdn (*or* **Sqdn**) squadron

Sqdn Ldr Squadron Leader

sq ft square feet (*or* foot)

sq in square inch(es)

sq km square kilometre(s)

SQL *Computing* standard query language • *Computing* structured query language

sq m square metre(s)

sq mi square mile(s)

sq mm square millimetre(s)

sqn (*or* **Sqn**) squadron

Sqn Ldr Squadron Leader

sqq. sequentia (*see under* seqq.)

sq yd square yard

sr *Maths., symbol for* steradian

Sr Senhor (Portuguese: Mr, Sir) • Senior (after a name) • Señor (Spanish: Mr, Sir) • Sir • Sister (religious) • *Chem., symbol for* strontium

SR Saudi riyal (Saudi Arabian monetary unit) • Saunders Roe (aircraft) • *symbol for* Seychelles rupee (monetary unit) • Society of Radiographers • (USA) Sons of the Revolution • Southern Railway (now Region) • *Military* Special Reserve • *postcode for* Sunderland

S/R sale or return

Sra Senhora (Portuguese: Mrs) • Señora (Spanish: Mrs)

SRA Squash Rackets Association

SRAM short-range attack missile • *Computing* static random access memory

SR & CC strikes, riot, and civil commotion

SRBC *Med.* sheep red blood cell(s)

SRBM short-range ballistic missile

SRC Science Research Council (*see* SERC) • Students' Representative Council

SRCh State Registered Chiropodist

SRCN (formerly) State Registered Children's Nurse (*see* RSCN)

SRG Strategic Research Group (marketing research company)

SRHE Society for Research into Higher Education

SRI Sacrum Romanum Imperium (Latin: Holy Roman Empire)

SRIS Science Reference Information Service

SRls *symbol for* Saudi riyal (monetary unit of Saudi Arabia)

SRN (formerly) State Registered Nurse (*see* RGN)

sRNA *Biochem.* soluble RNA

SRNA Shipbuilders and Repairers National Association

SRO *Finance* self-regulatory organization • (USA) single-room occupancy (as in **SRO hotel**) • standing room only • Statutory Rules and Orders • Supplementary Reserve of Officers

SRP State Registered Physiotherapist • suggested retail price

SRS Fellow of the Royal Society (Latin *Societatis Regiae Sodalis*)

SRSA *Immunol.* slow-reacting substance A (of anaphylaxis)

Srta Senhorita (Portuguese: Miss) • Señorita (Spanish: Miss)

SRU Scottish Rugby Union

SRY Sherwood Rangers Yeomanry

ss. sections • *Med.* semis (Latin: half; in prescriptions) • subsection

s.s. screw steamer • sensu stricto (Latin: in the strict sense) • *Music* senza sordini (Italian: without mutes) • steamship

SS Sacra Scriptura (Latin: Holy Scripture) • Saints • Schutzstaffel (German: protection squad; Nazi paramilitary organization) • Secretary of State • secret service • security service • social security • *postcode for* Southend-on-Sea • steamship • Straits Settlements • Sunday school

S/S steamship

SSA Society of Scottish Artists • standard spending assessment (in local government)

SSAC Social Security Advisory Committee

SSAE stamped self-addressed envelope

SSAFA (*or* **SS&AFA**) Soldiers', Sailors', and Airmen's Families Association

SSAP Statement of Standard Accounting Practice

SSBN *US Navy* strategic submarine, ballistic nuclear

SSC Scottish Ski Club • Sculptors' Society of Canada • (India) Secondary School Certificate • Short Service Commission • Society of the Holy Cross (Latin *Societas Sanctae Crucis*) • (Scotland) Solicitor before the Supreme Court • Species Survival Commission

SSD Doctor of Sacred Scripture (Latin *Sacrae*

Scripturae Doctor) • Social Services Department

SS.D Sanctissimus Dominus (Latin: Most Holy Lord; the pope)

SSE south-southeast

SSEB South of Scotland Electricity Board

S-SEED *Optics* symmetric self-electro-optic-effect device

SSEES School of Slavonic and East European Studies (University of London)

SSF *Military* single-seater fighter (aircraft) • Society of St Francis

S/Sgt (*or* **S.Sgt**) Staff Sergeant

SSHA Scottish Special Housing Association

SSI Scottish Symphony Orchestra • site of scientific interest • *Electronics* small-scale integration • Social Services Inspectorate • Society of Scribes and Illuminators

SSJE Society of St John the Evangelist

SSM Society of the Sacred Mission • *Military* surface-to-surface missile

SSN severely subnormal • Standard Serial Number

SSO Senior Scientific Officer • Senior Supply Officer

ssp. *Biology* subspecies

SSP statutory sick pay

SSPCA Scottish Society for the Prevention of Cruelty to Animals

SSPE *Med.* subacute sclerosing panencephalitis

sspp. *Biology* subspecies (plural)

SS.PP. Sancti Patres (Latin: Holy Fathers)

SSR secondary surveillance radar • (formerly) Soviet Socialist Republic

SSRC Social Science Research Council (*see under* ESRC)

SSS *Golf* standard scratch score

SSSI site of special scientific interest

SSStJ Serving Sister, Order of St John of Jerusalem

SST Society of Surveying Technicians • supersonic transport

SSTA Scottish Secondary Teachers' Association

SSW south-southwest

st. stanza • state • statute • stem • *Printing* stet • Knit-

ting stitch • stone (weight) • strait • street • *Prosody* strophe • *Cricket* stumped by

s.t. short ton • steam trawler

St Saint • *Physics, symbol for* stokes

St. Statute • Strait • Street

ST septic tank • (Hubble) Space Telescope • speech therapist • spring tide • Standard Time • *postcode for* Stoke-on-Trent • Summer Time

sta. (*or* **Sta.**) station

Sta Santa (Italian, Spanish, Portuguese: Saint (female))

STA Sail Training Association

stab. stabilization • stabilizer • stable

stacc. *Music* staccato

Staffs Staffordshire

STAGS (stægz) Sterling Transferable Accruing Government Securities

START (stɑːt) Strategic Arms Reduction Talks

stat. statics • *Med.* statim (Latin: immediately; in prescriptions) • stationary • statuary • statue • statute

STB Bachelor of Sacred Theology (Latin *Sacrae Theologiae Baccalaureus*)

stbd starboard

STC Senior Training Corps • Short-Title Catalogue • (India) State Trading Corporation

std standard • started

STD Doctor of Sacred Theology (Latin *Sacrae Theologiae Doctor*) • *Med.* sexually transmitted disease • (New Zealand) subscriber toll dialling • subscriber trunk dialling

Ste Sainte (French: Saint (female))

Sté (*or* **Sᵗᵉ**) société (French: company; Co.)

STE Society of Telecom Executives (trade union)

STEM (stɛm) scanning transmission electron microscope (*or* microscopy)

sten. stenographer • stenography

Sten Shepherd and Turpin (inventors), Enfield (in **Sten gun**)

steno. (*or* **stenog.**) stenographer • stenographic • stenography

STEP (stɛp) Special Temporary Employment Programme

ster. (*or* **stereo.**) stereophonic • (*or* **stereo.**) stereotype • sterling

St. Ex. Stock Exchange

stg sterling

stge storage

Sth South

STh Scholar in Theology

STI Straits Times Index (of the Singapore Stock Exchange)

STIM scanning transmission ion microscope

stip. stipend • (*or* **Stip.**) stipendiary

stk stock

STL Licentiate in Sacred Theology (Latin *Sacrae Theologiae Licentiatus*)

stlg sterling

STM Master of Sacred Theology (Latin *Sacrae Theologiae Magister*) • scanning tunnelling microscope (*or* microscopy) • *Med., Psychiatry* short-term memory

STMS *Finance* short-term monetary support (within the EMS)

stmt statement

stn (*or* **Stn**) station

STOL (stɒl) *Aeronautics* short takeoff and landing

S to S ship to shore

stp (*or* **s.t.p.**) *Physics* standard temperature and pressure

STP Professor of Sacred Theology (Latin *Sacrae Theologiae Professor*) • *Trademark* scientifically treated petroleum (an oil substitute; refers colloquially to a hallucinogenic drug) • *Physics* standard temperature and pressure

str steamer

str. straight • (*or* **Str.**) strait • (*or* **Str.**) street • *Music* strings (*or* stringed) • *Rowing* stroke (oar) • strong

stratig. stratigraphy

strd stranded

string. *Music* stringendo (Italian; intensifying)

STRIVE (straɪv) Society for the Preservation of Rural Industries and Village Enterprises

Sts Saints

STS Scottish Text Society

STSO Senior Technical Staff Officer

st. st. *Knitting* stocking stitch

STUC Scottish Trades Union Congress

stud. student

STV Scottish Television • single transferable vote

SU Scripture Union • *Physics, Maths.* special unitary (group; as in **SU₃**) • *Physics* strontium unit (of radioactive strontium)

sub. subeditor • *Music* subito (Italian: immediately, suddenly) • subject • submarine • subordinated • subscription • substitute • suburb(an) • subway

sub-ed. subeditor

subj. subject • subjective(ly) • subjunctive

Sub-Lt (*or* **Sub-Lieut.**) Sub-Lieutenant

subs. subsidiary • subsistence

subsc. subscription

subsp. *Biology* (pl. **subspp.**) subspecies

subst. substantive(ly) • substitute

suc. (*or* **succ.**) successor

suff. sufficient • (*or* **suf.**) suffix

Suff. Suffolk • (*or* **Suffr.**) Suffragan

sum. *Med.* sumat *or* sumendum (Latin: let him (*or* her) take *or* let it be taken; in prescriptions) • summer

SUM surface-to-underwater missile

Sun. (*or* **Sund.**) Sunday

SUNY State University of New York

sup *Maths.* supremum

sup. superfine • superior • superlative • *Grammar* supine (noun) • supplement(ary) • supply • supra (Latin: above) • supreme

sup. ben. supplementary benefit

Sup. Ct Superior Court • Supreme Court

super. superfine • superior • supernumerary

superl. superlative

supp. (*or* **suppl.**) supplement(ary)

Supp. Res. Supplementary Reserve (of officers)

supr. superior • (*or* **Supr.**) supreme

Supt Superintendent

supvr (*or* **supr**) supervisor

sur. surplus

surg. surgeon • surgery • surgical

surv. survey • (*or* **survey.**) surveying • surveyor

Surv. Gen. Surveyor General

Sus. Susanna (in the Apocrypha)

SUT Society for Underwater Technology

s.v. sailing vessel • side valve • sub verbo (*or* voce) (Latin: under the word *or* heading) • *Insurance* surrender value

Sv *Physics, symbol for* sievert

SV Sancta Virgo (Latin: Holy Virgin) • Sanctitas Vestra (Latin: Your Holiness) • stroke volume (of an engine)

svc. (*or* **svce**) service

SVD swine vesicular disease

svgs savings

S-VHS super-VHS

SVO *Linguistics* subject-verb-object (in **SVO language**)

s.v.p. s'il vous plaît (French: if you please)

s.v.r. *Med.* spiritus vini rectificatus (Latin: rectified spirit of wine; in prescriptions)

SVS still-camera video system

s.vv. sub verbis (Latin: under the words or headings)

Sw. Sweden • Swedish

SW shipper's weight • *Radio* short wave • small women (clothing size) • South Wales • south-west(ern) • *postcode for* southwest London

S/W *Computing* software

SWA *international vehicle registration for* Namibia (formerly South West Africa)

Swab. Swabia(n)

SWA(L)K (swɔːlk *or* swæk) sealed with a (loving) kiss (on envelopes)

SWANU ('swɑːuː) South West Africa National Union

SWAPO (*or* **Swapo**) ('swɑːpəʊ) South-West Africa People's Organization

S/WARE *Computing* software

SWCI *Computing* software configuration item

SWEB South Wales Electricity Board • Southwest Electricity Board

Swed. Sweden • Swedish

SWET Society of West End Theatre

SwF *symbol for* Swiss franc (monetary unit)

SWG standard wire gauge

SWIE South Wales Institute of Engineers

SWIFT (swɪft) Society for Worldwide Interbank Financial Transmission

Swing (swɪŋ) *Finance* Sterling warrant into gilt-edged stock

Switz. (*or* **Swit.**) Switzerland

SWLA (*or* **SWIA**) Society of Wildlife Artists

SWOT (swɒt) *Marketing* strengths, weaknesses, opportunities, and threats (of a new product)

SWPA South-West Pacific Area

SWR *Telecom.* standing-wave ratio

SWRB Sadler's Wells Royal Ballet (now the Royal Ballet)

Swtz. Switzerland

Sx Sussex

SX *Shipping* Sundays excepted

Sy. supply • Surrey

SY *international vehicle registration for* Seychelles • *postcode for* Shrewsbury • steam yacht

SYB (ital.) The Statesman's Year-Book

Syd. Sydney

SYHA Scottish Youth Hostels Association

syl. (*or* **syll.**) syllable • syllabus

sym. symbol • symphonic • symphony • symptom

symp. symposium

syn. synonym(ous) • synonymy

sync *Image technol.* synchronization (*or* synchronize)

synd. syndicate • syndicated

synop. synopsis

synth. *Music* synthesizer

syr. *Pharmacol.* syrup

Syr. Syria(n) • Syriac

SYR *international vehicle registration for* Syria

syst. system

sz. size

T

t (ital.) *Statistics, symbol for* Student's t distribution •

Music te (in tonic sol-fa) • (ital.) *Chem.* tertiary (isomer; as in **t-butane**) • *symbol for* tonne(s)

t. taken (from) • *Commerce* tare • teaspoon(ful) • *Music* tempo • tempore (Latin: in the time of) • tenor • *Grammar* tense • territory • thunder • time • ton(s) or tonne(s) • town • township • transit • *Grammar* transitive • troy • tun

T (ital.) *Physics*, symbol for kinetic energy • *Biochem.*, symbol for ribosylthymine • tera- (prefix indicating 10^{12} as in **TJ**, terajoule) • *Physics*, symbol for tesla(s) • *international vehicle registration for* Thailand • *Biochem.*, symbol for thymine • (bold ital.) *Physics, Engineering*, symbol for torque • trainer (aircraft; as in **T-37**) • *Chem.*, symbol for tritium

T. (or **T**) tablespoon(ful) • *Music* tace (Italian: be silent) • telephone • *Music* tenor • Territorial • Territory • Testament • Thursday • time • Tuesday

Ta *Chem.*, symbol for tantalum

TA postcode for Taunton • telegraphic address • temporary admission • Territorial Army • *Psychol.* transac-

tional analysis • Translators Association • travelling allowance

TAA Territorial Army Association • Trans-Australia Airlines

TA&VRA Territorial Auxiliary and Volunteer Reserve Association

tab. table (list or chart) • tablet • tabulation • tabulator

TAB tabulator (on a typewriter) • (Australia, New Zealand) Totalizator Administration (or Agency) Board • *Med.* typhoid, paratyphoid A, paratyphoid B (vaccine)

TAC The Athletics Congress

TACAN ('tækæn) tactical air navigation

TACV tracked air-cushion vehicle

TADA taking and driving away (police use)

Tads (tædz) *Military* target acquisition and designation sight

TAF Tactical Air Force

TAFE ('tæfɪ) technical and further education

tafu ('tæfuː) *Slang* things are fouled (or fucked) up

tafubar ('tæfuː,baː) *Slang* things are fouled (*or* fucked) up beyond all recognition

TALISMAN (*or* **Talisman**) ('tælɪzmən) *Stock exchange* Transfer Accounting Lodgement for Investors and Stock Management

tal. qual. talis qualis (Latin: average quality)

Tam. Tamil (language)

TAM (tæm) Television Audience Measurement (as in **TAM rating**)

Tamba ('tæmbə) Twins and Multiple Births Association

tan (tæn) *Maths.* tangent

T&AFA Territorial and Auxiliary Forces Association

T & AVR Territorial and Army Volunteer Reserve

T & E *Colloquial* tired and emotional (i.e. drunk) • travel and entertainment • trial and error

t. & g. *Carpentry* tongued and grooved

T & G Transport and General Workers' Union

t. & p. *Insurance* theft and pilferage

t. & s. toilet and shower

TANS Territorial Army Nursing Service (now merged with QARANC)

TANU ('tænuː) Tanganyika African National Union

TAP Transportes Aéreos Portugueses (Portuguese Airlines)

TAPS Trans-Alaska Pipeline System

TARO Territorial Army Reserve of Officers

Tas. Tasmania(n)

TAS torpedo antisubmarine (course) • *Aeronautics* true air speed

TASI *Telecom.* time-assignment speech interpolation

Tasm. Tasmania(n)

Tass (tæs) (formerly) Telegrafnoye Agentsvo Sovetskovo Soyuza (Soviet news agency)

TAT *Psychol.* thematic apperception test • *Med.* tired all the time

TAURUS ('tɔːrəs) *Stock exchange* Transfer and Automated Registration of Uncertified Stock

TAVR Territorial and Army Volunteer Reserve (1967–79)

TAVRA Territorial Auxiliary and Volunteer Reserve Association

tax. (*or* **taxn**) taxation

t.b. *Book-keeping* trial balance • tubercle bacillus • tuberculosis

Tb *Chem., symbol for* terbium

TB torpedo boat • training board • Treasury bill • *Book-keeping* trial balance • tuberculosis

t.b.a. *Commerce* to be advised • to be agreed • to be announced

TBC *Image technol.* time-based corrector

TBD torpedo-boat destroyer

TBF Teachers Benevolent Fund

TBG *Immunol.* thyroxine-binding globulin

TBI *Engineering* throttle-body injection • *Med.* total body irradiation

t.b.l. *Knitting* through back of loop

TBM *Military* tactical ballistic missile • tunnel-boring machine

TBO *Aeronautics* time between overhauls • *Theatre* total blackout

tbs. (*or* **tbsp.**) tablespoon(ful)

TBS talk between ships (radio apparatus) • tight building syndrome

TBT tributyl tin (used in marine paints)

tc. *Music* tierce (organ stop)

Tc *Chem., symbol for* technetium

TC *Law* Tax Cases • traveller's cheque • *Music* tre corde (Italian: three strings; i.e. release soft pedal) • (Trinidad and Tobago) (Order of the) Trinity Cross • Trusteeship Council (of the UN) • *Chem.* tungsten carbide • twin carburettors (on motor vehicles)

TCA *Biochem.* tricarboxylic acid (in **TCA cycle**) • trichloroacetic acid (herbicide) • tricyclic antidepressant (drug)

TCB *Chem.* tetrachlorobiphenyl

TCBM transcontinental ballistic missile

TCCB Test and County Cricket Board

TCD Trinity College, Dublin

TCDD tetrachlorodibenzodioxin (dioxin; environmental pollutant)

TCE *Chem.* trichloroeth(yl)ene (solvent)

tcf trillion cubic feet (measure of natural gas)

TCF Temporary Chaplain to the Forces · Touring Club de France

TCNQ *Chem.* tetracyanoquinodimethane

TCP *Computing* transmission control protocol · *Trademark* trichlorophenylmethyliodisalicyl (an antiseptic)

TCPA Town and Country Planning Association

TD *postcode for* Galashiel's · tank destroyer · *Med.* tardive dyskinesia · (Ireland) Teachta Dála (Gaelic: Member of the Dáil) · technical drawing · Territorial (Efficiency) Decoration (in the Territorial Army) · trust deed · Tunisian dinar (monetary unit)

TDA 2,4-toluene diamine (possible carcinogen released by breast implants)

TDC Temporary Detective Constable · (*or* **t.d.c.**) *Engineering* top dead centre

TDL tunable diode laser

TDMA *Telecom.* time-division multiple access

TDN total digestible nutrients

TDR *Finance* Treasury deposit receipt

TDRSS (*or* **TDRS**) tracking and data-relay satellite system

t.d.s. *Med.* ter die sumendum (Latin: to be taken three times a day; in prescriptions)

TDS *Computing* tabular data stream

t/e twin-engined

Te *Chem., symbol for* tellurium

TEAC Technical Educational Advisory Council

TEC (tek) Training and Enterprise Council

tech. (*or* **techn.**) technical(ly) · technician · technology

Tech(CEI) Technician (Council of Engineering Institutions)

technol. technological · technology

TEE Trans-Europe Express (train)

TEF toxicity equivalence factor

TEFL teaching (of) English as a foreign language

tel. telegram · telegraph(ic) · telephone

TEL tetraethyl lead (petrol additive)

telecom. telecommunication(s)

teleg. telegram • telegraph(ic) • telegraphy

telex ('tɛlɛks) teleprinter exchange

tel. no. telephone number

TEM Territorial Efficiency Medal

TEMA Telecommunications Engineering and Manufacturing Association

temp. temperate • temperature • temporary • tempore (Latin: in the time of)

Templar ('tɛmplə) tactical expert mission-planner (military computer)

ten. tenor • Music tenuto (Italian: held, sustained)

Tenn. Tennessee

TENS (tɛnz) Med. transcutaneous electrical nerve stimulation

TeolD Doctor of Theology

TEPP tetraethyl pyrophosphate (pesticide)

ter. (or **Ter.**) terrace • territory

terat. teratology

TERCOM ('tɜːkɒm) Aeronautics terrain contour matching (or mapping)

term. terminal • termination

terr. (or **Terr.**) terrace • territorial • territory

TES thermal-energy storage • (ital.) Times Educational Supplement

TESL teaching (of) English as a second language

TESOL ('tiːsɒl) teaching (or teacher) of English to speakers of other languages

Tessa ('tɛsə) Tax-Exempt Special Savings Account

TET Teacher of Electrotherapy

TEU Shipping twenty-foot equivalent unit

Teut. Teuton(ic)

TEWT (or **Tewt**) (tjuːt) Military tactical exercise without troops

Tex. Texan • Texas

text. rec. textus receptus (Latin: the received text)

TF postcode for Telford • Territorial Force

TFAP Tropical Forestry Action Plan

TFD Electronics thin-film detector

tfr transfer

TFR Territorial Force Reserve

TFSC (or **TFSK**) Turkish Federated State of Cyprus (Turkish *Kibris*)

TFW *Military* tactical fighter wing

TFX tactical fighter experimental (aircraft)

tg *Maths.* tangent

t.g. *Biology* type genus

TG temporary gentleman • *Colloquial* thank God • *international vehicle registration for* Togo • transformational-generative (grammar) • transformational grammar

TGAT ('ti:gæt) *Education* Task Group on Assessment and Testing

T-gate *Computing* ternary selector gate

TGEW Timber Growers England and Wales Ltd

TGF *Med.* transforming growth factor

TGI *Marketing* Target Group Index

TGIF *Colloquial* thank God it's Friday

T-group training group

TGV (France) train à grande vitesse (high-speed passenger train)

TGWU Transport and General Workers' Union

Th *Chem., symbol for* thorium

Th. Thursday

TH Territory of Hawaii

ThB Bachelor of Theology (Latin *Theologicae Baccalaureus*)

THC tetrahydrocannabinol (cannabis component) • (New Zealand) Tourist Hotel Corporation

ThD Doctor of Theology (Latin *Theologicae Doctor*)

THD total harmonic distortion (in sound recording)

theat. theatrical

THELEP Therapy of Leprosy

theol. theologian • theological • theology

theor. theorem • (or **theoret.**) theoretical

theos. theosophical • theosophist • theosophy

therap. (or **therapeut.**) therapeutic(s)

therm. thermometer

thermom. thermometer • thermometry

THES (ital.) Times Higher Education Supplement

Thess. *Bible* Thessalonians

THF Trusthouse Forte plc

THI temperature–humidity index

ThL Theological Licentiate

ThM Master of Theology (Latin *Theologiae Magister*)

thou. thousand

thr. through

Thr (*or* **thr**) *Biochem.* threonine

THR *Med.* total hip replacement

3i Investors in Industry

3M Minnesota Mining and Manufacturing Company

three (*or* **3**) **Rs** reading, (w)riting, and (a)rithmetic

ThSchol Scholar in Theology

Thurs. (*or* **Thur.**) Thursday

THWM Trinity (House) high-water mark

THz *Physics, symbol for* terahertz

Ti *Chem., symbol for* titanium

TI *Med.* thermal imaging

TIA *Med.* transient ischaemic attack

TIBOR ('ti:bɔ:) *Finance* Tokyo InterBank Offered Rate

TIC (*or* **tic**) *Law* taken into consideration (of an offence) • total inorganic carbon (in chemical analysis)

t.i.d. *Med.* ter in die (Latin: three times a day; in prescriptions)

TIE theatre in education

TIG tungsten inert gas (welding)

TIGR ('taɪgə) Treasury Investment Growth Receipts (type of bond)

TIH Their Imperial Highnesses

Tim. *Bible* Timothy

TIM transient intermodulation distortion (in sound recording)

timp. *Music* timpani

TIMS The Institute of Management Sciences

TINA ('ti:nə) *Politics, colloquial* there is no alternative (usually referring to Margaret Thatcher)

tinct. tincture

TIP *Computing* terminal interface processor

TIR Transport International Routier (French: International Road Transport; on continental lorries)

tit. title

Tit. *Bible* Titus

TJ (*or* **t.j.**) talk jockey • *Athletics* triple jump

tk tank • truck

Tk *symbol for* taka (monetary unit of Bangladesh)

TKO (*or* **t.k.o.**) *Boxing* technical knockout

tkt ticket

t.l. *Insurance* total loss • trade list

Tl *Chem., symbol for* thallium

TL target language • thermoluminescent (as in **TL-dating**) • *Insurance* total loss • transmission line • Turkish lira (monetary unit)

T/L *Banking* time loan • *Insurance* total loss

TLA three-letter abbreviation (*or* acronym)

TLC tender loving care • *Chem.* thin-layer chromatography • *Med.* total lung capacity • (Australia) Trades and Labour Council

TLG Theatrical Ladies' Guild

t.l.o. *Insurance* total loss only

TLR Times Law Reports • *Photog.* twin-lens reflex

TLS (*ital.*) Times Literary Supplement • typed letter, signed

TLWM Trinity (House) low-water mark

t.m. true mean

Tm *Chem., symbol for* thulium

TM trademark • transcendental meditation • trench mortar

TMA Theatrical Management Association • Trans-Mediterranean Airways (Lebanese national airline) • *Chem.* trimellitic acid

TMD *Military* theatre missile defence

TMJ *Med.* temporomandibular joint (as in **TMJ syndrome**)

TMMG Teacher of Massage and Medical Gymnastics

TMO telegraph(ic) money order

tn ton (*or* tonne) • town • train

TN *US postcode for* Tennessee • *postcode for* Tonbridge • *international vehicle registration for* Tunisia

TNC Theatres National Committee • transnational corporation

TNF *Military* theatre nuclear forces • *Med.* tumour necrosis factor

tng training

TNM *Med.* tumour (size), (lymph) node (involvement), metastasis (in **TNM classification**)

T-note *Finance* Treasury note

tnpk. turnpike

TNT 2,4,6-trinitrotoluene (explosive)

t.o. turnover

TO *Management* table of organization • telegraph office • Transport Officer • turn over (page)

T/O turnover

Tob. *Old Testament* Tobit

Toc H Talbot House (obsolete telegraphic code for its initials; original headquarters of the movement)

TOE *Physics* theory of everything

TOEFL test(ing) of English as a foreign language

TOFC trailer on flat car (type of freight container)

tom. (*or* **tomat.**) tomato • tomus (Latin: volume)

tonn. tonnage

TOO (*or* **t.o.o.**) time of origin • *Commerce* to order only

TOP (tɒp) *Computing* technical office protocol • temporarily out of print

TOPIC ('tɒpɪk) *Stock exchange* Teletext Output

Price Information Computer

topog. topographer • topographical • topography

TOPS (tɒps) Training Opportunities Scheme

TOSD Tertiary Order of St Dominic

Toshiba (tɒˈʃiːbə) Tokyo Shibaura Denki KK (Japanese corporation)

tot. total

TOTC time-on-target computation (military computer)

TOTP Top of the Pops (television programme)

TOW (təʊ) tube-launched optically tracked wire-guided (antitank missile)

toxicol. toxicological • toxicologist • (*or* **tox.**) toxicology

tp township • troop

t.p. teaching practice • title page

TP *Insurance* third party • Transvaal Province • *Surveying* trigonometric point • *Surveying* turning point

TPA (*or* **tPA**) *Med.* tissue plasminogen activator

TPC (Australia) Trade Practices Commission

tpd (*or* **TPD**) tons per day

tph (*or* **TPH**) tons per hour

tpi *Engineering* teeth per inch • *Computing* tracks per inch • *Engineering* turns per inch

TPI tax and price index • *Engineering* threads per inch • *Shipping* tons per inch (immersion) • (Australia) totally and permanently incapacitated • Tropical Products Institute

tpk. turnpike

TPM (*or* **tpm**) tons per minute

TPN *Med.* total parenteral nutrition

Tpr *Military* Trooper

TPR *Med.* temperature, pulse, respiration

tpt *Music* trumpet

TQ (*or* **t.q.**) *Banking* tel quel (exchange rate) • *postcode for* Torquay • total quality (quality control)

TQM total quality management

tr. *Med.* tinctura (Latin: tincture) • trace • train • transaction • transitive • translate(d) • translator • *Printing* transpose • transposition • treasurer • *Music* treble • *Music* trill • troop • trust • trustee

TR tempore regis *or* reginae (Latin: in the time of the king *or* queen) • tons registered • *Telecom.* transmit–receive (as in **TR switch**) • *postcode for* Truro • trust receipt • *international vehicle registration for* Turkey

TRACE (treɪs) *Aeronautics* test equipment for rapid automatic checkout evaluation

trad. tradition(al)

trans. transaction • transfer(red) • transit • transitive • translate(d) • translation • translator • transparent • transport(ation) • *Printing* transpose • transverse

transcr. transcribed (by *or* for) • transcription

transf. transferred

transl. translate(d) • translation • translator

transp. transport(ation)

trav. traveller • travels

trbn. *Music* trombone

TRC Thames Rowing Club

TRDA Timber Research and Development Association

treas. treasurer • (*or* **Treas.**) treasury

tree. trustee

trem. *Music* tremolando

(Italian: trembling) • *Music* tremulant (device in an organ)

TRF tuned radio frequency

TRH Their Royal Highnesses

TRIC Television and Radio Industries Club

trid. *Med.* triduum (Latin: three days; in prescriptions)

trig. trigonometric(al) • trigonometry

trike (traɪk) *Chem.* trichloroeth(yl)ene (solvent)

Trin. Trinity

tripl. triplicate

triple A (*or* **AAA**) antiaircraft artillery

TRJ turboramjet (engine)

trlr trawler

TRM trademark

tRNA *Biochem.* transfer RNA

TRO *Law* temporary restraining order

trop. tropic(al)

Trp (*or* **trp**) *Military* troop • *Biochem.* tryptophan

TRRL Transport and Road Research Laboratory

trs. transfer • *Printing* transpose • trustees

Truron. Truronensis (Latin: (Bishop) of Truro)

t.s. turbine ship • twin screw

TS *postcode for* Cleveland • *Music* tasto solo (Italian: one key alone; in figured-bass playing) • Theosophical Society (in England) • *Slang* tough shit • training ship • Treasury Solicitor • tub-sized (paper) • typescript

TSA The Securities Association Ltd • total surface area • Training Services Agency (now called Training Agency)

TSB Trustee Savings Bank

tsc *indicating* passed a Territorial Army course in staff duties

TSD Tertiary of St Dominic

TSE Tokyo Stock Exchange • Toronto Stock Exchange • *Med.* transmissible spongiform encephalopathy

T.Sgt Technical Sergeant

TSh *symbol for* Tanzanian shilling (monetary unit)

TSH Their Serene Highnesses • *Biochem.* thyroid-stimulating hormone

tsi tons per square inch

TSO Trading Standards Officer

tsp. teaspoon(ful)

TSR *Computing* terminate and stay resident (program)

TSS *Med.* toxic shock syndrome • twin-screw steamer (*or* steamship, ship) • typescripts

TSSA Transport Salaried Staffs' Association

TSW Television South West

TT technical training • teetotal(ler) • *Banking* telegraphic transfer • *Motorcycling* Tourist Trophy (races) • *international vehicle registration for* Trinidad and Tobago • Trust Territories (abbrev. *or* postcode) • tuberculin-tested (as in **TT milk**)

TTB tetragonal tungsten bronze

TTBT Threshold Test Ban Treaty

TTC technical training centre

TTF Timber Trade Federation

TTFN *Colloquial* ta-ta for now

TTL *Photog.* through the lens • (*or* **t.t.l.**) to take leave • *Electronics* transistor-transistor logic • (Zimbabwe) tribal trust land

TTS teletypesetter (*or* teletypesetting)

Tu. Tuesday

TU toxic unit • trade union • *Telecom.* traffic unit • training unit • *Acoustics, Telecom.* transmission unit • Tupolev (aircraft; as in **TU-104**)

TUC Trades Union Congress

Tues. Tuesday

TUG Telephone Users' Group

TULRA Trade Union and Labour Relations Act (1974)

Turk. Turkey • Turkish

TV television

TVEI Technical and Vocational Educational Initiative

Tvl Transvaal

TVO tractor vaporizing oil

TVP textured vegetable protein (a meat substitute)

TVR television rating

TVRO television receive only (type of antenna)

TW *Telecom.* travelling wave (in **TW antenna**) • *postcode for* Twickenham

TWA Thames Water Authority • time-weighted average • Trans-World Airlines

TWh (*or* **TW h**) *Electricity, symbol for* terawatt hour(s)

TWIMC to whom it may concern

twocky take without owner's consent (of a person who takes away a car without the owner's consent)

TX *US postcode for* Texas

Ty Territory

typ. typographer • typographic(al) • typography

typh. typhoon

typo. (*or* **typog.**) typographer • typographic(al) • typography

typw. typewriter • typewriting • typewritten

Tyr (*or* **tyr**) *Biochem.* tyrosine

U

u (*ital.*) *Electricity, symbol for* instantaneous potential difference • *Physics* up (a quark flavour) • (*ital.*) *Physics, symbol for* a velocity component or speed

u. uncle • unit • unsatisfactory • upper

U (*ital.*) *Electricity, symbol for* potential difference • *symbol for* rate of heat loss (measured in British thermal units; in **U** value, a measure of insulating power) • *Films* universal (certification) • *Colloquial* upper class (of characteristics, language habits, etc.; also in **non-U**) • *Biochem., symbol for* uracil • *Chem., symbol for* uranium • *Biochem., symbol for* uridine • you (from phonetic spelling, as in **IOU, while U wait**)

U. (*or* **U**) Union • Unionist • United • University • unsatisfactory • upper

U/a *Insurance* underwriting account

UAB Unemployment Assistance Board

UAE United Arab Emirates

UAM underwater-to-air missile

u. & l.c. *Printing* upper and lower case

UAR United Arab Republic (1958–71)

UARS upper-atmosphere research satellite

UART ('juː,ɑːt) *Electronics, Computing* universal asynchronous receiver/transmitter

UAU Universities Athletic Union

UB *postcode for* Southall

UB40 *indicating* the index card used for unemployment benefit

UBI Understanding British Industry (organization)

U-boat *indicating* a German submarine during the World Wars (German *Unterseeboot*)

UBR *Taxation* Uniform Business Rate

u.c. *Music* una chorda (*see under* UC) • *Printing* upper case

u/c *Commerce* undercharge

UC *Music* una corda (Italian: on one string; i.e. use soft pedal) • under construction • undercover • *Civil engineering* upcast shaft • *Theatre* up centre (of stage) • Upper Canada • *Obstetrics* uterine contraction

U$_c$ *Films* universal, particularly suitable for children (certification)

UCATT (*or* **Ucatt**) ('juː,kæt) Union of Construction, Allied Trades, and Technicians

UCBSA United Cricket Board of South Africa

UCCA (*or* **Ucca**) ('ʌkə) Universities Central Council on Admissions

UCET Universities Council for Education of Teachers

UCH University College Hospital (London)

UCITS *Finance* Undertakings for Collective Investment in Transferable Securities

UCMSM University College and Middlesex School of Medicine

UCNS Universities' Council for Nonacademic Staff

UCR *Physiol., Psychol.* unconditioned reflex (*or* response)

UCS *Physiol., Psychol.* unconditioned stimulus

UCTA United Commercial Travellers' Association

(now part of the MSF union)

UCW Union of Communication Workers

u.d. *Med.* ut dictum (Latin: as directed; in prescriptions)

UDA Ulster Defence Association

UDC universal decimal classification • Urban Development Corporation • Urban District Council

UDF Ulster Defence Force • (South Africa) Union Defence Force • (South Africa) United Democratic Front

UDI unilateral declaration of independence

UDM Union of Democratic Mineworkers

UDN ulcerative dermal necrosis (fish disease)

UDR Ulster Defence Regiment

UE (New Zealand) university entrance (examination)

UEA University of East Anglia

UED University Education Diploma

u.e.f. universal extra fine (screw)

UEFA (juːˈeɪfə) Union of European Football Associations

UF United Free (Church, of Scotland) • urea–formaldehyde (as in **UF resin**)

UFAW Universities Federation for Animal Welfare

UFC United Free Church (of Scotland) • University Funding Council

UFF Ulster Freedom Fighters

UFO (ˈjuː ˈɛf ˈəʊ *or* ˈjuːfəʊ) unidentified flying object

UFT *Physics* unified field theory

UHB *Colloquial* urban haute bourgeoisie

UHF ultrahigh frequency

UHT ultra-heat-treated (as in **UHT milk**) • ultrahigh temperature

UHV ultrahigh vacuum

u.i. ut infra (Latin: as below)

u/i under instruction

UIL United Irish League

UIT unit investment trust

UJ Union Jack • *Engineering* universal joint

UJC Union Jack Club (London)

UJD Utriusque Juris Doctor (Latin: Doctor of Civil and Canon Law)

UK United Kingdom

UK(A) *Athletics* United Kingdom Allcomers

UKA United Kingdom Alliance

UKAC United Kingdom Automation Council

UKADGE United Kingdom Air Defence Ground Environment

UKAEA United Kingdom Atomic Energy Authority

UKAPE United Kingdom Association of Professional Engineers

UKCC United Kingdom Central Council for Nursing, Midwifery, and Health Visiting

UKCIS United Kingdom Chemical Information Service

UKCOSA (juː'kəuzə) United Kingdom Council for Overseas Students' Affairs

UKCSBS United Kingdom Civil Service Benefit Society

UKDA United Kingdom Dairy Association

UKFBPW United Kingdom Federation of Business and Professional Women

UKgal *symbol for* UK gallon

UKIAS (*or* **Ukias**) (juː-'kaɪəs) United Kingdom Immigrants' Advisory Service

UKISC United Kingdom Industrial Space Committee

UKLF United Kingdom Land Forces

UKMF(L) United Kingdom Military Forces (Land)

UKMIS United Kingdom Mission

UKOOA United Kingdom Offshore Operators Association

UKPIA United Kingdom Petroleum Industry Association Ltd

Ukr. Ukraine • Ukrainian

UKSLS United Kingdom Services Liaison Staff

UKSMA United Kingdom Sugar Merchant Association Ltd

UL *Theatre* up left (of stage)

ULC *Theatre* up left centre (of stage)

ULCC ultralarge crude carrier (oil tanker)

ULCI Union of Lancashire and Cheshire Institutes

ULF *Radio, etc.* ultralow frequency

ULMS underwater long-range missile system

ULSEB University of

London School Examinations Board

ult. ultimate(ly) • (*or* **ulto.**) ultimo (Latin: in (*or* of) the last (month); in correspondence)

ULT United Lodge of Theosophists

ULV ultralow volume (as in **ULV sprayer**)

u/m undermentioned

UM *symbol for* Mauritanian ouguiya (monetary unit)

UMB *Computing* upper memory block

UMDS United Medical and Dental Schools

UMIST (*or* **Umist**) ('juː,mɪst) University of Manchester Institute of Science and Technology

UMNO United Malays (later Malaysia) National Organization

UMT universal military training

UN United Nations

UNA United Nations Association

unab. unabridged

unacc. (*or* **unaccomp.**) unaccompanied

unattrib. unattributed

unauthd unauthorized

unb. (*or* **unbd**) unbound

UNBRO (*or* **Unbro**) ('ʌnbrəʊ) United Nations Border Relief Operation

UNC United Nations Command

UNCAST United Nations Conference on the Applications of Science and Technology

UNCDF United Nations Capital Development Fund

UNCED United Nations Conference on Environment and Development

UNCIO United Nations Conference on International Organization

UNCITRAL United Nations Commission on International Trade Law

unclas. (*or* **unclass.**) unclassified

UNCLE ('ʌŋkᵊl) United Network Command for Law Enforcement (fictional organization in TV series 'The Man from UNCLE')

UNCLOS United Nations Conference on the Law of the Sea

UNCSTD United Nations Conference on Science and Technology for Development

UNCTAD (*or* **Unctad**) ('ʌŋk,tæd) United Nations

Conference on Trade and Development

UNDP United Nations Development Programme

UNDRO (*or* **Undro**) (ˈʌnˌdrəʊ) United Nations Disaster Relief Organization

UNECA United Nations Economic Commission for Asia

UNEF (ˈjuːˌnɛf) United Nations Emergency Force

UNEP (ˈjuːˌnɛp) United Nations Environment Programme

UNESCO (*or* **Unesco**) (juːˈnɛskəʊ) United Nations Educational, Scientific, and Cultural Organization

UNFAO United Nations Food and Agriculture Organization

UNFICYP United Nations (Peace-Keeping) Force in Cyprus

UNFPA United Nations Fund for Population Activities

ung. *Med.* unguentum (Latin: ointment)

UNHCR United Nations High Commissioner for Refugees

UNIA (USA) Universal Negro Improvement Association

UNICEF (*or* **Unicef**) (ˈjuːnɪˌsɛf) United Nations Children's Fund (formerly United Nations International Children's Emergency Fund)

UNIDO (*or* **Unido**) (juːˈniːdəʊ) United Nations Industrial Development Organization

UNIFIL (*or* **Unifil**) (ˈjuːnɪˌfɪl) United Nations Interim Force in Lebanon

UNIP (*or* **Unip**) (ˈjuːnɪp) (Zambia) United National Independence Party

UNISIST (*or* **Unisist**) (ˈjuːnɪˌsɪst) Universal System for Information in Science and Technology

Unit. Unitarian(ism)

UNITA (*or* **Unita**) (juːˈniːtə) União Nacional para a Independência Total de Angola (Portuguese: National Union for the Total Independence of Angola)

UNITAR United Nations Institute for Training and Research

univ. universal(ly) • university

Univ. Universalist • University

UNIVAC ('juːnɪˌvæk) universal automatic computer

UNIX ('juːnɪks) *Trademark, indicating* a type of computer operating system

UNO United Nations Organization

unpub. (*or* **unpubd**) unpublished

UNREF (*or* **Unref**) ('ʌnrɛf) United Nations Refugee Emergency Fund

UNRISD United Nations Research Institute for Social Development

UNRRA (*or* **Unrra**) ('ʌnrə) United Nations Relief and Rehabilitation Administration

UNRWA (*or* **Unrwa**) ('ʌnrə) United Nations Relief and Works Agency

UNSCOB United Nations Special Committee on the Balkans

UNSCOP United Nations Special Committee on Palestine

UNTAC (*or* **Untac**) ('ʌntæk) United Nations Transitional Authority for Cambodia

up. (*or* **u.p.**) underproof (of alcohol) • upper

UP United Party (esp. in South Africa) • United Presbyterian • United Press (news agency) • University Press • Uttar Pradesh (formerly United Provinces)

UPC Uganda People's Congress • United Presbyterian Church • universal product code (bar code)

UPI United Press International

UPNI Unionist Party of Northern Ireland

UPR *Insurance* unearned premiums reserve

UPS uninterruptible power supply (to computers, etc.)

UPU Universal Postal Union (UN agency; formerly General Postal Union, GPU)

UPUP Ulster Popular Unionist Party

uPVC unplasticized polyvinyl chloride

UR *Physiol., Psychol.* unconditioned reflex (*or* response) • *Theatre* up right (of stage)

URC United Reformed Church • *Theatre* up right centre (of stage)

URI *Med.* upper respiratory infection

URTI *Med.* upper respiratory tract infection

URTU United Road Transport Union

Uru. Uruguay(an)

u.s. ubi supra (Latin: where (mentioned *or* cited) above) • ut supra (Latin: as above)

u/s unserviceable • useless

US *Med.* ultrasound (*or* ultrasonic) scanning • Undersecretary • United States • United States highway (as in **US66**)

U/S unserviceable • useless

USA United States Army • United States of America (abbrev. *or* IVR)

USAF United States Air Force

USC Ulster Special Constabulary • United Somali Congress

USCL United Society for Christian Literature

USDAW (*or* **Usdaw**) ('ʌz,dɔː) Union of Shop, Distributive, and Allied Workers

USgal *symbol for* US gallon

USh *symbol for* Uganda shilling (monetary unit)

USI United Service Institution

USIA United States Information Agency

USM underwater-to-surface missile • *Stock exchange* unlisted securities market

USN United States Navy

USO (USA) United Service Organization

US of A *Colloquial* United States of America

USP *Advertising* unique selling proposition (of a product) • United States Pharmacopeia

USPG United Society for the Propagation of the Gospel (formerly SPG)

USR Universities' Statistical Record

USS United States Senate • United States Ship • United States Steamer (*or* Steamship)

USSR (formerly) Union of Soviet Socialist Republics

usu. usual(ly)

USW *Radio, etc.* ultrashort wave

Ut. Utah

UT unit trust • *Astronomy* universal time • *US postcode for* Utah

U/T under trust

UTA Unit Trust Association

UTC Coordinated Universal Time (French *universel*

temps coordonné) • University Training Corps

Utd United

ut dict. *Med.* ut dictum (Latin: as directed; in prescriptions)

utend. *Med.* utendus (Latin: to be used)

U3A University of the Third Age

UTI *Med.* urinary-tract infection

ut inf. ut infra (Latin: as below)

UTS ultimate tensile strength

ut sup. ut supra (Latin: as above)

UU Ulster Unionist

UUM underwater-to-underwater missile

UUUC United Ulster Unionist Coalition (*or* Council)

UUUP United Ulster Unionist Party

UV ultraviolet

UV-A (*or* **UVA**) *indicating* ultraviolet radiation of wavelength 320–380 m

UV-B (*or* **UVB**) *indicating* ultraviolet radiation of wavelength 280–320 m

UVF Ulster Volunteer Force

U/W *Law* under will • (*or* **U/w**) underwriter

UWC Ulster Workers' Council

UWIST (*or* **Uwist**) ('juː‚wɪst) University of Wales Institute of Science and Technology

UWT Union of Women Teachers (now merged with NAS/UWT)

ux. uxor (Latin: wife)

UXB unexploded bomb

V

v *Physics, symbol for* instantaneous voltage • (bold ital.) *Physics, symbol for* velocity • (ital.) *Physics, symbol for* a velocity component *or* speed

v. valve • vein • ventral • verb(al) • verse • version • *Printing* verso • versus • very • via • vice (Latin: in place of) • vide (Latin: see) • village • violin • virus • *Med.* vision • *Grammar* vocative • *Music* voice • volume • von (German: of; in names)

V (ital.) *Electricity, symbol for* electric potential • *Roman numeral for* five • (ital.) *Physics, symbol for* luminous efficiency • (ital.) *Electricity, symbol for* potential difference • (ital.) *Physics, symbol for* potential energy • *Chem., symbol for* vanadium • *international vehicle registration for* Vatican City • verb (in transformational grammar) • Vergeltungswaffe (German: reprisal weapon, as in **V-1** and **V-2**, World War II missiles) • victory (as in **V-Day**, **V-sign**) • *symbol for* volt • (ital.) *symbol for* volume (capacity) • *indicating types of aircraft (see* V bomber)

V. (*or* **V**) Venerable • version • Very (in titles) • Via (Italian: Street) • Vicar • Vice (in titles) • Viscount

(*or* Viscountess) • Volunteer(s)

V1 (*or* **V-1**) Vergeltungswaffe 1 (*see under* V)

V2 (*or* **V-2**) Vergeltungswaffe 2 (*see under* V)

va *Music* viola

v.a. value analysis • verb active • verbal adjective

Va. Virginia (USA)

VA value-added • *Commerce* value analysis • (USA) Veterans' Administration • Vicar Apostolic • Vice-Admiral • (Order of) Victoria and Albert • *US postcode for* Virginia • *Med.* visual acuity

VAB *Astronautics* vehicle assembly building (of NASA)

vac. vacancy • vacant • vacation • vacuum

VAD (member of the) Voluntary Aid Detachment

VADAS *Med.* voice-activated domestic appliance system

V-Adm Vice-Admiral

val. valley • valuation • value(d)

Val (*or* **val**) *Biochem.* valine

van (væn) *Tennis* advantage

V&A Victoria and Albert Museum

V & V *Computing* verification and validation

var. variable • variant • variation • *Botany* variety • variometer • various

VAR visual aural range

Varig (*or* **VARIG**) ('værɪg) (Empresa de) Viação Aérea Rio Grandense (Brazilian airline)

var. lect. varia lectio (Latin: a variant reading)

Vascar (*or* **VASCAR**) ('væskɑː) visual average speed computer and recorder

VASP Viação Aérea São Paulo (Brazilian airline)

Vat. Vatican

VAT ('viː 'eɪ 'tiː *or* væt) value-added tax

v. aux. auxiliary verb

VAV variable air volume (in **VAV** (air-conditioning) **system**)

VAX *Computing, trademark* virtual address extension (range of computers manufactured by DEC)

VAX/VMS *Trademark, indicating* the standard operating system for VAX processors. (*see under* VAX; VMS)

vb (*or* **vb.**) verb(al)

VB verbal constituent (in transformational grammar)

V bomber *indicating* various types of aircraft (named after the types Victor, Vulcan, and Valiant)

vc. *Music* cello (from *violoncello*)

VC *Finance* venture capital • Vice-Chairman • Vice-Chancellor • Vice-Consul • Vickers Commercial (aircraft, as in **VC10**) • Victoria Cross • Viet Cong • *Med., Physiol.* vital capacity

VCAS Vice-Chief of the Air Staff

VCDS Vice-Chief of the Defence Staff

VCE variable-cycle engine

VCGS Vice-Chief of the General Staff

VCH Victoria County History (reference book)

vcl. *Music* cello (from *violoncello*)

VCNS Vice-Chief of the Naval Staff

VCO (India) Viceroy's Commissioned Officer

VCPI *Computing* virtual control program interface

VCR video-cassette recorder • visual control room (at an airfield)

v.d. various dates

VD venereal disease • Victorian Decoration • Volunteer Decoration (formerly awarded in the Territorial Army or the Royal Naval Volunteer Reserve)

V-Day Victory Day

VDC Volunteer Defence Corps

v. dep. verb deponent

VDH valvular disease of the heart

VDI *Computing* virtual device interface

VDJ video disc jockey

VDQS vin délimité de qualité supérieure (French; superior-quality wine; wine classification)

VDR video-disc recording

VDRL venereal disease research laboratory (in **VDRL test**, for syphilis)

VDT *Computing* visual display terminal

VDU *Computing* visual display unit

VE Victory in Europe (in **VE Day**, 8 May 1945)

VEB (formerly, in East Germany) Volkseigener Betrieb (German: People's Concern; state-owned company)

veg. vegetable • vegetation

veh. vehicle • vehicular

vel. vellum • velocity

Ven. Venerable • (*or* **Venet.**) Venetian • (*or* **Venez.**) Venezuela(n) • Venice

ver. verse • version

VERA ('vɪərə) vision electronic recording apparatus

verb. et lit. *Law* verbatim et literatim (Latin: word for word and letter for letter)

verb. sap. (*or* **sat.**) verbum sapienti satis (Latin: a word is enough to the wise)

vers *Maths.* versed sine (*or* versine)

vers. version

vert. vertical

Very Rev. (*or* **Very Revd**) Very Reverend

ves. (*or* **vesp.**) *Med.* vespere (Latin: in the evening; in prescriptions) • vessel

vet. veteran • (*or* **veter.**) veterinarian • (*or* **veter.**) veterinary

vet. sci. veterinary science

vet. surg. veterinary surgeon

v.f. very fair

VF *Med.* ventricular fibrillation • RC Church

Vicar Forane • video frequency • *Telecom.* voice frequency

VFA (Australia) Victorian Football Association

VFL (Australia) Victorian Football League

VFM *Accounting* value for money (audit)

VFT (Australia) very fast train

VFW (USA) Veterans of Foreign Wars

v.g. verbi gratia (Latin: for example) • very good

VG very good • Vicar General

VGA *Computing* video graphics array

v.g.c. very good condition

VHC (*or* **v.h.c.**) very highly commended

VHD video high density (system)

VHE very high energy

VHF *Radio, etc.* very high frequency

VHP (India) Vishwa Hindu Parishad (militant Hindu group)

VHS *Trademark* Video Home System

VHT very high temperature

v.i. verb intransitive • vide infra (Latin: see below)

VI Vancouver Island • Virgin Islands

VIASA Venezolana Internacional de Aviácion, SA (Venezuelan International Airways)

vib. *Music* vibraphone

vic. vicar • vicarage • vicinity

Vic. Victoria (Australia)

VIC Victoria Institute of Colleges

Vice-Adm. Vice-Admiral

vid. vide (Latin: see)

VID *Computing* virtual image display

vil. village

VIP very important person

VIR Victoria Imperatrix Regina (Latin: Victoria, Empress and Queen)

Virg. Virginia (USA)

v. irr. verb irregular

vis. visibility • visual

Vis. Viscount (*or* Viscountess)

visc. viscosity

VISTA ('vɪstə) Volunteers in Service to America

viz videlicet (Latin: namely; *z* is medieval Latin symbol of contraction)

VJ (Australia) Vaucluse Junior (yacht) • Victory over Japan (in **VJ Day**, 15 Aug.

or 2 Sept. 1945) • video jockey

v.l. varia lectio (Latin: a variant reading)

VL Vulgar Latin

VLBW *Med.* very low birth weight

VLCC very large crude carrier (oil tanker)

vle *Music* violone (double-bass viol)

VLF *Radio, etc.* very low frequency

VLLW very low-level (radioactive) waste

vln violin

VLR very long range (aircraft) • Victoria Law Reports

VLSI *Electronics* very large-scale integration

VM Victory Medal • Virgin Mary • *Computing* virtual machine

V-Mail *Military* (USA) victory mail

VM/CMS *Computing, trademark* virtual machine, conversational monitor system

VMD Doctor of Veterinary Medicine (Latin *Veterinariae Medicinae Doctor*)

VMH Victoria Medal of

Honour (awarded by the Royal Horticultural Society)

VMS *Computing* virtual machine system (*see also* VAX/VMS)

vn violin

v.n. verb neuter

VN Vietnam (abbrev. or IVR)

vo. verso

VO very old (of brandy, whisky, etc.) • Veterinary Officer • (Royal) Victorian Order

VOA *Radio* Voice of America

voc. *Grammar* vocative

vocab. vocabulary

vocat. *Grammar* vocative

voc-ed (ˌvɒkˈɛd) vocational education

vol. volcano • (*or* **Vol.**) volume • voluntary • (*or* **Vol.**) volunteer

vols (*or* **Vols**) volumes

VOP very oldest procurable (of brandy, port, etc.)

VOR very-high-frequency omnirange *or* omnidirectional radio range (navigation aid)

vox pop (vɒks pɒp) vox populi (Latin: voice of the people)

v.p. verb passive

VP verb phrase (in transformational grammar) • Vice-President • Vice-Principal • *vita patris* (Latin: during the life of his (*or* her) father)

VPP (India) value payable post • Volunteer Political Party

VPRP Vice-President of the Royal Society of Portrait Painters

VQMG Vice-Quartermaster-General

v.r. variant reading • verb reflexive

VR variant reading • *Physics* velocity ratio • Victoria Regina (Latin: Queen Victoria) • *Computing* virtual reality • voltage regulator • Volunteer Reserve

VRAM *Computing* video random access memory

VRD Royal Naval Volunteer Reserve Officers' Decoration

v. refl. verb reflexive

V. Rev. Very Reverend

VRI Victoria Regina et Imperatrix (Latin: Victoria, Queen and Empress)

VRO vehicle registration office

vs. versus

v.s. vide supra (Latin: see above)

VS Veterinary Surgeon • *Music* volti subito (Italian: turn over quickly)

VSB *Telecom.* vestigial sideband

VSI *Navigation* vertical speed indicator

V-sign victory sign

VSO *Linguistics* verb-subject-object (as in **VSO language**) • very superior old (of brandy, port, etc.) • Voluntary Service Overseas

VSOP very special (*or* superior) old pale (of brandy, port, etc.)

VSR very special reserve (of wine)

V/STOL (*or* **V-STOL, VSTOL**) ('viːˌstɒl) vertical and short takeoff and landing (aircraft)

v.t. verb transitive

Vt Vermont

VT variable time (as in **VT fuse**) • *symbol for* vatu (monetary unit of Vanuatu) • *Med.* ventricular tachycardia • *US postcode for* Vermont

VTC Volunteer Training Corps

VTE *Psychol.* vicarious trial and error

VTO vertical takeoff (aircraft)

VTOL ('vi:,tɒl) vertical takeoff and landing (aircraft)

VTR videotape recorder

VU *Acoustics* volume unit (as in **VU meter**)

Vul *Astronomy* Vulpecula

Vul. (*or* **Vulg.**) Vulgate

vulg. vulgar(ly)

vv. verbs • verses • *Music* (first and second) violins • *Music* voices • volumes

v.v. vice versa

VVO very very old (of brandy, port, etc.)

VW Very Worshipful • Volkswagen

v.y. *Bibliog.* various years

W

w (ital.) *Physics, symbol for* a velocity component

w. water • week • weight • white • *Cricket* wicket • *Cricket* wide • width • wife • win • with • won • word

W (ital.) *Engineering, symbol for* load • *Chem., symbol for* tungsten (formerly wolfram) • *Colloquial* water closet; WC • *symbol for* watt • (ital.) *Physics, symbol for* weight • *Genetics* Weigle (in **W reactivation**) • west(ern) • *postcode for* west London • *Shipping* winter loading (on load line) • women's (clothing size) • *symbol for* won (South Korean monetary unit) • (ital.) *Physics, symbol for* work

W. (*or* **W**) Wales • Warden • Wednesday • Welsh • Wesleyan • west(ern) • white • wide • widow(er) • widowed

WA *postcode for* Warrington • *US postcode for* Washington (state) • West Africa(n) • Western Australia • *Insurance* with average

WAAAF (wæf) Women's Auxiliary Australian Air Force

WAAC (wæk) Women's Army Auxiliary Corps

WAAF (wæf) Women's Auxiliary Air Force • Women's Auxiliary Australian Air Force

WAC (wæk) (USA) Women's Army Corps (in World War II)

WACC World Association for Christian Communications

WAF (*or* **w.a.f.**) with all faults • (USA) Women in the Air Force

W. Afr. West Africa(n)

WAG *international vehicle registration for* (West Africa) Gambia

WAGBI Wildfowl Association of Great Britain and Ireland

WAGGGS World Association of Girl Guides and Girl Scouts

WAIS *Psychol.* Wechsler Adult Intelligence Scale

WAIS-R *Psychol.* Wechsler Adult Intelligence Scale – Revised

Wal. Walloon

WAL *international vehicle registration for* (West Africa) Sierra Leone

WAN (wæn) *international vehicle registration for* (West Africa) Nigeria • *Computing* wide-area network

W & S whisky and soda

W & T *Taxation* wear and tear

war. warrant

War. Warwickshire

WARC World Administrative Radio Conference • World Alliance of Reformed Churches

Warks Warwickshire

Wash. Washington

WASP (wɒsp) (*or* **Wasp**) (USA) white Anglo-Saxon Protestant • (USA) Women Airforce Service Pilots

WAT *Aeronautics* weight, altitude, temperature (as in **WAT curves**) • *Psychol.* word association test

WATFOR ('wɒtfɔː) *Computing* University of Waterloo Fortran (Fortran compiler)

W. Aus. (*or* **W. Aust.**) Western Australia

WAVES (*or* **Waves**) (weɪvz) *US Navy* Women

Accepted for Volunteer Emergency Service

w.b. water ballast • waybill • westbound • *Knitting* wool back

Wb *Magnetism, symbol for* weber

WB Warner Brothers (Pictures, Incorporated) • (*or* **W/B**) *Telecom.* waveband • (*or* **W/B**) *Commerce* waybill • *Psychol.* Wechsler–Bellevue (Intelligence Scale)

WBA West Bromwich Albion (Football Club) • World Boxing Association

WBC *Med.* white blood cell • *Med.* white blood (cell) count • World Boxing Council

WBF World Bridge Federation

WbN west by north

w.b.s. *Insurance* without benefit of salvage

WbS west by south

w.c. water closet • without charge

WC water closet • Wesleyan chapel • *postcode for* west central London

WCC World Council of Churches

W/Cdr (*or* **W. Cdr**) Wing Commander

WCEU World Christian Endeavour Union

WCL World Confederation of Labour

WCT World Championship Tennis

WCTU (USA, Canada) Women's Christian Temperance Union

wd ward • warranted • wood • word • would

w/d warranted

WD *international vehicle registration for* (Windward Islands) Dominica • War Department • *postcode for* Watford • Works Department

W/D *Banking* withdrawal

WDA *Taxation* writing-down allowance

WDC Woman Detective Constable

WDM *Telecom.* wavelength division multiplex

WDS Woman Detective Sergeant

WDV *Taxation* written-down value

w/e weekend • week ending

WEA Royal West of England Academy • Workers' Educational Association

Wed. Wednesday

Weds. Wednesday

w.e.f. with effect from

WEFT (weft) *Aeronautics* wings, engine, fuselage, tail

WEN (*or* **Wen**) (wɛn) Women's Environmental Network

WES Women's Engineering Society

WES/PNEU Worldwide Education Service of Parents' National Educational Union

Westm. Westminster

WET West(ern) European Time

WEU Western European Union (for defence policy)

wf (*or* **w.f.**) *Printing* wrong fount

WF *postcode for* Wakefield

WFA White Fish Authority

w factor *Psychol.* will factor

WFC World Food Council

w.fd *Knitting* wool forward

WFEO World Federation of Engineering Organizations

wff *Logic* well-formed formula

WFP World Food Programme (of the FAO)

WFSW World Federation of Scientific Workers

WFTU World Federation of Trade Unions

w.fwd *Knitting* wool forward

WG *international vehicle registration for* (Windward Islands) Grenada • (*or* **w.g.**) water gauge • (*or* **w.g.**) weight guaranteed • *Colloquial* W(illiam) G(ilbert) Grace (1848–1915, English cricketer) • (*or* **w.g.**) wire gauge • Working Group

WGA Writers' Guild of America

WGC Welwyn Garden City

Wg/Cdr (*or* **Wg Comdr**) Wing Commander

W. Ger. West German(y) • West Germanic (language group)

W. Glam. West Glamorgan

WGmc West Germanic (language group)

wh. white

W h *Electricity, symbol for* watt hour(s)

WH (*or* **w/h**) *Banking* withholding

WHA World Hockey Association

w.h.b. wash-hand basin

whf. wharf

WhF Whitworth Fellow

WHO World Health Organization

whs. (or **whse**) warehouse

WhSch Whitworth Scholar

whsle wholesale

whs. rec. warehouse receipt

whs. stk warehouse stock

w.i. *Finance* when issued

WI West Indian · West Indies · *US postcode for* Wisconsin · Women's Institute

WIA wounded in action

WICA Warsaw International Consumer Association

wid. widow(er)

Wigorn. Wigorniensis (Latin: (Bishop) of Worcester)

wilco ('wɪlˌkəʊ) will comply (in radio communications, etc.)

Wilts Wiltshire

WIMP (wɪmp) *Physics* weakly interacting massive particle · (or **wimp**) *Computing* windows icons menus pointers

W. Ind. West Indian · West Indies

Wind. I. Windward Islands

Wing Cdr Wing Commander

wint. winter

WIP work in progress

WIPO (or **Wipo**) ('waɪpəʊ) World Intellectual Property Organization

Wis. Wisconsin

WISC *Psychol.* Wechsler Intelligence Scale for Children

WISC-R *Psychol.* Wechsler Intelligence Scale for Children – Revised

Wisd. *Old Testament* Wisdom of Solomon

WITA Women's International Tennis Association

Wits. Witwatersrand

WIZO (or **Wizo**) ('waɪtzəʊ) Women's International Zionist Organization

WJC World Jewish Congress

WJEC Welsh Joint Education Committee

wk weak · week · work

Wk Walk (in place names)

WKB *Physics* Wentzel-Kramers–Brillouin (as in **WKB solution** of the Schrödinger equation)

wkly weekly

wks weeks

wkt *Cricket* wicket

WL *international vehicle registration for* (Windward Islands) St Lucia • wagon-lit (French: sleeping car) • (*or* **w.l.**) water line • (*or* **W/L**) wavelength

WLA Women's Land Army

wld would

WLF Women's Liberal Federation

wl fwd *Knitting* wool forward

WLHB Women's League of Health and Beauty

WLM Women's Liberation Movement

W. long. west longitude

WLR Weekly Law Reports

W/M (*or* **w/m**) *Shipping* weight or measurement

WMA Working Mothers' Association • World Medical Association

WMC Working Men's College

WMCIU Working Men's Club and Institute Union Ltd

wmk watermark

WMO World Meteorological Organization

WN *postcode for* Wigan

WNA *Shipping* winter North Atlantic loading (on load line)

WNO Welsh National Opera

WNP Welsh Nationalist Party

WNW west-northwest

w.o. walkover • *Commerce* written order

w/o without • *Accounting* written off

WO War Office • Warrant Officer • welfare officer • wireless operator • written order

w.o.b. washed overboard

w.o.c. without compensation

WOC(S) *Building trades* waiting on cement (to set)

WOF (New Zealand) Warrant of Fitness (for vehicles)

W/offr welfare officer

w.o.g. with other goods

Worcs Worcestershire

WORM (*or* **worm**) (wɜːm) *Computing* write once read many (times)

WOSB ('wɒzbɪ) War Office Selection Board

WOW waiting on weather • Women Against the Ordination of Women

w.p. weather permitting • word processing (*or* processor)

Wp. Worship • Worshipful

WP weather permitting •

Government White Paper • word processing (*or* processor) • working pressure

WPA Western Provident Association • World Pool-Billiard Association

WPB (*or* **w.p.b.**) wastepaper basket

WPBSA World Professional Billiards and Snooker Association

WPC Woman Police Constable

WPESS within pulse electronic sector scanning (in **WPESS sonar**)

WPI wholesale price index • World Press Institute

w.p.m. words per minute

WPMSF World Professional Marathon Swimming Federation

wpn weapon

WPPSI *Psychol.* Wechsler Preschool and Primary Scale of Intelligence

WPT Women's Playhouse Trust

w.r. warehouse receipt • *Insurance* war risk

WR warehouse receipt • *Med.* Wassermann reaction • *Railways* Western Region • Willelmus Rex (Latin: King William) • (*or*

W–R) *Astronomy* Wolf-Rayet (in **WR stars**) • *postcode for* Worcester

WRAAC (ræk) Women's Royal Australian Army Corps

WRAAF (ræf) Women's Royal Australian Air Force

WRAC (ræk) Women's Royal Army Corps

WRAF (ræf) Women's Royal Air Force

WRANS (rænz) Women's Royal Australian Naval Service

WRC Water Research Centre

WRI Women's Rural Institute

WRNS Women's Royal Naval Service

wrnt warrant

w.r.o. *Insurance* war risks only

WRP Worker's Revolutionary Party

w.r.t. with respect to

WRU Welsh Rugby Union

WRVS Women's Royal Voluntary Service (formerly WVS)

WS *postcode for* Walsall • *international vehicle registration for* Western Samoa • West Saxon • wind speed •

Law (Scotland) Writer to the Signet

WSCF World Student Christian Federation

WSPU Women's Social and Political Union

WSTN World Service Television News

WSTV World Service Television

WSW west-southwest

wt weight

WT (*or* **W/T**) wireless telegraphy (*or* telephony)

WTA winner takes all • Women's Tennis Association

wtd warranted

WTN Worldwide Television News

WTO Warsaw Treaty Organization

WTS Women's Transport Service (now amalgamated with FANY)

WUF World Underwater Federation

WUS World University Service

WV *international vehicle registration for* (Windward Islands) St Vincent and the Grenadines • *US postcode for* West Virginia • *postcode for* Wolverhampton

W. Va. West Virginia

WVS Women's Voluntary Service (*see* WRVS)

WW (*or* **W/W**) wall-to-wall (in estate agency) • (*or* **W/W**) warehouse warrant • (ital.) Who's Who • World War (*see* WW1, WW2)

WW1 (*or* **WWI**) World War One (1914–18)

WW2 (*or* **WWII**) World War Two (1939–45)

WWF Worldwide Fund for Nature (formerly World Wildlife Fund)

WWMCCS World Wide Military Command and Control System

WWSSN worldwide standard seismograph network

WWSU World Water Ski Union

WWW World Weather Watch (of the WMO)

WX women's extra-large (clothing size)

Wy. Wyoming

WY *US postcode for* Wyoming

Wyo. Wyoming

WYSIWYG (*or* **wysiwyg**) ('wɪzɪ,wɪg) *Computing* what you see (on the screen) is what you get (from the printer)

X

x *Genetics*, symbol for the basic number of chromosomes in a genome • (ital.) *Maths.*, symbol for a Cartesian coordinate (usually horizontal, as in **x-axis**) • *Bridge*, symbol for any card other than an honour • symbol for cross (as in **x-cut**, **x'd out**) • *Commerce, Finance, etc.* ex • extra • (ital.) *Maths.*, symbol for an algebraic variable

X *Films*, symbol for adults only (former certification, still used in **X-rated**, **X-rating**) • symbol for beer strength (in **XX**, **XXX**, etc.) • symbol for choice (on a ballot paper) • Christ (from Greek letter X (chi), representing *ch*) • symbol for Cross (as in **King's X**) • symbol for error • experiment(al) • (ital.) *Physics*, symbol for exposure dose • extra • *Chem.*, symbol for a halogen (as in **MgX**) • symbol for a kiss • symbol for the location of a place or point on a map, diagram, etc • symbol for his (or her) mark • (ital.) *Electricity*, symbol for reactance • *Roman numeral for* ten • symbol for any unknown, unspecified, or variable thing, factor, number, or person. *See also* X-ray • X-ray • *Genetics*, indicating a sex chromosome in humans and most animals (as in **X chromosome**, **X-linked**, **XYY syndrome**)

xa *Finance* ex all (without any benefits)

xb *Finance* ex bonus (i.e. without bonus shares)

XBT expendable bathythermograph

xc *Finance* ex capitalization (without capitalization) • *Finance* ex coupon (without the interest on the coupon)

XC (or **X-C**) (USA, Canada) cross-country (in **XC skiing**)

x.c.l. *Insurance* excess current liabilities

xcp (*or* **x.cp.**) *Finance* ex coupon (*see under* xc)

xd (*or* **xdiv**) *Finance* ex dividend (without dividend)

XDR extended dynamic range (of cassettes)

Xe *Chem.*, symbol for xenon

x-height *Printing, indicating* typesize of lower-case letters excluding ascenders and descenders (from the height of the lower-case x)

xi (*or* **x in**) *Finance* ex interest (without interest)

XL extra large (clothing size)

Xmas ('ɛksməs) Christmas

XMS *Computing* extended memory specification

xn *Finance* ex new (without right to new shares)

Xn Christian

Xnty Christianity

XO executive officer • *indicating* a cognac of superior quality

XOR (*or* **xor**) ('ɛksɔː) *Electronics, Computing* exclusive-OR (as in **XOR gate**)

XP symbol or monogram for Christ or Christianity (from X (chi) and P (rho), the first two letters of the Greek word for Christ) • (*or* **x.p.**) express paid

XPS X-ray photoelectron spectroscopy

xq (*or* **XQ**) cross-question

xr *Finance* ex rights (without rights)

XR X-ray(s)

X-ray *indicating* electromagnetic radiation of very short wavelength (*X* refers to its unknown nature at the time of its discovery)

x ref. (*or* **X ref.**) cross reference

XRF X-ray fluorescence

x.rts *Finance* ex rights (without rights)

xs expenses

Xt Christ

Xtian Christian

Xty Christianity

xw *Finance* ex warrants (without warrants)

X-Windows *Computing, trademark indicating* a precisely defined form of windowing mechanism developed by MIT

xyl. xylophone

Y

y (ital.) *Maths.*, symbol for a Cartesian coordinate (usually vertical, as in **y-axis**) • (ital.) *Maths.*, symbol for an algebraic variable

y. yard • year • young • youngest

Y (ital.) *Electricity*, symbol for admittance • symbol for yen (Japanese monetary unit) • (or **Y.**) Yeomanry • *Colloquial* YMCA, YWCA, YMHA, or YWHA • *Chem.*, symbol for yttrium • symbol for yuan (Chinese monetary unit; *see also* RMB) • (or **Y.**) Yugoslavia • *Genetics*, indicating a sex chromosome of humans and most animals (as in **Y chromosome, Y-linked, XYY syndrome**)

YA (or **Y/A**) *Marine insurance* York–Antwerp (Rules) • (USA) young adult

YAC *Genetics* yeast artificial chromosome(s)

YACC (jæk) *Computing* yet another compiler-compiler

YAG (or **yag**) (jæg) *Elec-*tronics yttrium–aluminium garnet

YAR *Marine insurance* York–Antwerp Rules

YAS Yorkshire Agricultural Society

Yb *Chem.*, symbol for ytterbium

YB yearbook

YC Young Conservative

YC&UO Young Conservative and Unionist Organization

YCNAC Young Conservative National Advisory Committee

yd yard

YD symbol for Yemeni dinar (monetary unit)

yds yards

YE Your Excellency

yeo. (or **Yeo.**) yeoman • yeomanry

YER (or **y.e.r.**) *Finance* yearly effective rate (of interest)

YES Youth Employment Service • Youth Enterprise Scheme

YFC Young Farmers' Club

YHA Youth Hostels Association

YHANI Youth Hostels Association of Northern Ireland

YIG (jɪg) *Electronics* yttrium–iron garnet

YM *Colloquial* YMCA (*or* a YMCA hostel)

YMCA Young Men's Christian Association

YMHA Young Men's Hebrew Association

y.o. *Knitting* yarn over • year(s) old (following a number)

YO *postcode for* York

YOB (*or* **y.o.b.**) year of birth

YOP (*or* **Yops**) (jɒp; jɒps) Youth Opportunities Programme (replaced by Youth Training Scheme, YTS)

Yorks Yorkshire

YP young prisoner

YPTES Young People's Trust for Endangered Species

yr year • younger • your

yrbk yearbook

YRls *symbol for* Yemen riyal (monetary unit)

yrs years • (*or* **Yrs**) yours (in correspondence)

yt yacht

YT Yukon Territory

y.t.b. *Knitting* yarn to back

YTD *Accounting* year to date

y.t.f. *Knitting* yarn to front

YTS Youth Training Scheme

YU *international vehicle registration for* Yugoslavia

Yugo. Yugoslavia

yuppie (*or* **yuppy**) ('jʌpɪ) *Colloquial* young urban (*or* upwardly mobile) professional

YV *international vehicle registration for* Venezuela

YVFF Young Volunteer Force Foundation

YWCA Young Women's Christian Association

YWHA Young Women's Hebrew Association

Z

z (ital.) *Maths.*, *symbol for* a Cartesian coordinate (as in **z-axis**) • (ital.) *Maths.*, *symbol for* an algebraic variable

z. zero • zone

Z (ital.) *Electricity*, *symbol for* impedance • (ital.) *Physics*, *symbol for* proton number • *symbol for* zaïre (monetary unit of Zaïre) • *international vehicle registration for* Zambia • *Genetics*, *indicating* a sex chromosome in birds and some insects

Z. (*or* Z) zero (as in **Z-day**) • zone

ZA *international vehicle registration for* South Africa

ZANU (*or* Zanu) ('zænu:) Zimbabwe African National Union

ZANU (PF) (*or* Zanu (PF)) ('zænu: 'pi: 'εf) Zimbabwe African National Union (Patriotic Front)

ZAPU (*or* Zapu) ('zæpu:) Zimbabwe African People's Union

Z-car *indicating* a police patrol car (from *zulu*, radio call sign)

ZE *postcode for* Lerwick

Zech. *Bible* Zechariah

Zeep (zi:p) *Nuclear engineering* zero-energy experimental pile

ZEG zero economic growth

Zeph. *Bible* Zephaniah

ZETA ('zi:tə) *Nuclear engineering* zero-energy thermonuclear apparatus (*or* assembly)

ZFGBI Zionist Federation of Great Britain and Ireland

ZI *Military* zone of interior

ZIF (zɪf) *Electronics* zero insertion force (in **ZIF socket**)

ZIFT (zɪft) *Med.* zygote intrafallopian transfer (treatment for infertility)

zip (*or* Zip) (zɪp) (USA) zone improvement plan (in **zip code**, US postcode)

Zł *symbol for* zloty (Polish monetary unit)

Zn *Chem.*, *symbol for* zinc

zod. zodiac

, zoological • zoolo-
  zoology
  zero population
th
hem., symbol for zirconium
*international vehicle
tration for* Zaïre

ZS Zoological Society
ZST zone standard time
ZW *international vehicle registration for* Zimbabwe
zz zigzag
Zz. *Med., Pharmacol.* ginger
  (Latin *zingiber*)